UNION INTERNATIONALE DES SCIENCES PRÉHISTORIQUES ET PROTOHISTORIQUES
INTERNATIONAL UNION FOR PREHISTORIC AND PROTOHISTORIC SCIENCES

PROCEEDINGS OF THE XV WORLD CONGRESS (LISBON, 4-9 SEPTEMBER 2006)
ACTES DU XV CONGRÈS MONDIAL (LISBONNE, 4-9 SEPTEMBRE 2006)

Series Editor: Luiz Oosterbeek

VOL. 19

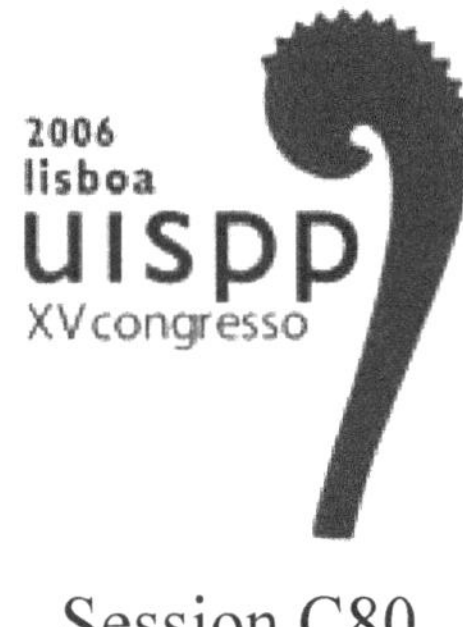

Session C80

Pleistocene Palaeoart of the World

Edited by

Robert G. Bednarik
Derek Hodgston

BAR International Series 1804
2008

Published in 2016 by
BAR Publishing, Oxford

BAR International Series 1804

Proceedings of the XV World Congress of the International Union for Prehistoric and Protohistoric Sciences / Actes du XV Congrès Mondial de l'Union Internationale des Sciences Préhistoriques et Protohistoriques
Pleistocene Palaeoart of the World. Vol. 19, Session C80

ISBN 978 1 4073 0291 1

Outgoing President: Vítor Oliveira Jorge
Outgoing Secretary General: Jean Bourgeois
Congress Secretary General: Luiz Oosterbeek (Series Editor)
Incoming President: Pedro Ignacio Shmitz
Incoming Secretary General: Luiz Oosterbeek
Signed papers are the responsibility of their authors alone.
Les texts signés sont de la seule responsabilité de ses auteurs.
Contacts : Secretary of U.I.S.P.P. – International Union for Prehistoric and Protohistoric Sciences
Instituto Politécnico de Tomar, Av. Dr. Cândido Madureira 13, 2300 TOMAR
Email: uispp@ipt.pt www.uispp.ipt.pt

BAR Publishing is the trading name of British Archaeological Reports (Oxford) Ltd. British Archaeological Reports was first incorporated in 1974 to publish the BAR Series, International and British. In 1992 Hadrian Books Ltd became part of the BAR group. This volume was originally published by Archaeopress in conjunction with British Archaeological Reports (Oxford) Ltd / Hadrian Books Ltd, the Series principal publisher, in 2008. This present volume is published by BAR Publishing, 2016.

Printed in England

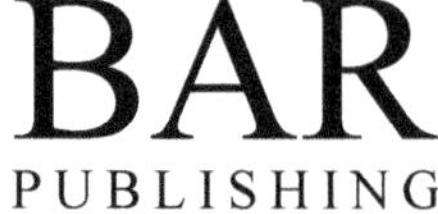

BAR titles are available from:

BAR Publishing
122 Banbury Rd, Oxford, OX2 7BP, UK
EMAIL info@barpublishing.com
PHONE +44 (0)1865 310431
FAX +44 (0)1865 316916
www.barpublishing.com

NOTE OF THE SERIES EDITOR

The present volume is part of a series of proceedings of the XV world congress of the International Union for Prehistoric and Protohistoric Sciences (UISPP / IUPPS), held in September 2006, in Lisbon.

The Union is the international organization that represents the prehistoric and protohistoric research, involving thousands of archaeologists from all over the world. It holds a major congress every five years, to present a "state of the art" in its various domains. It also includes a series of scientific commissions that pursue the Union's goals in the various specialities, in between congresses. Aiming at promoting a multidisciplinary approach to prehistory, it has several regional or thematic associations as affiliates, and on its turn it is a member of the International Council for Philosophy and Human Sciences (an organism supported by UNESCO).

Over 2500 authors have contributed to c. 1500 papers presented in 101 sessions during the XVth world Congress of UISPP, held under the organisation of the Polytechnic Institute of Tomar. 25% of these papers dealt with Palaeolithic societies, and an extra 5% were related to Human evolution and environmental adaptations. The sessions on the origins and spread of hominids, on the origins of modern humans in Europe and on the middle / upper Palaeolithic transition, attracted the largest number of contributions. The papers on Post-Palaeolithic contexts were 22% of the total, with those focusing in the early farmers and metallurgists corresponding to 12,5%. Among these, the largest session was focused on prehistoric mounds across the world. The remaining sessions crossed these chronological boundaries, and within them were most represented the regional studies (14%), the prehistoric art papers (12%) and the technological studies (mostly on lithics – 10%).

The Congress staged the participation of many other international organisations (such as IFRAO, INQUA, WAC, CAA or HERITY) stressing the value of IUPPS as the common ground representative of prehistoric and protohistoric research. It also served for a relevant renewal of the Union: the fact that more than 50% of the sessions were organised by younger scholars, and the support of 150 volunteers (with the support of the European Forum of Heritage Organisations) were in line with the renewal of the Permanent Council (40 new members) and of the Executive Committee (5 new members). Several Scientific Commissions were also established.

Finally, the Congress decided to hold its next world congress in Brazil, in 2011. It elected Pe. Ignácio Shmitz as new President, Luiz Oosterbeek as Secretary General and Rossano Lopes Bastos as Congress secretary.

L.O.

TABLE OF CONTENTS

LIST OF FIGURES

LIST OF TABLES

PLEISTOCENE PALAEOART OF THE WORLD
INTRODUCTION AND SUMMARY

Robert G. BEDNARIK

The symposium "Pleistocene palaeoart of the world" was held on Saturday 9 September 2006 at the XVth UISPP Congress, in Lisbon. Chaired by Robert G. Bednarik (Australia) and Derek Hodgson (United Kingdom), its purpose had been to present recent advances in the study of human evolution that have shown the need for greater attention to the cognitive and cultural development of humans. Traditionally, the study of hominin evolution is dominated by skeletal morphology, especially cranial architecture, and recently, to a lesser degree, by genetics. In both these approaches it is completely ignored that being human is not so much related to skeletal or genetic indices, but to cognition, intellect and culture, the factors that have made us human. This imbalance is at last being addressed.

In the Pleistocene record, cognition and culture are primarily accessible through the study of palaeoart, which consists of rock art and portable art-like productions. Cognitive evolution, informed by recent advances in neuroscience and psychology, is increasingly becoming relevant to the understanding of Pleistocene palaeoart. The potential for gaining new insights into the significance of these surviving materials from the perspective of cognition is therefore most promising. Correspondingly, archaeological finds from this period can provide evidence that may help substantiate particular models as to how human cognition may have eventuated. Collaboration between these disciplines can be viewed as mutually beneficial and sustaining. As research into cognition and brain functioning continues apace, the need to assimilate the various findings in relation to palaeoart becomes all the more imperative. Where Pleistocene artefacts are subjects of controversy, cognitive studies can supply useful suggestions as to interpretation, thereby providing the proper context for the determination of such items. It can also help to disentangle the complex ways by which culture and evolutionary factors interact so that a clearer understanding of their respective roles and influences can be gauged in relation to Pleistocene artefacts.

To render Pleistocene palaeoart scientifically useful, evidence needs to be studied as global rather than regional phenomena. Underlying principles and universals need to be identified, and the material of the Middle and Early Upper Pleistocene requires much more attention than has been evident in the 20th century. This symposium was therefore intended to bring together some of the latest key evidence deriving from the archaeological record, cognitive studies and neuroscience to reflect the current change from traditional preoccupations to new approaches. It was endeavoured to place Pleistocene palaeoart into the context of cognitive evolution, explore its semiotic dimensions, consider implications for technology and culture during the Palaeolithic periods, and present new empirical evidence of Pleistocene palaeoart.

The main results of this symposium appear in the following small but valuable collection of papers. It is immediately evident that most of the key objectives were successfully met. Semiotic and neuroscientific data were presented, some of the most important empirical evidence of relevance to the cognitive status of early hominins was contributed, and highly innovative analytical and baffling information on early cognition was offered for consideration. In fact it is amazing that so much new and signifycant material could be crammed into such a relatively short session and volume.

Perhaps the greatest surprise came in the shape of a presentation by John Feliks, whose unconventional approach to research questions caused him to investigate the geometric properties of some of the world's oldest engravings we currently know of. Feliks noted mind-boggling regularities which, if valid indicators, would suggest that some Lower Palaeolithic hominins possessed concepts of spatiality significantly different from ours, and apparently much more sophisticated.

Derek Hodgson presented a neurovisual perspective of Pleistocene palaeoart, a general subject he has excelled in before. He contended convincingly that there must be a connection between the visual cortex of hominins and the initial markings they produced. His work connects neatly with that of Feliks, even though his approach is very different.

In terms of new relevant empirical evidence, the two directors of the Early Indian Petroglyphs Project presented a summing up of their research at the two oldest rock art sites currently known, both in central India. One of them, Giriraj Kumar, also gave a separate paper on one of these two sites, Daraki-Chattan Cave, reporting the results of the ongoing excavation that is recovering petroglyphs from well below Lower Palaeolithic occupation strata.

A key issue in the question of art beginnings in Europe concerns the identity of the producers of Aurignacian palaeoart of that continent. Robert G. Bednarik reviewed the current palaeoanthropological evidence, arriving at the conclusion that the Aurignacian was probably a tradition of Neanderthaloid humans. Another paper addressing an important issue in rock art research is by Yann-Pierre Montelle, dealing with the possibilities of behavioural studies through the analysis of the tools used in making rock art. Like the approaches sketched out by Feliks and Hodgson, Montelle thus offers one more unique and new way of exploring palaeoart. Paul Bouissac, who represents the semiotic approach to rock art, focuses on an evaluation of the work of two pioneers of palaeoart and semiotics, Edouard Piette and William Flinders Petrie. He poignantly notices that the debate the former experienced a century ago is now being replayed under surprisingly similar conditions. Indeed, history often does repeat itself in archaeology.

The advent of the 21st century has brought with it noticeable changes in the way the palaeoart of the Pleistocene is perceived and studied, and the proceedings of this symposium bear witness to these changes. The first aspect we notice of this collection is that there are no papers about the traditional obsession of Palaeolithic "art" specialists, with meaning and the cultural role of the art. Simplistic interpretation of this corpus of evidence has been the discipline's hallmark throughout the 20th century, and even the more realistic question of antiquity is not much dwelt on in the papers in this collection. Rather, we note a distinctive heterogeneity in research approaches, an acceptance that there are more ways than one to skin a cat. The most obvious change in research direction, then, is away from the monomania with meaning to a tacit acceptance that the science has to come first, and that science involves refutation, deep probing and methodological pluralism. Despite a number of precursors in such areas, this development is rather new and probably in its very early stages, but already it illustrates the benefits of such a more inclusive and multifarious approach. It is clear enough from this collection of papers that an outdated model of palaeoart is now under sustained challenge, and that some of the most cherished ideas of the past will have to fall by the wayside. Much of what we have come to think the palaeoart of the Pleistocene tells us about the people who made it could well be false. The probable corollary is that much of what has during the 20th century become the received dogma of Pleistocene history will need to be challenged.

These are exciting times in the study of Pleistocene palaeoart!

30 March 2007

WHERE ARE THE MUR-E?: A BEHAVIOURAL APPROACH TO ROCK ART RESEARCH

Yann-Pierre MONTELLE
140A Condell Avenue, Papanui, Christchurch 8005, New Zealand, yann_montelle@mac.com

***Abstract**: With increasing attention to behavioural 'details', and by shifting some of rock art research's paradigmatic concerns, our young discipline could be effectively upgraded. In this article, the hermeneutic frenzy is being readjusted and redirected towards a more phenomenological attitude where questions of epistemology, ontology and behaviour are carefully examined. The author lays out the foundation for an alternative approach to rock art that is a work-in-progress towards understanding the behavioural motivations involved in one of the most shared and ubiquitous anthropic manifestation around the world - rock art.*
***Keywords**: Iconocentrism; mur-e; replicative experiment; behavioural archaeology*

***Résumé**: Avec une attention croissante pour le "détail" et avec un changement paridagmatique de l'art rupestre et pariétal, les recherches actuelles pourraient être efficacement amélioré. Dans cet article, la frénésie interprétative est réajustée et réorientée vers une position plus phénoménologique ou des questions importantes concernant l'épistémologie, l'ontologie et les comportements sont prudemment examinés. L'auteur introduit les fondations pour une approche complémentaire de l'art rupestre et pariétal axée essentiellement vers la compréhension des motivations comportementales impliquées dans l'emplacement et la production de l'art rupestre et pariétal.*
***Mots clés**: Iconocentrisme; mur-e; reconstructions expérimentales; archéologie du comportement humain*

'*Scientific concepts must have a behavioral basis* [and] *have to be grounded in observations of people performing activities*' (Marvin Harris in *The nature of cultural things* – 1964)

Prolegomenon – There seems to be a barely perceptible innovative breeze blowing gently in the field of rock art research. Hidden in the tall grass, and among the caterpillars, is a new specimen still struggling out of its chrysalis. Helped by the wind of change, the caterpillar transforms into a butterfly, and the humble flapping of its wings could soon become a reformative storm showering rock art research with objective descriptions, falsifiable propositions, testable hypotheses, suppression of unsubstantiated beliefs, and perhaps trigger a promising methodological renaissance. Hidden in the folds of this, admittedly, lyrical introduction is a critical discussion about the future of our prematurely aging discipline. To diagnose this premature aging of what is still a young discipline, rock art research will need to equip itself with a new entry in its official glossary: *iconocentrism*. In the context of rock art research, *iconocentrism* defines a logocentric attitude towards extant parietal manifestations (all types included). *Iconocentrism* describes the paralysing lack of interest, from past and current researchers, in a variety of so-called peripheral phenomena that, in fact, are what provides most of the context for the iconography (and yes, rock art is iconographic in that it is a set of images used in a particular context and recognised by people as having a particular meaning).

Rock art sites, as cultural reservoirs, are complex repositories of anthropic traces that, until recently, have been excavated with antiquarian discriminations. The systematic destructions of the palaeo-floors have resulted in a series of biased investigations focused mainly on one obvious evidential body, the so-called 'cave art'. The recent efforts to preserve the floors and to pay attention to the 'details' have already made major breakthroughs and elevated rock art research beyond the limitations of the *iconocentric* approach – the site (a cave, a shelter, a boulder) is approached as a complex platform where a variety of human behavioural traces can be detected[1]. Parietal iconography is brought down from its pedestal and becomes a part of a more intricate behavioural system. This traumatic shift of investigative loci (from an iconographic-based investigation to a context–based one) marks the affirmation of a new line of reforms in rock art research. The reforms begin with a mature attitude towards progress. It starts with accepting the difficult reality that what is considered empirical today will be obsolete tomorrow. The (almost obsessive) focus on iconography is slowly shifting and rock art researchers are becoming gradually more concerned with the environments/contexts (cognitive, cultural, technological and behavioural) that were conducive to the production of these anthropic manifestations.

As a rock art researcher interested primarily in human behaviour, I believe that the iconocentric approach is responsible for the irreversible destruction of many micro- and macro-behavioural evidences. These were the repositories of behavioural patterns responsible for the production of rock art images. By systematically destroying such evidence, the iconocentrists terminated all future empirical investigations. In fact, the iconocentrist paid no attention to 'details' and provided his readers with fictitious narratives that are at best 'emically' unacceptable, and at worst 'etically' paralysing. A brief review of the impact of iconocentrism on rock art research (in preparation) will show that the iconocentric approach has

[1] Taphonomically speaking, deep caves are more suitable candidates for a thorough analysis of a palaeo-floor than are open-air sites.

been the dominant paradigm in our discipline since its inception. This, I will argue, is the consequence of a historical phenomenon. Rock art research was conceived through the dogmatic lenses of the clergy as well as the antiquarian follies of museum collectors. What the 'founding fathers' were after was not a scientific explanation for a how, but a frantic determination to provide the public with some dogmatic 'when' and 'why.'

Even with the anti-clerical 'art for art's sake' discourses, the cave was never the target; it was the image – the icon – that instantly became the focus of all investigations. The cave quickly became a commercial container – a ready-made and lucrative museum. But even in the heydays of iconcentrism, the image was never approached as the end product of a chain of actions – a behavioural container – rather it was understood as the vestige of some exotic and primitive thought processes. To 'translate' these sedimentted thought-processes, the investigators were quick to draw parallels with 'living vestiges.' They too were reliant on iconography for lack of a coherent writing system. Fortunately, this historical emphasis on the icon was challenged. The icon became sign and the signs are today sophisticated semiotical segments – syntactic entities. The shift to semiotics was effective, but quickly became as 'loaded' with assumptions as any of the other hermeneutic attempts. While semiotics does offer one of the most intelligible and coherent approach to rock art imagery, it fails to provide a workable framework to investigate the behavioural choices that led to the production of these images.

MUR-E ANYONE?

> 'This word is from the Booandik language of the Mt Gambier – Portland region in Australia [...] In its scientific usage, mur-e (singular and plural) refers generically to a tool that has been used in fashioning a petroglyph [...] such a tool may be of any material, but in most cases stone was used. Mur-e include percussion tools, abrasion tools, human fingers [...]' (Bednarik 1998: 27).

In 1998, Robert Bednarik[2] raised a warning flag when he wrote that

> [...] archaeologists who lack the ability to recognise and study mur-e need to be discouraged from excavating at and near petroglyph sites unless they can secure the collaboration of a specialist for this purpose' (Bednarik 1998: 32).

In fact, and according to Bednarik, a condemnable form,

> [...] of archaeological site vandalism is the excavation of sediments near petroglyph panels if the excavator lacks the knowledge support for identifying mur-e (petroglyph-making tools), leading to this key-evidence being discarded' (Bednarik 2001: 98).

A noticeable aspect of this evidential loss (which I am going to discuss only briefly) concerns the possibility of using systematically excavated mur-e to 'estimate the age of a series of petroglyphs without excavating any sediments' (Bednarik 1998: 32). This obviously presents a very efficient and non-destructive approach that, combined with stereomicroscopy, laser scanning, mapping with a total station, photogrammetry, ImageJ, ArchaeoCAD and 3D reconstruction software (to name a few) provides a very effective package for rock art research. By monitoring the replicated petroglyphs, researchers can also establish some basic (but empirical) taphonomic database about weathering, patination and exfoliation. With the loss of this paramount evidence, it is a whole chain of behavioural investigations that is being suppressed.

Replicative experiments have been attempted by a number of researchers for decades. Replication is an investigative framework that allows a recontextualisation of objects and subjects within a body of testable hypotheses. When it comes to pre-History, hypothesis is really the only suitable investigative tool. Absence of evidence in the majority of investigated domains systematically aborts the possibility for empirical knowledge. If this is accepted, then 'replication' becomes an adequate mode of investigation. This is important because the core of this article is based on proposed methodologies, the aim of which is to recontextualise through replications the behaviour inherent to specific tasks in specific conditions. 'The great significance of replicative experimentation in the study of petroglyph technology has been emphasised repeatedly in papers on fundamental rock art science' (Bednarik 2001: 43).

But these pioneering efforts have not followed any standardised and systematic guidelines.

> The ad hoc approach to the need of replicative experimentation that seems evident from the literature needs to be replaced with a systematic program of research. Such program could be guided or even administered by the International Federation of Rock Art Organisations (IFRAO) (Bednarik 2001: 45).

This is a brilliant proposal and one that should be endorsed by IFRAO without delay. By establishing a 'central repository' for these replicative experiments, IFRAO would provide rock art research with a seminal database 'so that future taphonomic studies of petroglyphs can be based on sound information rather than conjecture' (Bednarik 1998: 31). Bednarik suggests that the standarddised records of these replicative experiments comprise:

- Precise location, so that the actual marking(s) can be found again. The location must be referenced to permanent features, not vegetation, sediment or unstable rock features.

[2] The reliance on Robert Bednarik's pioneering work is not just a preferential choice, but also illustrates the discrepancy of intelligible, cohesive, and scientific discourses in our discipline.

- Condition and aspects of the rock surface at the time: depth of weathering rind; detail of patination; exposure to rain; insulation and wind. Is the rock dry or wet? Which direction is the replica petroglyph facing?
- Petrology of support rock substrate; rainwater acidity at the site; annual precipitation details.
- Type and material of mur-e used; their weight; microscopic description of tool wear.
- Description of manufacturing technique used; time taken.
- Recording of true colours by photography with a [IFRAO] colour scale calibrated for digitised colour reconstitution (Bednarik 1998: 31).

Basically, replicative experiments which are somewhat analogous to experiments conducted in the field of experimental archaeology can be divided into five interconnected areas of investigation:

- Testing the validity of hypotheses and methodological assumptions.
- Controlled replication of recovered artefacts (mur-e).
- Controlled replication of associated petroglyphs.
- Taphonomic analysis.
- Controlled replication of activities (behaviour).

Consider the following:

> When I visited a petroglyph and occupation site [...] in the company of four Indjibandi men in early 1968, one of the men, who was in his seventies then, spontaneously produced a new petroglyph. He made a linear, to me non-iconic, motif within ten or twelve minutes. I was curious about several aspect of this event, including whether he had seen this done before. He stated, through a translator, that he had seen the old people do it when he was very young, and that he had himself as a child. On the occasion I observed then he used only a single tool, an untrimmed quartz cobble with a pointed end, about seven centimetres long, to strike the rock panel directly [...] I had not attempted any replication work prior to 1968, and I had simply assumed that to create the impact necessary to achieve the indentations on hard rock (such as diorite [...]), a tool mass well in excess of a kilogram would be required. I was surprised to see such a small tool (of about 150 to 200 g) used so effectively, and subsequently looked for suitable tools at petroglyph sites [...] (Bednarik 1998: 26).

In this excerpt, Bednarik managed to by-pass replicative experiments in order to rid himself of a methodological assumption that was probably shared across the field. But not everyone has this kind of unexpected encounter, and most of us rely on decontextualised evidence and conjectural narratives. This being established, Bednarik's recollection of his informant's spontaneous behaviour demonstrates how critical the falsifiability of our hypotheses really is. If Bednarik had postulated the following hypothesis: indentations on hard rock surface requires a tool mass well in excess of a 1kg, and if no opposing evidence were provided, then we would still be working under the assumption that mur-e used on hard surfaces were chipped large pebbles in excess of one kilogram. Because a mur-e fitting the description would not have been found, and other potential mur-e would have been discarded based on insufficient tool mass, we would not only still be operating under false assumptions, but we would still be discarding most (if not all) mur-e. In order to ensure that we, fieldworkers and researchers, do not perpetuate this methodological havoc, our hypotheses need to be falsifiable and our methodological assumptions tested under strict and controlled conditions. The proposed replicative methodology is, in my mind, the most effective forum to test assumptions and hypotheses.

The replication phase starts with the recovery of mur-e and a careful description of the mur-e's relationship with adjacent petroglyphs. Once the mur-e has been systematically recorded *in situ* (preferably using a total station), it can then be collected and brought to the lab. The next stage is to perform a lithic analysis (Odell 2003) where questions about geomorphic characteristics, procurement, manufacture, variability, taphonomy, and typology are being thoroughly investigated. Empirical database will result from this lithic analysis, enabling experimental knappers to reproduce in controlled environments workable facsimile(s) of the mur-e. Once the replicative implement (the mur-e) has reached a satisfactory level of duplication, it can then be tested. To maximize the collection of empirical data, the surface onto which the mur-e is to be used should replicate the exact mineral composition and taphonomy of the surface the mur-e was found adjacent to. On a slab (either found in the outcrop where both petroglyph and mur-e originated, or matched in terms of mineral makeup and weathering) a facsimile of the petroglyphs can be attempted under rigorous control. The final stage of the replication stage would be to return the mur-e in its original archaeological context, and to compare in situ original petroglyphs and facsimile. 'I have found such replicas, including those I made decades ago, most useful in studying weathering and patination processes. Such studies, in turn, may be relevant to dating research and conservation' (Bednarik 2001: 44).

Ethnographic observations concerning mur-e are extremely rare. As it stands, ethnographic observations, related to the manufacture and use of mur-e, are mostly anecdotal and can only provide minimum information. To palliate the impact such absence of behavioural data has on rock art research, I propose an addendum to Bednarik's proposal for '*a central repository*' of replicative experiments of mur-e and petroglyphs. This addendum is primarily concerned with what I can only refer to as 'behavioural archaeology' – a recycled version of

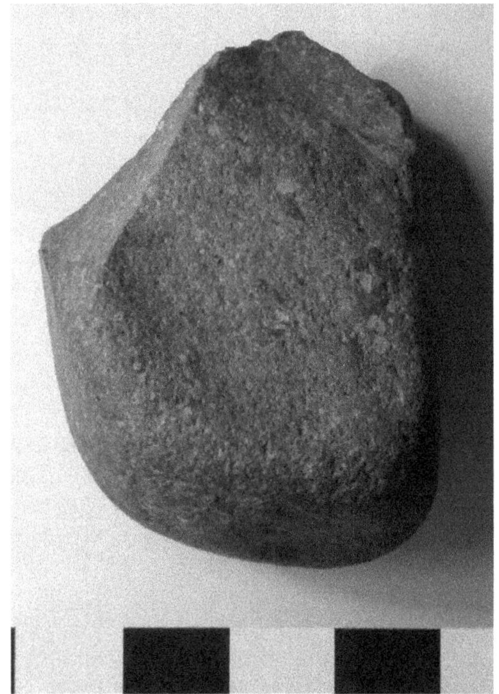

Figure 1.1. Mur-e of coarse quartzite from Mexico. © Robert Bednarik

Michael B. Schiffer's[3] behavioural archaeology (Schiffer 1995) but obviously tailored for rock art research. As defined by Schiffer, behavioural archaeology is '*an approach to cultural phenomena that privileged the study of human behavior – especially making, using, and discarding artifacts*' (1995: 10). Somewhere else he adds that the core of behavioural archaeology, the relationship between human behaviour and material culture, needs to be investigated 'in all times and all places' (1999: 166). It is the ubiquitous nature of the relationship between behaviour and artefact that I wish to pursue further in this article. Its ultimate aim is to provide rock art research with a workable behavioural past – a past seen through complex patterns of activities involving interactions between people and artefacts.

As a theoretical program, it privileges behavior – what people actually do, recognizing that all behavior (defined as activities) consists of people-artifact interactions. Also implied is an interest in the life histories of artifacts, whether one represents these as flow models or activities in behavioral chains. Behavioral archaeology is also concerned to understand and take into account, in archaeological inference, all relevant cultural and noncultural formation processes of the archaeological record' (Schiffer, unpublished material).

[3] In regards to the 'recycling' of Michael Schiffer's behavioural archaeology, I must preface this forthcoming discussion with an anecdote. In my graduate years at Brown University, I titled a short think piece: *Behavioural archaeology: looking ahead*. There was no grade on the piece, just a suggestion: 'Ask Schiffer!' Rude awakening, but memorable encounter with a discourse that I still find incredibly inspirational and, in my mind, begs to be adapted to rock art research.

Assuming that the patterning of archaeological remains in rock art sites reflects 'spatial patterning of past activities', (Schiffer 1995: 25), then behavioural archaeology can help answer the following critical question: 'How is the archaeological record formed by behaviour in a cultural system?' (Schiffer ibid.)

RECYCLING BEHAVIOURAL ARCHAEOLOGY

Rock art science has been very successful lately in providing a remarkable volume of paradigms and frameworks to generate scientific inferences about dating and taphonomic processes, but has done very little with the kinetic and biomechanical (read: behavioural) aspects of rock art production. It is my intention to gradually develop an empirical methodology to analyse the behavioural patterns related to:

- The human use of caves, shelters and boulders.
- The manufacture of rock art imagery.

Ultimately this effort should be seen as a springboard for constructing a new approach to rock art research that, benefiting from the pioneering work of Bednarik and others, could open new investigative horizons.

To 'recycle' effectively Schiffer's behavioural archaeology, I must disengage from one of Schiffer's primary aims: '[...] the study of present material objects in ongoing cultural systems to describe and explain present human behaviour' (Schiffer 1995: 72). Instead, I will focus on empirical artefacts and contexts, implicit kinetics/biomechanics, and deduced behavioural patterns from the archaeological remains of the past. This, however, excludes only one of the methodological approaches provided by behavioural archaeology ('strategies' in Schiffer's terminology), leaving us with three other options that are *a propos* for a discussion about replicative experiments:

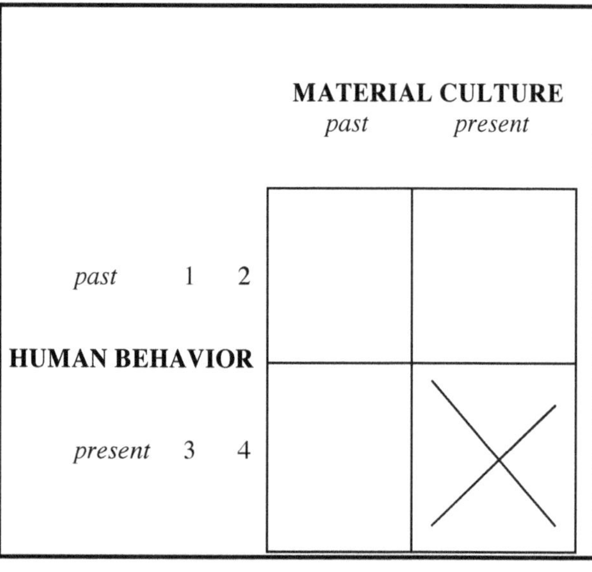

STRATEGY 1: Past human behaviour/past material culture – '[...] using material culture that was made in the past to answer specific descriptive and explanatory questions about the behavioural and organizational properties of past cultural systems' (Schiffer 1995: 69). This could easily be rephrased as: using extant evidence to postulate behaviourally testable hypothesis concerning past behavioural patterns [palaeo-quarrying, for example].

STRATEGY 2: Past human behaviour/present material culture – '[elaborate] general questions in present material culture in order to acquire laws useful for the study of the past' (Schiffer 1995: 70). In the context of rock art research, this is where one could be using extant behavioural remains (such as rock art imagery) to perform rigorous replications using analogic historical models.

STRATEGY 3: Present human behaviour/past material culture – '[...] the pursuit of general questions in the study of past material remains to derive behavioral laws of wide applicability that illuminate past as well as present human behaviour' (Schiffer 1995: 71). The replication here could be using historically and carefully recorded behaviour as a behavioural model for the replication of archaeological remains from pre-History.

Keeping these three strategies in mind, I wish to discuss behavioural investigations in the context of rock art research as essentially concerned with the following three behavioural stages:

1. Conception (template/cognitive behaviour)

2. Manufacture (biomechanical behaviour/kinetics)

3. Practice (behavioural patterns/social behaviour)

Conception, in terms of behaviour, includes the whole chain of actions that is potentially generated in cultural innovation, transited through the trials and errors inherent to retention, and finally found a more permanent status as template in the cultural index. Inherent to the notion of 'conception' are all the cognitive stages inherent to location, appropriation, and transformation of a space into a place (Montelle 2003). This stage of conception is inherent to all archaeological remains. As an investigation, it relies heavily on the researchers' current epistemological understanding of how the absent agents behaved in a reality constructed through both intellectual and material means. This, however, finds a strong resonance with Bednarik's position that the ultimate purpose for the study of rock art is an epistemological investigation about '*the origins of the human model of reality*'. Here, the scientific discourse could support the behavioural inferences and provide an innovative body of coherent and falsifiable hypotheses.

Manufacture is where behavioural archaeology can make its most noticeable contribution. The biomechanical and cognitive requirements inherent to the manufacture of an artefact can be identified and tested (Stout *et al.* 2000). In 2000, Stout, Toth and Schick pioneered an investigative technique that should be a standard today, but unfortunately remains an isolated occurrence. '*The functional brain imaging technique employed, Positron Emission Tomography (PET), examines task-related brain activity by assessing changes in regional cerebral blood flow during specific task*'(Stout et al. 2000: 1215). In the context of rock art research, this type of investigation could reveal a great deal of fundamental information regarding the brain activity of an individual involved in the manufacturing of a mur-e; the making of a paint recipe; the conception and making of rock art images under a variety of conditions; etc ... Needless to say that these comprehensive studies could generate seminal data that could help determine specific areas of neurological (motor, somatosensory, etc...) and biomechanical activetions. Testing the type of muscular input, and biomechanical patterns during specific tasks (such as the manufacture of a petroglyph) in specific conditions could help us determine the overall energy expenditure required for the task as well a basic calculation of time expenditure.

Another input behavioural archaeology could provide to rock art research is an index of 'gestures' based on replicative experiments. Gestures are biomechanical sequences that produce archaeological remains. Gestures as '*techne*' escape the ethnographic paralysis and provide another empirical venue for rock art research. Unfortunately, '[n]*o consensual definition can be proposed in regards to gesture*' (Bouissac 2004).

Despite this major setback, I will propose that gestures (in the context of rock art research):

- are strips of behaviour,
- are biomechanical patterns that are subjected to the laws of aesthetics, economy and efficiency,
- are performed as a response to exterior stimuli (threat, needs, manufacture, signals),
- are 'loaded' with intention,
- are *restored* (that is they have been retained, refined and indexed).

I believe that the way a restored gesture is performed has more to do with biomechanical and kinetics requirements than cultural standards per se. That the artefact/image signifies a specific cultural period is undeniable. But the same gesture is also an independent product of some evolutionary stages of the human body. Obviously, the culturally conditioned individual is programmed to perform sets of pre-established gestural patterns, but at the end of the process the result is an artefact/image that has been manufactured using muscular and neurological activities that are different only in the light of cultural variations.

The biomechanical aspects of absent gestures from the past become relevant only when contextualised. In other words, the trace, the discarded artefact, the broken bone, the heated blade etc., all do generate a logical biomechanics that can be replicated and indexed. Indexing gestures then would generate a database that would be, I argue, as efficient in determining phylogenetic progressions as any existing models. At this point, I wish to endorse, and somewhat expand another of Bednarik's pioneering ideas: his cultural chronology (2002). The biomechanic database generated by the replicative experiments could substantiate empirically Bednarik's cultural phases:

ROBERT BEDNARIK'S CULTURAL CHRONOLOGY

Paleolithic 1 (2.4 million years to 900 ka ago): lithic implements, expansion out of Africa, incipient ability to detect some forms of iconicity.

Paleolithic 2 (900 ka to 350 ka ago): archaic seafaring, pigment use, probably dwellings, discrimination of common and exotic entities.

Paleolithic 3 (350 ka to 60 ka ago): linear, radial and form-prompted engravings, probably cupules, inland navigation and improved seafaring, developed wooden and composite artefacts, dwellings, beads and pendants, proto-figurines.

Paleolithic 4: (60 ka to 12–8 ka ago): seafaring beyond visual range, underground mining, complex graphic markings, ritual, interment, developed garments, later figurative sculpted and graphic palaeoarts [*omission of the Mesolithic period*].

Neolithic 1: domestication, sporadic pottery.

Neolithic 2: 'High' Neolithic, general pottery use.

Neolithic 3: Late Neolithic or Chalcolithic, copper use.

> *Ref: Bednarik, Robert 'The human ascent: a critical review', Anthropologie, XL/2. 2002: 101-105*

For the purpose of this discussion, I only want to emphasise the critical function of cultural phases in a phylogenetic progression based on the evolution of material culture and human behaviour. Consider, for example, the fourth period of the Palaeolithic. Now, let me conveniently target one of these paramount innovations: underground mining. This particular aspect of human behaviour has been discussed elsewhere (Bednarik 1992; Montelle 2006), and presents rock art research with a very effective prototype for future research. Bednarik has already thoroughly described Pleistocene lithic quarrying in some of the Australian deep caves. The same prosaic behaviour, but this time concerned with the quarrying of calcium carbonate, seems to have been one the factors that engaged Palaeolithic 4 individuals in a new relationship with the deep caves, especially in the cave of Cosquer. The restoration of behavioural and gestural patterns involved in the quarrying of calcium carbonate in Cosquer (Clottes 2005), for example, can be experimentally replicated and tested. The chain of actions inherent to behavioural processes such as mining and quarrying follow a logical biomechanics adapted to specific environments. Therefore a certain degree of variability is expected and the replication obviously needs to be structured on a per case basis. But once all the variables are in place, replicative experiments can provide a body of evidential data that can then be transposed into other sites and potentially help discern new functional venues for analogous anthropic manifestations. Finger markings come to mind. At the moment, it is approached mostly on an iconographic basis. Without providing evidence, I will suggest that perhaps many of these finger tracings/flutings were initially performed for testing the calcium carbonate without, necessarily, the intervention of any iconographic templates. That the criss-crossing of these test marks ended-up producing recognisable shapes and, hence were retouched so as to conform to the iconographic index of the time is entirely possible. With the help of on-going investigations[4] and of the proposed behavioural and gestural index, it will become possible to determine which finger flutings were testing the calcium carbonate and which were the products of an aesthetic desire to construct specific formulaic applications.

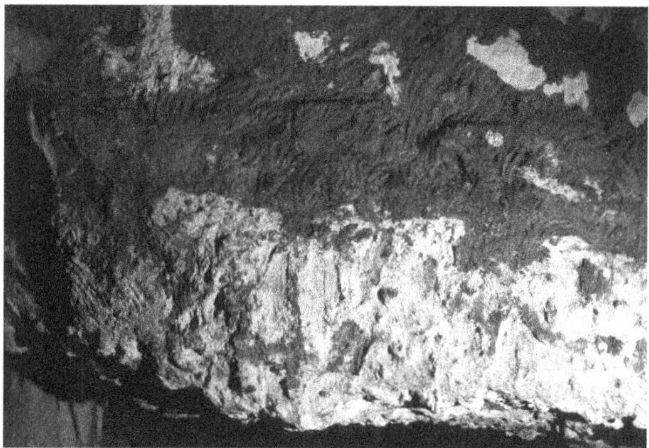

Figure 1.2. Testing calcium carbonate in Cosquer. © Jean Clottes.

The kinetic potential of a restored gesture is that its 'concatenate' nature is replicable. In other words, the progression in the cave, the struggle for access, the position adopted during manufacture of images, and the dynamic involved in the production of the image can be reconstructed at varying empirical degrees. The artefact,

[4] Kevin Sharpe and some of his colleagues have made remarkable progress in terms of replicative analysis. In the context of their investigations of finger flutings in deep caves, '[they propose] a language and systematic methodology for their study based on theory, experiment, field research, and analysis. [...] From this, we endeavour to gather sufficient information from each site to replicate the markings as the original fluters made them and to describe their ages, genders, handedness and sizes, and numbers. Analysing their flutings, what can we know about the people who used the cave?' (Sharpe and van Gelder, 2006).

image, remains of material culture are all embodiments of restored behaviours (a variation on the theme of the *chaîne opératoire*). This restoration of behavioural bits or strips is a process that can be replicated (even if only at the minimal unit of biomechanical logic). Replication of restored gestures provide the empirical grounds for the replication of restored behaviour – formulaic strips of behaviour that, through specific chains of actions, result in the production of an artefact. In the context of rock art research, replicative experiments of restored behaviour have been attempted but, in most cases, lacked the cohesiveness of a standardised and systematic approach.

It is in the spirit of 'rigour' that I wish to discuss the final stage of a replicative experiment – the analogic reasoning based on ethnographic parallels and the reconstruction of (pre)historic social practices. This final stage is, to put it mildly, problematic. To begin with, I believe that there is nothing emic about rock art research. And yet, it is a common practice to hop back and forth a few thousand years at a time in order to create analogies that help explain palaeo-behaviour using historical ethnographic models. The question of ethnographic analogies has tormented the field of rock art research since its emergence. Ethnographic research, in the context of pre-History, is a synthesis of published ethnological studies followed by an attempt at re-contextualising the assumed provenance, function and socio-economic aspects of an artefact. The data in most cases generate unfalsifiable explanations about fragmentary evidence based in a problematic ethnographic present. As it stands, rock art researchers are, for the most part, merchants of alterity, engineers of a manufactured otherness. To disguise the etic nature of rock art research, the researchers are expected to provide fictional emic narratives to satisfy a growing readership thirsty for sensational discoveries about how the Other behaved in the hostile environments of, say, the Pleistocene. They are the champions in making the unfamiliar familiar and absence a presence. In fact, if the anthropologist specialises in difference, the rock art researcher specialises in absence.

To push this argument further, I believe that in rock art research the constructed Other's empirical absence turns into his theoretical presence (hence the desire to situate this constructed Other in the present tense). And so while the ethnographer is busy trying to come to terms with the dialectic of sameness and difference, the rock art researcher thrills in a discursive mode where, for authoritative sake, he can deny autonomy and agency (read: historicity) to his fictional Other. The researcher emulates the Other by a subtle play between alterity and mimesis. The Invented Primitive (to borrow from Fabian's terminology) becomes an idealised projection of the researcher himself. He moves, strategises, and behaves according to patterns that are directly borrowed from the researcher's index. His artefacts become assemblages categorised in arbitrarily constructed taxonomies. Operating from a more clinical perspective, the researcher humanises the absent Other to such a degree that he (the Other) quickly transforms into yet another exotic fetish absorbed in a fictitious narrative of presence, sameness and continuity – when obviously, pre-History and, by association, rock art research, should be about absence, difference, change and discontinuity.

At this point I wish to synthesise my discussion about the three stages inherent to a replicative experiment. Consider the following excerpt describing Michel Lorblanchet's pioneering parietal experiments:

> Following the aboriginal practices he had witnessed, Lorblanchet first made a light outline sketch of the horses with a charred stick. Then he prepared black pigment for the painting. [...] To turn the charcoal into paint, Lorblanchet ground it with a limestone block, put the powder in his mouth, and diluted it to the right consistency with saliva and water. For red pigment he used ocher from the local iron-rich clay. He started with the dark mane of the right-hand horse. I spat a series of dots and fused them together to represent tufts of hair, he says, unself-consciously reproducing the spitting action as he talks. Then I painted the horse's back by blowing the pigment below my hand held so – he holds his hand flat against the rock with his thumb tucked in to form a straight line – and used it like a stencil to produce a sharp upper edge and a diffused lower edge. You get an illusion of the animal's rounded flank this way. He experimented as he went. You see the angular rump?, he says, pointing to the original painting. I reproduced that by holding my hand perpendicular to the rock, with my palm slightly bent, and I spat along the edge formed by my hand and the rock. He found he could produce sharp lines, such as those in the tail and in the upper hind leg, by spitting into the gap between parallel hands. The belly demanded more ingenuity; he spat paint into a V-shape formed by his two splayed hands, rubbed it into a curved swath to shape the belly's outline, then finger-painted short protruding lines to suggest the animals' shaggy hair. Neatly outlined dots, he found, could not be made by blowing a thin jet of charcoal onto the wall – he had to spit pigment through a hole made in an animal skin. I spent seven hours a day for a week, he says. Puff . . . puff . . . puff . . . [...] But you experience something special, painting like that. You feel you are breathing the image onto the rock – projecting your spirit from the deepest part of your body onto the rock surface. Was that what the Palaeolithic painter felt when creating this image? Yes, I know it doesn't sound very scientific (Lewin, *http://www.discover.com/issues/jul-93/features/paleolithicpaint240/*).

While Lorblanchet's overall concerns are, I would suggest, rather outside scientific interests, his methodology as described provides a workable blueprint for a new approach to replicative experiments. Unfortunately, Lorblanchet's attempt at 'going native' was an ethnographic absurdity that is a common occurrence in certain archaeological circles. '*Breathing the image*' is a lovely metaphor, but confers to Lorblanchet's experiment both an ethnocentric dimension and methodological *naiveté* that is regrettable. According to Lorblanchet, the main concern for his experimentation was to re-experience the type of internal feelings the palaeo-painters were subjected to while manufacturing parietal images. While this might be a noble and genuine concern, it is subjective and unscientific. This obvious lack of rigour is an unfortunate departure from what could have easily been a seminal scientific investigation. Replicative experiments of restored behaviour must be performed in controlled environment and under rigorous methodological parameters. Obviously, the more controlled and the more scientific the experiment(s), then the more rigorous the testing of the hypotheses.

In this article, I have tried to show that paying attention to behavioural 'details', and shifting some of rock art research paradigmatic concerns could result in providing rock art research with an improved set of investigative tools for the 21st century. The hermeneutic frenzy is being readjusted and redirected towards a more phenomenological attitude where questions of epistemology, ontology and behaviour are carefully examined. The emerging discourse is still embryonic, but is already more empirical than most of the past efforts that have relied on 'perennial' facts that were in fact as temporal as the era they were issued in. I believe that it is through changes in trends and through paradigmatic shifts that progress is made. Even if it hurts, this inescapable reality must be the guiding force of rock art research.

References

BEDNARIK, R.G. (1992) – Early subterranean chert mining. *The Artefact*. Melbourne. 15, p. 11-24.

BEDNARIK, R.G. (1998) – The technology of petroglyphs. *Rock Art Research*. Melbourne. 15: 1, p. 23-35.

BEDNARIK, R.G. (2001) – *Rock art science: the scientific study of palaeoart*. Tournhout: Brepols, 219 p.

BEDNARIK, R.G. (2002) – The human ascent: a critical review. *Anthropologie*. Brno. 40: 2, p. 101-105.

BOUISSAC, P. Gestures in evolutionary perspective. *http://www.semioticon.com/virtuals/evolutionofgestures.2.pdf*

CLOTTES, J. (2005) – Prehistoric images and medicines under the sea. *International Newsletter of Rock Art*. Foix. 42, p. 1-8.

HARRIS, M. (1964) – *The nature of cultural things*. New York: Random House.

MONTELLE, Y.-P. (2006) – 'Cosquer redécouvert', Book review for *Rock Art Research*. Melbourne. 23, p. 130-132.

MONTELLE, Y.-P. (2003) – Rock art as mapping. *Before Farming* 2003: 2(4).

ODELL, G. (2003) – *Lithic analysis*. New York: Springer.

SHARPE, K. & L. VAN GELDER (2006) – The study of finger flutings. *Cambridge Archaeological Journal*. Cambridge. 16, p. 281-295.

SCHIFFER, M.B. (1995) – *Behavioral archaeology – first principles*. Utah: University of Utah Press.

SCHIFFER, M.B. (1999) – Behavioral archaeology: some clarifications. *American Antiquity* 64, p. 166-168.

STOUT, D., TOTH, N., SCHICK, K., STOUT, J.C. & HUTCHINS, G. (2000) – Stone tool-making and brain activation: Positron Emission Tomography (PET) studies'. *Journal of Archaeological Science* 27, p. 1215-1223.

PHI IN THE ACHEULIAN: LOWER PALAEOLITHIC INTUITION AND THE NATURAL ORIGINS OF ANALOGY*

John FELIKS

32619 Dover St., Garden City, MI 48135, U.S.A., feliks@umich.edu

Abstract: *The ratio 1.618, commonly known as the golden ratio or phi, has fascinated the modern mind since the beginnings of Greek science and philosophy, and many have made cases for its use as early as the Sumerian and Egyptian civilizations. In this paper, however, I hope to demonstrate that interest in the ratio extends much farther back in time than a mere four or five thousand years, being already highly developed during the Lower Palaeolithic. At whatever point it first occurred, I suggest that interest in phi was an essential human trait that grew in tandem with the human capacity for analogy. With the cranial ratios of Turkana Boy (Walker and Leakey 1993) and the stone handaxe ratios of Gowlett (1984, 1993) serving as stable early references, I provide evidence of phi spanning 1.6 million years time. In the central studies, I expand on the work of Mania and Mania (1988) and Bednarik (1995), and demonstrate that the hominins at Bilzingsleben, Germany, 350,000 years ago, continued the long established phi tradition in ways that prove its existence beyond the long-debated handaxe ratio issue into microlithic tools and intricate bone engravings, adhering more accurately and more consistently to the ratio than the most often cited examples in modern culture. The intense concentration of phi in so many forms within Bilzingsleben is well beyond any expectations of chance. Based on the evidence, I suggest that phi was not only a centralizing element in general Acheulian culture but due to its intrinsic analogical quality played a defining role in the actual development of human cognition. Deliberate use of phi suggests that human understanding of analogy occurred much earlier in our history than ever anticipated, and by way of a "mathematical idea" which has remained firmly rooted in human thought to this very day.*

Keywords: *Cognitive Archaeology, Bilzingsleben, Phi, Analogy, Linguistics*

Résumé: *Le rapport 1.618, communément connu comme le "rapport d'or" ou "phi", a fasciné l'esprit moderne depuis les débuts de science grecque et de philosophie, et beaucoup ont fait des cas pour son usage dès les civilisations de Sumerian et l'égyptien. Dans ce papier, pourtant, j'espère démontrer que l'intérêt pour le rapport prolonge un beaucoup plus lointain à temps que seul quatre ou cinq mille ans, étant déjà hautement développé pendant le Palaeolithic inférieur. À n'importe quel point il s'est d'abord produit, je suggère que l'intérêt pour phi était un trait humain essentiel qui a grandi dans de tandem avec la capacité humaine pour analogie. Avec les rapports crâniens du "Garçon de Turkana" (Walker et Leakey 1993) et la continuité d'Acheulian handaxe rapports (Gowlett 1984, 1993) être les fortes premières références, je fournis l'évidence du rapport phi enjambant la période de 1.6 million d'ans. Dans les études centrales, j'exame le travail de Mania et Mania (1988) et Bednarik (1995), et démontre que les hominids chez Bilzingsleben, Allemagne, il y a 350.000 ans, ont continué la longue tradition établie de phi des manières qui prouvent son existence au delà des détails souvent discutés de rapport de handaxes vers le contexte des outils microlithic et des gravures complexes d'os, adhérant plus exactement et plus uniformément au rapport que les exemples le plus souvent cités dans la culture moderne. La concentration intense de phi dans tant de formes dans Bilzingsleben est bien au delà de toutes les espérances de chance. Basé sur l'évidence, je suggère que phi n'était pas seulement un élément centralisant en général la culture d'Acheulian mais en raison de son qualité analogique intrinsèque il a joué un définissant rôle dans le développement réel de cognition humaine. L'utilisation délibérée de rapport de phi suggère que la compréhension humaine d'analogie se soit produit beaucoup plus tôt dans notre histoire que jamais prévue, et par guise d'une "idée mathématique" qui est demeurée fermement établie dans pensée humaine même jusqu'à aujourd'hui.*

Mots clés: *Archéologie Cognitive, Bilzingsleben, Phi, Analogie, Linguistique*

INTRODUCTION

Archaeology has typically been reluctant to attribute conscious mathematical skills to any peoples other than our own species, *Homo sapiens*. The most advanced mathematical attribution even remotely considered for early peoples such as *Homo erectus*, *Homo ergaster*, Neanderthals, and *Homo heidelbergensis*, is that of sequential counting. And although this counting is sometimes extended to include the concept of "calendar," more often than not considerations never go beyond matters of simple tallying. This has been a difficult perspective for archaeology to break away from because in our zeal to see *Homo sapiens* as an intellectual pinnacle, viewing early peoples as less intelligent than us enables them to conveniently serve as "half-way-there" links in a developmental chain. In this paper, I hope to demonstrate that one advanced mathematical concept at least–that of ratio–was well understood by all of the early humans listed above, and that it was their natural inclination toward the specific ratio of phi that led to the human cognitive attribute known as analogy.

Acknowledging the capacity for analogy in early peoples is significant because it is through analogy that nearly all aspects of advanced cognition become possible; whereas to acknowledge only sequential counting need attribute nothing more to these peoples than understanding the concepts of

* This paper is the second half of a two-part program which the author presented at the XVth UISPP Congress. The first half was Program #C80-05, 'The graphics of Bilzingsleben: Sophistication and subtlety in the mind of Homo erectus.'

accumulation, reduction, or simple references to time. I suggest that our tendency to view sequentially engraved lines in artifacts as mere tallies (if anything at all) has caused us to miss the most meaningful core of mathematics, the double-serving rational concept and intuitive sense of ratio.

It is not the purpose of this paper to focus on the association between ratio (a mathematical term) and analogy (a much broader term encompassing virtually every form of human cognition, in that all cognition is based upon relationships between abstract points). Rather, its purpose is to offer refutable archaeological and morphological evidence that the capacity for analogy developed during the Lower Palaeolithic as suggested by the mirror concept of ratio–especially fractal ratio. Since the paper was originally conceived as a visual program rather than thesis paper, it will proceed simply by way of its Figures, but will also include brief explanations of how the material fits into a larger system of analysis. The figures offered represent approximately one third of those produced for the Lisbon *Phi* program, so the reader may rest assured that there already exists substantially more evidence in support of the thesis forwarded.

INFLUENCES AND POSITION IN A LARGER SYSTEM

The theoretical aspects of this paper were inspired by the work of Gowlett (1984, 1993), Mania and Mania (1988, 2005), Bednarik (1995), Mandelbrot (1982), Eglash (1999), Mikiten *et al.* (2000), Chomsky (1972), Sacks (1999, 2002), Capra (1982) and others. However, the thesis revolves around three core ideas or observations: (1) Gowlett's observation that Acheulian people were remarkably consistent in the length-to-width ratios of their handaxes, a fact which he regards as a sign of "mathematical transformations" (Gowlett 1984: 185), (2) Mania and Mania's and Bednarik's observations that engraved artifacts at Bilzingsleben represent the earliest graphic evidence of language, and (3) various associations between seemingly unrelated elements, fractal structures, systems, etc., influenced by the work of Eglash, Mikiten, Chomsky, Pinker, Sacks, Greene, Capra, Bohm, and others (as listed in the references).

To be detailed in a later publication, I will explain here that the evidence offered is part of a fractal system fully capable of translating the "core ideas" of Lower and Middle Palaeolithic peoples. In this system, facts work as concepts rather than traditionally like letters of an alphabet, enabling access to complex Palaeolithic ideas without the need for text or standard representational images. And while presently not common in archaeology, the system also quite reasonably provides access to ideas regarding various dimensions of time.

Bednarik and Mania and Mania have long promoted the idea that *Homo erectus* and other early hominins had capabilities not far removed from our own. It is through conclusions reached by thorough study and confidence in their work that I decided to approach the matter from the top down rather than the bottom up, and suggest that once a single profoundly advanced capability is proven, no matter how esoteric it may seem (e.g., use of a "dimensionless fundamental constant" such as phi), the floodgates will open, and before long, discussions of Lower Palaeolithic "philosophy" will be far more scientific than discussions of whether or not these people were intelligent enough to throw a stick, which is essentially where the issue has been stuck for the past one hundred years. Twenty years ago the idea of "cognitive archaeology" itself (a term coined by Colin Renfrew) seemed an impossible pursuit. This is obviously no longer the case as researchers are coming into the field in droves from every other field imaginable.

To clarify an earlier point, the challenge that phi and other ideas in the new paradigm presents for anthropology is that early hominins can no longer be used as convenient "half-way-there" links between the lowly *Ardipithecus* and the allegedly superior modern *Homo sapiens*. Other perspectives will need to be adopted because in light of all the evidence for higher culture beginning to surface the smaller-than-*sapiens* brain of *Homo erectus* now creates as much of a problem for the idea of gradually evolving intelligence as did the larger-than-*sapiens* Neanderthal brain. Brain configuration theories are equally weakened as they too position evolving intellectual ability as a given. Bednarik has long stated that human intellectual development had nothing to do with physical evolution. I concur, but am compelled one step further, and suggest that the very idea of gradually increasing intellectual ability (not accumulation of knowledge) is itself a myth. In other words, once someone brought out the football, in this case, consciousness based on analogy, there were plenty who could already instantly run with it. Analogy, as I propose, was the idea that engendered other ideas. The hard part was the initial idea or spark. Assimilation of the idea into culturally-preserved cognition, and subsequent rapid accumulation of other ideas was comparatively effortless. The Acheulian age discovery of phi by *Homo erectus* engendered a "mathematical" idea which had a profound effect on all subsequent human species and which suggests that the completely modern human mind began 2 million years ago rather than a mere 40, 100, or even 350 thousand years ago. For these reasons I suggest that phi is the oldest abstract knowledge passed down intact by way of culture, and support this proposition with its unique testability. It is regarded a significant related matter that the oldest large-scale non-hemispheric ratio within the human brain is also phi (as demonstrated below). Accrediting phi and analogy appropriately to *Homo erectus* solves many problems that have long hindered cognitive archaeology, not the least of which was the specific ability to create fire. As another critical example, the aptitude for analogy also makes the island hopping of this species over 800,000 years ago (an idea fully developed in Bednarik's [1997] open sea bamboo raft voyages) not the least bit difficult to accept; otherwise we are stuck with old paradigm views such that

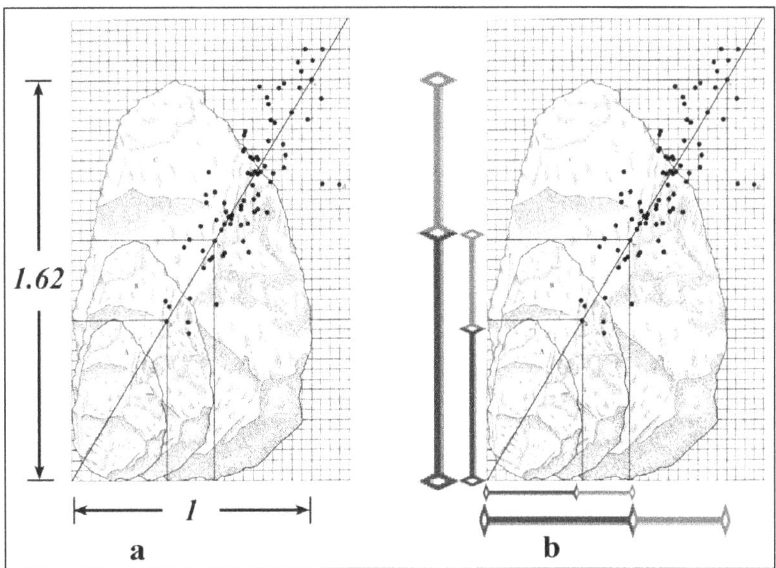

Figure 2.1. Long-time awareness and use of the Phi ratio, 1.618. (a) Gowlett's observation regarding consistency of handaxe ratios from Kilombe, Kenya, over a wide range of sizes (the largest is 17cm), c. 700,000 BP. (Graphic by John Gowlett 1993. Ascent to Civilization: The Archaeology of Early Humans. Used with permission of The McGraw-Hill Companies. Ratio numbers were added for clarity.) While not identified as the "golden ratio," it is now known as the general ratio of choice for handaxes during the Acheulian. (b) Gowlett's homage to the ratio in his graphic layout choices, representing the most efficient example of Phi's ubiquitous role in human creativity.

Homo erectus could only have accomplished this profound task on mats of floating vegetation.

DISCLAIMERS AND NOMENCLATURE

All geometric studies are of the utmost accuracy and exactly as stated. The tolerances applied are clearly visible. However, Mania and Mania's original drawings were not made with such meticulous studies in mind, so qualities of the actual artifacts may vary slightly.

While attempting to navigate the maze of ever-changing and debated hominin names, I will occasionally generalize by referring to early or Lower Palaeolithic peoples as a single group rather than specify whether or not certain researchers regard local populations as *erectus*, *ergaster*, *heidelbergensis*, etc. Since virtually all of the literature cited in this paper (as recent as 2005) uses the name *Homo erectus*, I will not feel any sense of obligation to spell out every alternative interpretation when referring to these texts, and will adhere essentially to the name used in the original publications. To be certain, this paper is about Lower Palaeolithic cognition regardless of the species involved.

Conventionally, uppercase "Phi" is used to denote the ratio 1.618 (or positive form), while lower case "phi" is used to denote its reciprocal .618 (or negative form). Not everyone adheres to this convention, and in this paper's present version, phi may appear in either form. The most significant point is that Phi is the only number whose "reciprocal" (the number which when multiplied by equals 1; also known as "multiplicative inverse") is itself plus 1. [Note for mathematics purists only: The phrase "phi ratio" is used as a catch-all term and may be written in this paper as 1.618, .618, .382, .618/.382, .382/.618, or 1/2 phi ratio .309, and for the sake of convenience, etc., .618/1.618 may be used instead of .618/1 or 1/1.618. The author, whose background is in the arts rather than mathematics, went for simplification and poetry.]

"Phi-based conceptual units," Part 1: the ratio that crosses time and species (Figure 2.1)

Although Gowlett did not describe it as such, phi is the first archaeologically identifiable ratio to cross over from the natural world into the world of human ideas. It might perhaps be understood as one of the earliest "cognitive archetypes", having been with humanity from the beginning. Complete within a single three-point phi line segment is a ratio and a fractal–the fractal suggesting its own self-similar replication into realms of the infinitely large and the infinitely small, hence, an analogy. As such, phi is the single most efficient concept capable of opening the human mind to every other area of intellectual inquiry. It is from this perspective that I propose that Lower Palaeolithic thoughts may be accessed in reference to what I am calling "phi-based conceptual units."

However, as demonstrated in Figures 2.1 and 2.2, phi does not end as a line. The phi "line" represents only its one-dimensional aspect. Phi was employed in the handaxe technologies of all Acheulian and Mousterian peoples as a "two-dimensional" ratio. This fact makes phi the ratio

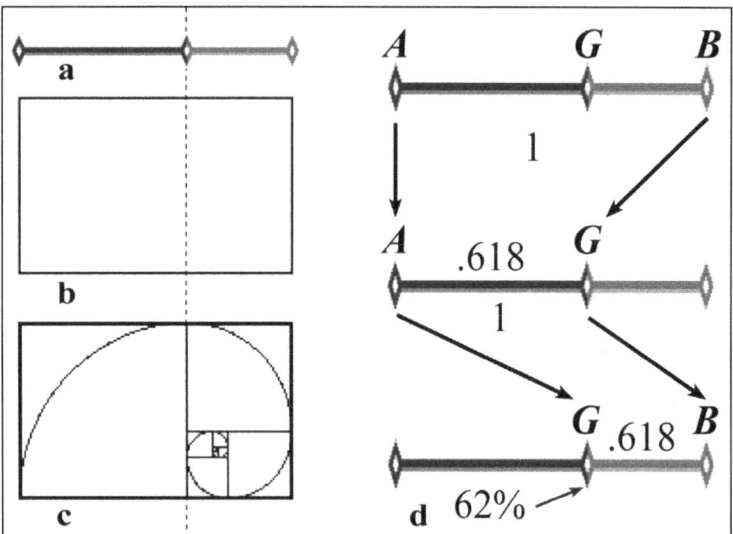

Figure 2.2. Phi measuring tools. These shapes are based on the ratio 1.618, and are commonly known as (a) "golden line, (b) "golden rectangle," and (c) "golden spiral." Each of these tools measure by ratio. Measuring by ratio is more transparent than measuring by any equal-increment system as relationships between and within objects are visible instantly and unambiguously. (d) General explanation of phi and the phi line measuring tool. This tool will be used to test if any "three" significant points demonstrate phi or the golden mean. The unique quality of phi can be described like this: The complete line (AB) is to the larger portion (AG) what the larger portion is to the smaller portion (GB). "G" is a convention referring to the phi point or "gold" point. Phi can also be thought of as a point around 62% into the line. Euclid described it as "dividing a line between extreme and mean ratio." The "line" tool is from a public domain graphic by Eisnel.

equally representing the cognition of all post-*habilis* early human species from *ergaster* and *erectus* through *heidelbergensis* and Neanderthal (its use by modern *Homo sapiens* is, of course, well known). Phi can also be represented in three and four dimensions including time, and if one is open to such as string theory, a great deal more dimensions useful in cognitive archaeology, as well.

It has long been agreed that the Acheulian handaxe represents one of the most important milestones in human cognitive development. It is hard to believe with all the knowledge now gleaned from handaxes, that when they were first discovered many archaeologists regarded them as "worthless pebbles" (R. Bednarik, pers. comm.). The list of researchers who now study handaxes has grown immensely, with many profound implications being suggested regarding the handaxe makers. For instance, in addition to the uncountable survival–related perspectives, handaxes have also been interpreted in regards to religion, e.g., Harrod 2003; and sexuality, e.g., Mithen 2003. See also Feliks 1998a, 1998b, and 2006 for the "earliest iconic image framed by a human being" (detailed geometric studies of a fossil scallop shell located in the exact center of a 250,000 year old handaxe). The aspect focused on in this paper is Gowlett's observation that the handaxe demonstrates a remarkably unexpected consistency of ratio over a vast range of sizes and spanning a million years time. Among other things, Gowlett regards this consistency of ratio as nothing less than the foundation of mathematics (Gowlett 1984: 183–85). Most archaeologists are willing to admit something of this nature now, albeit, reservedly, but after his own extensive systematic studies, Gowlett had no reservations:

> "Making hand-axes in the same proportions at different sizes provides the earliest practical demonstration of principles treated hundreds of thousands of years later in Euclid's *Elements of Geometry*" (Gowlett 1993: 71).

It is perhaps no coincidence in Gowlett's point-of-view that Euclid is also regarded as the first to offer a clear definition of the golden mean, referring to it as "dividing a line between extreme and mean ratio" (Euclid, c. 300 B.C.). Euclid's line and the two other main phi measuring tools used in this paper will now be introduced.

Phi measuring tools: how the "phi-based conceptual units" will be demonstrated (Figure 2.2)

Figure 2.2 gives a brief overview of the line, rectangle, and spiral phi tools by which the ratio relationships in this paper will be visually measured. Means of calculating the Palaeolithic phi "decimal" will be introduced separately. Apart from the one-dimensional, two-dimensional, and decimal forms of phi demonstrated in this paper, there are many other means by which the value of Phi may be demonstrated in the work of Lower and Middle Palaeolithic peoples.

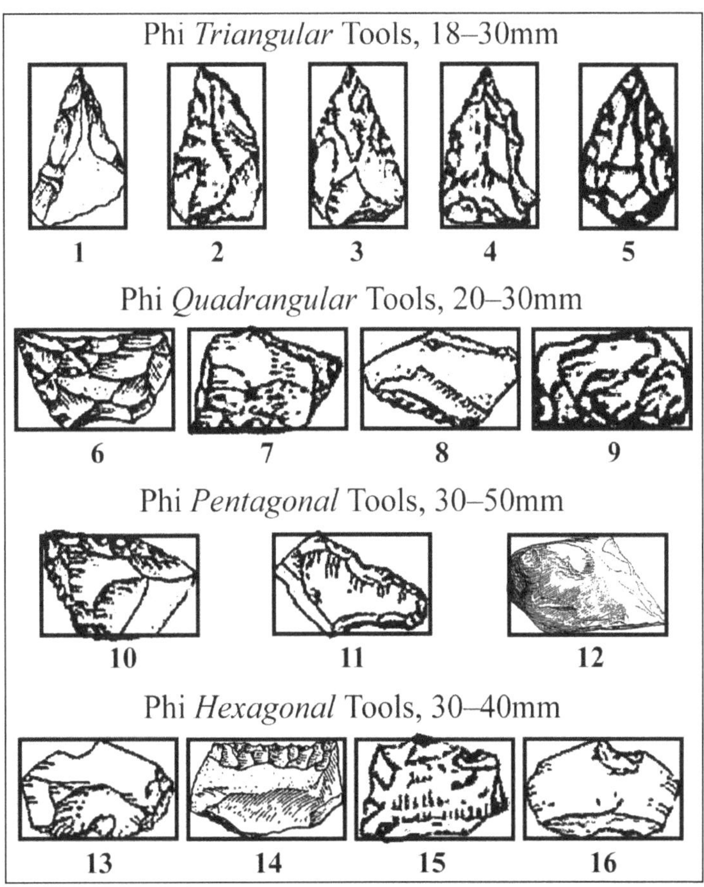

Figure 2.3. Phi in the Bilzingsleben microliths. (#s 1–11 & 13–16) Compiled from J. Svoboda, 1987. Lithic industries of the Arago, Vértesszöllös, and Bilzingsleben hominids: Comparison and evolutionary interpretation. Current Anthropology 28(2): 219–27. Used with permission of The University of Chicago Press. (#12) D. Mania and U. Mania 2003. Bilzingsleben - Homo erectus, his culture and his environment. The most important results of research. In Lower Palaeolithic Small Tools in Europe and The Levant. Edited by J.M. Burdukiewicz and A. Ronen, BAR S1115, 2003:29–48. Used with permission.

"Phi-based conceptual units," Part 2: Phi fractals in the Bilzingsleben microliths (Figure 2.3)

Bilzingsleben has sometimes been classified as an Acheulian site that lacks the standard Acheulian handaxe. However, as Mania and Mania point out (2005: 105–6), many of the microlithic tools are "reminiscent" of bifaces (tools worked on both front and back like handaxes, and often patterned in the well-known tear shape). This is actually an understatement, as many of the microliths are *exact replicas* of Acheulian handaxes only in miniature. Although there are many ratios represented in the Bilzingsleben microliths, for this paper I have only isolated a few that specifically demonstrate perfection of the phi ratio.

The earliest perfection of miniaturization: Seeing the miniature phi ratio at 10x magnification (Figure 2.4)

While the microliths are not the smallest example of Phi at Bilzingsleben (for the measure presently holding this position see Fig. 2.17), they are certainly the smallest examples of a standardized 2-D phi-based shape with a proven creative history of over a million years. They represent "flawless" variations on a standard whose duration of existence has never been surpassed, nor, likely, ever will be.

This early example of a technology's progression from extremely large to extremely small (i.e. Acheulian phi handaxes to Acheulian phi microliths) is not at all unlike innumerable examples in our own time such as evidenced in the similar developments of gears and microchips. And considering the restricting factors with which Lower Palaeolithic peoples were working–such as the slower spread of ideas due to smaller populations, lack of "easy access" to externally-stored knowledge (Donald 1991), or the fact of there not being any great need driving miniaturization (e.g., such as overpopulation)–that it occurred at such a high level of refinement despite these factors is perfectly comparable to our own transition from building room-sized computers to building microcom-

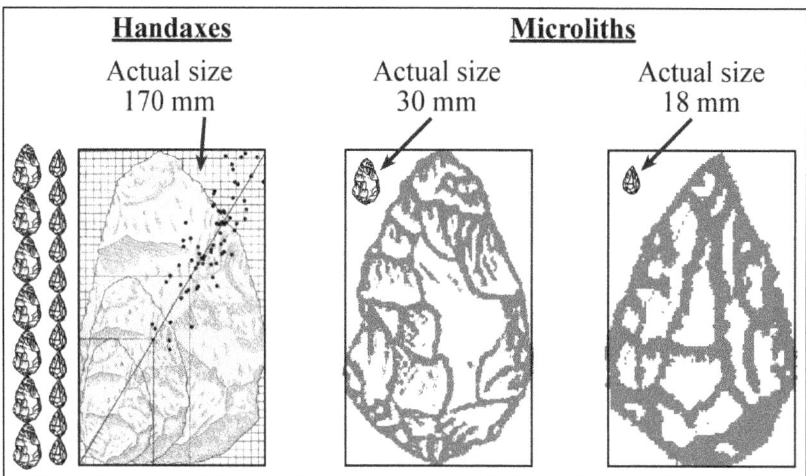

Figure 2.4. Gowlett's phi ratio discovery demonstrated to perfection by the Bilzingsleben microliths. This is the earliest evidence of miniaturization adhering to an identifiable mathematical ratio. Each enclosing rectangle is a "golden rectangle" in the ratio 1.618. The microliths and largest Acheulian handaxe have been equalized in size so that their identical ratios are readily seen. The several insets show the microliths as they compare in actual size to the handaxes, being up to 11 times smaller. (Kilombe handaxes, Gowlett 1993. Bilzingsleben microliths, Svoboda 1987.) The microliths also represent the earliest evidence for miniaturization of a pre-established technology, 350,000 years before the comparable histories of gears and microchips. Since microlithic tools are traditionally associated with highly advanced cultures, their presence at Bilzingsleben helps to confirm deliberate sophistication of the site's engravings.

puters. In fact, since we have always had knowledge of earlier technologies to guide us, while Lower Palaeolithic peoples started everything from scratch, the analogy should probably be extended to include our as-yet-to-be nanocomputer. I predict that population math, etc., will bear these assertions out. In case the point is not clear, the microlith/microcomputer comparison is another way of saying that we as modern "individuals" are really no more intelligent than the average Lower Palaeolithic individual.

"Phi-based conceptual units," Part 3: The golden groups: A starting point for linguistics and mathematics (Figures 2.5–2.9)

I will now proceed to what I regard as one of the most profound leaps in human creativity–*transformation of a specific and "measurable" idea from one medium into an entirely different and unrelated medium.* The engraved artifact sets offered here lend support to the idea that the ratio common to handaxes does indeed represent a "mental template," because the ratios inherent in engraved artifacts cannot be explained away as the necessary result of stone tool structural mechanics. Figures 2.5–2.9 are self-explanatory and may be considered with the next few paragraphs of text which is developed in parallel.

From the evidence currently available, it may be regarded as fact that at Bilzingsleben the long-established phi ratio of the Acheulian handaxe was transferred into intricately complex bone engravings. There are so many examples of the ratio at this small site, and in so many different forms and sizes that it is not at all difficult to see that by the time of Bilzingsleben, phi had become, at the very least, a superbly developed intuition, expressing itself in far from obvious terms. These terms cannot be explained away by simple concepts such as efficiency, etc., as though the makers of such things as handaxes were incapable of doing anything beyond putting the least amount of effort required into any project in order to get a quick result. This leads to the idea that phi, in abstract terms, was a "universal motif" expressing itself in one way or another across the entire range of Acheulian cultural groups that used the handaxe. The acknowledged range of this culture (or toolkit designation, if preferred) has been expanding in recent years. In particular, it was once thought that handaxe technology did not extend into eastern Asia, a perspective that was marked off by a boundary known as the "Movius Line." However, this line is continuously being adjusted. At the time this paper was submitted, the author had access to only two images of the recently discovered handaxes from China's Bose Basin. However, that was enough, momentarily at least, to discover that the average length-to-width ratio between the two handaxes was 1.642, easily comparable to the 1.618 of Phi.

The search for universal motifs is not new, being explored by early writers such as Plato, and many later writers such as Chomsky (who formulated his universal grammars long before physical evidence was available to corroborate any of his ideas archaeologically). However, it is only during the past 15 years or so that shared motifs have been discussed in the context of dissimilar human species. This

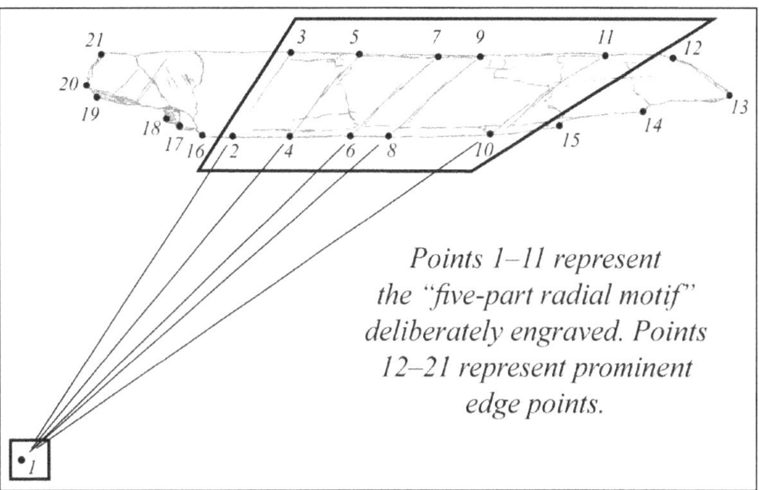

Figure 2.5. Numbering system used in studies associated with the radial motif of Artifact 2. Note #1: Lines which do not participate in the radial motif are not focused upon in this particular series. Note #2: Although part of a larger set including triangles, trapezoids, parallelograms, only studies related to phi via circles and rectangles are focused upon in this paper. Artifact 2 after Mania and Mania 1988. Artifact 2 is the flat rib bone of a large mammal, and measures 286mm in length by 36mm in width.

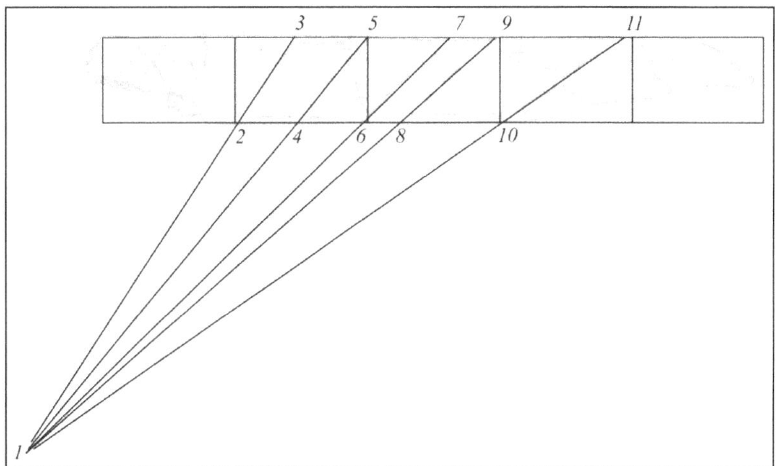

Figure 2.6. "Golden groups" division of the Artifact 2 radial motif via three identical golden rectangles. Artifact 2 "radials" were introduced in Musings on the Palaeolithic Fan Motif.

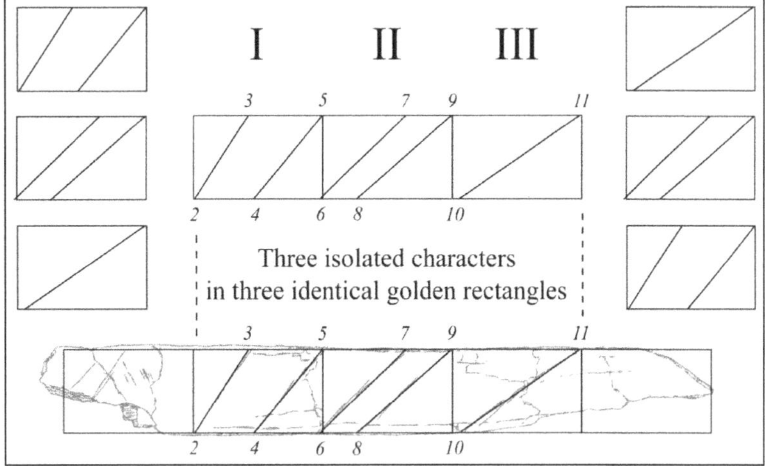

Figure 2.7. The "golden groups" as isolated characters.

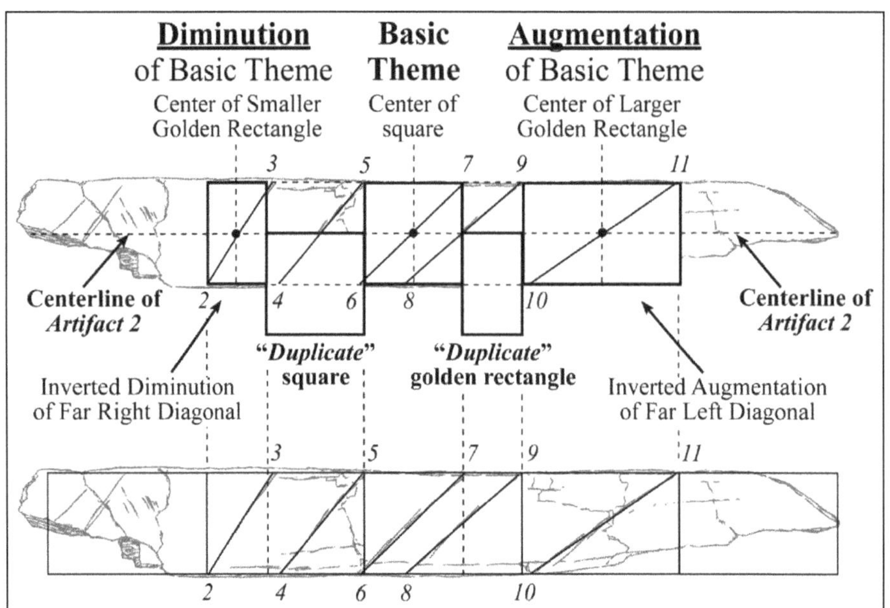

Figure 2.8. Diminution and augmentation in the Artifact 2 golden groups. These and other terms were appropriated from Bach fugue writing and are useful tools for exploring analog structures in language (e.g., revisiting the deep and surface structure of Chomsky's "universal grammar") and mathematics (e.g., progressive fractals, logarithm), to name only two. They can provide insights into many other disparate areas of the pre-sapiens psyche.

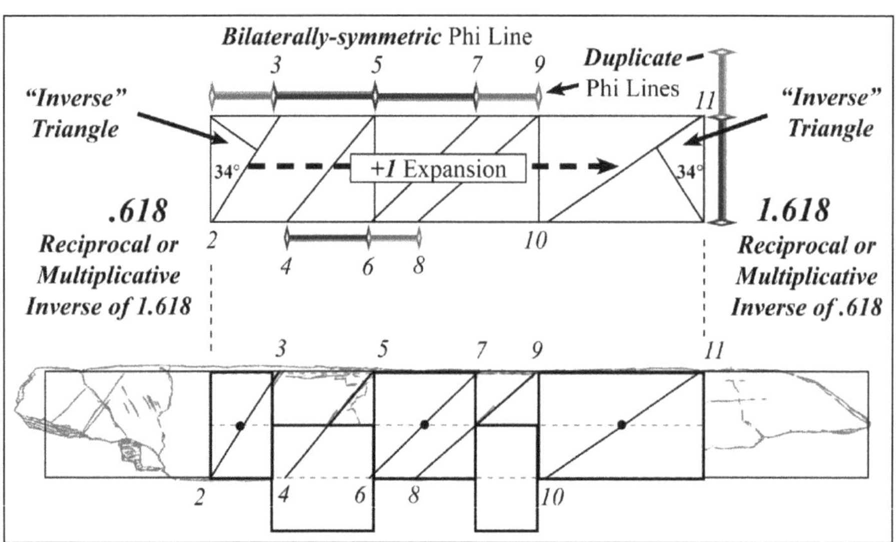

Figure 2.9. Inverse triangles in the Artifact 2 golden groups. This is another example of how fractals offer access to multiple levels of pre-sapiens knowledge simultaneously. It is not unlike how a musical composition may be appreciated on the level of sound, but can also be understood silently by way of a musical score. The fractal qualities of this particular artifact are detailed in Part I, The Graphics of Bilzingsleben, and extend even further to the compound structure of each individual line. Like music, geometry such as that of Artifact 2 communicates universally, and has no dependence upon text or representational images. This supports Chomsky's idea that language is separate from thought (see also Pinker 1994).

important addition was most succinctly introduced in Bednarik's 1995, *Concept-mediated marking in the Lower Palaeolithic*, where he compared Acheulian and Mousterian evidence side-by-side. (See Feliks 1997, 1998 and 2006 for expansion of these and related ideas and for some background on how this line of thought also involved the work of Leroi-Gourhan [1961, 1964], Oakley [1973, 1981], Marshack [1977, 1990], White [1989, 1993], Dissanayake etc.) The present paper was written for the UISPP session chaired by Bednarik and Hodgson (who approaches the field from the perspective of neuroscience) which included a specific call for researchers to begin identifying universals in the archaeological record.

A most important new approach toward understanding early human thought involves fractals, as brought to the fore by researchers such as Eglash and Mikiten. Fractals are patterns which exhibit repeating "self-similar structure" at larger or smaller sizes (i.e. "fractal levels"), and can be expressed in many different ways including abstract terms; but they are most easily visualized two-dimensionally such as seen in the branches and leaves of ferns. Most of the math regarding fractals has only been developed during the past 25 years or so beginning with the landmark work of Mandelbrot (e.g., 1982). Since then, fractals have transformed every field of science, and the influence of fractals on ideas in philosophy, psychology and neuroscience is profound. It is from this perspective that I am proposing the phi fractal as an early cognitive archetype via "phi-based conceptual units." Phi has the ability to serve such a role because it has proven cohesive enough to cross from its already critical role in the natural world into the cognitive world of human creativity. The following perspective, while not specifically referring to phi, adds support to the idea of phi-based conceptual units:

> "When a fractal system generates a new system, it has the same attributes and characteristics as the generator… Thus, mental associations that would appear at first to require enormous lengths of code (and consequently be termed complex) may in fact be handled by very short codes. If that is indeed the case, then the human mind could be using fractal encoding as a standard way of coding enormous chains of related thought into a single fractal entity" (Mikiten *et. al.* 2000).

The fractal system I am proposing revolves around how a single ratio, namely Phi, can have major cognitive implications on uncountable sub-levels (or supra-levels as used in analogy). This is born out by the many subtle variations on this single theme demonstrated in Figures 2.5–2.18.

Beyond the obvious examples of "perfect" phi, I suggest that minor deviations from the ratio (e.g., as visible in the off-diagonal points of Gowlett's graph, Fig. 2.1) reflect the natural tendency of all peoples to develop subtleties of discernment according to their specific geographic or cultural environments. One of the best ethnographic examples is how cultures with no history of vertical development in music (i.e. chordal, contrapuntal) develop extremely subtle horizontal (i.e. melodic) sensitivity. To take this particular example one step further, the entire "Western" system of music is based on simple half-tones, which can never compare in melodic subtlety to cultures whose music uses extensive quarter-tones such as that of various Arabic and Indian cultures. Western-trained ears are scarcely able to grasp it beyond the sensual level of sound, and psychologically may attempt to "round off" the quarter tones to the nearest half-tone, or relate such things to ornamental bending effects, etc. What I am suggesting by all of this is that we may have mistakenly interpreted the Acheulian as a "static" culture (or technology) when, in reality, it may actually represent a culture of refined subtleties, indicating high intelligence rather than the low intelligence we have traditionally ascribed to Acheulian peoples. I suggest (after e.g., Capra 1982, Bohm and Peat 1987) that a primary reason we see such things as reflecting crudeness rather than refinement has a Western science bias at its core, reflecting, among other things, our longtime preoccupation with the Cartesian grid system. It is interesting to note that since the current expansion of fractal awareness in Western science, all manner of sensibilities are being discovered where before, we could only see chaos.

Although fractal techniques have great potential for Palaeolithic linguistics (as introduced in Feliks 2006 and in the *Graphics* paper), the primary focus in this paper and the larger fractal system in general is to approach concepts which do not require text or representational images in order to be understood, i.e. cognitive archetypes. Cognitive archetypes can take many different forms, not the least of which are those present in music. Music, like words, need not be "heard" in order to be understood. In fact, as hard to believe as it may seem, someone born deaf, who has never experienced on any level can learn to compose music–even music of a complex contrapuntal texture–all by way of "theory" to such a degree that even a trained listener could not distinguish a piece written by a deaf person from one written by someone with normal hearing, hence, the following interpretations of Bilzingsleben *Artifact 2* in the terms of Western classical music (Figs. 2.8–2.9). (Note: In *The graphics of Bilzingsleben* and *Musings on the Palaeolithic fan motif*, I demonstrated how this particular artifact can also be read in terms of musical scales and rhythms, which has immediate application potential to Lower Palaeolithic spoken language.)

The golden mean in Artifact 2 circle studies, and an appeal to physics and astronomy (Figure 2.10)

Once it is understood that the influence of phi extends well beyond visible shapes or abstract numbers, much more information can be gleaned from the few Acheulian (or Mousterian) artifacts we have available for study. As noted in the *Graphics* paper, by employing extensions of engraved lines, we can access the geometric mind behind and beyond the artifacts themselves. This is possible because geometric extensions make accessible an invisible field of information outside of, but within the vicinity of, any given artifact. The extent of this field is more limited in some artifacts than in others, and the further out we go from various artifacts the more speculative the interpretations may be. However, depending on what specific information we are seeking, and despite what may be presumed, this is *not necessarily the case*, as demonstrated in the section of *Graphics* called "Proof of association between an abstract point and infinity." Depending on how the lines are organized, many interpretations of a surrounding field are perfectly safe.

If all of this seems absurd, I appeal to a well-established scientific field which, in reality, has no direct contact whatsoever with 99% of the objects it studies–namely, astronomy. Astronomers, astrophysicists, cosmologists assume

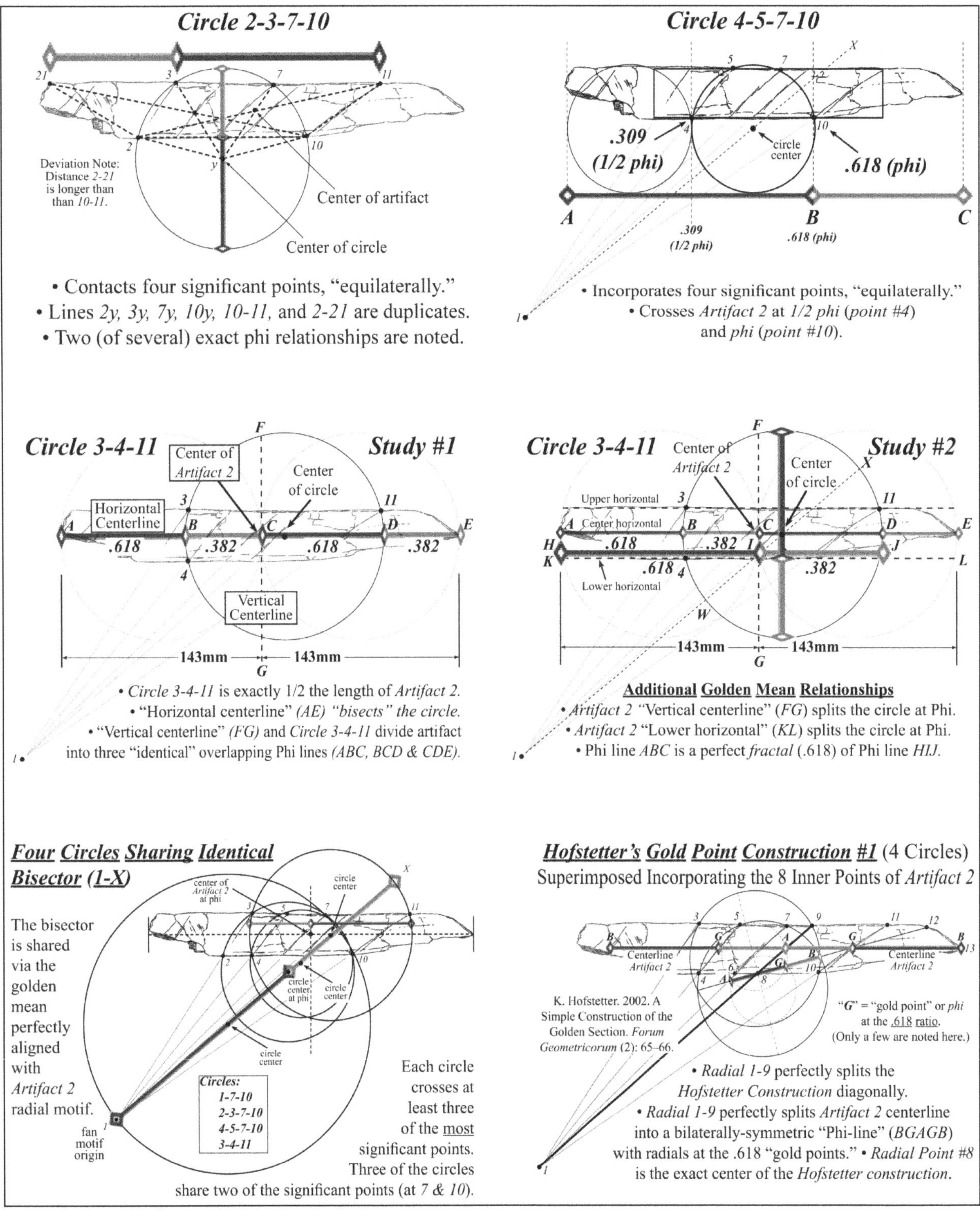

Figure 2.10. The golden mean in Artifact 2 circle studies. Whether or not it is the golden mean which is used or some other ratio is inconsequential, for it is the general idea and value of syntax based on ratio that is being proposed here. Theoretically, any ratio will offer the same kind of access to the cognition of our ancient predecessors. These studies are not offering any particular explanation for the alignments, only the knowledge that they exist. Artifact 2 after Mania and Mania 1988.

that physics works the same on the other side of the universe as it does on this side of the universe, or that various qualities do not undergo change in the process of movement from one side of the universe to the other. If astronomers and cosmologists didn't rely on these "safe" assumptions, astronomical studies based on electromag-

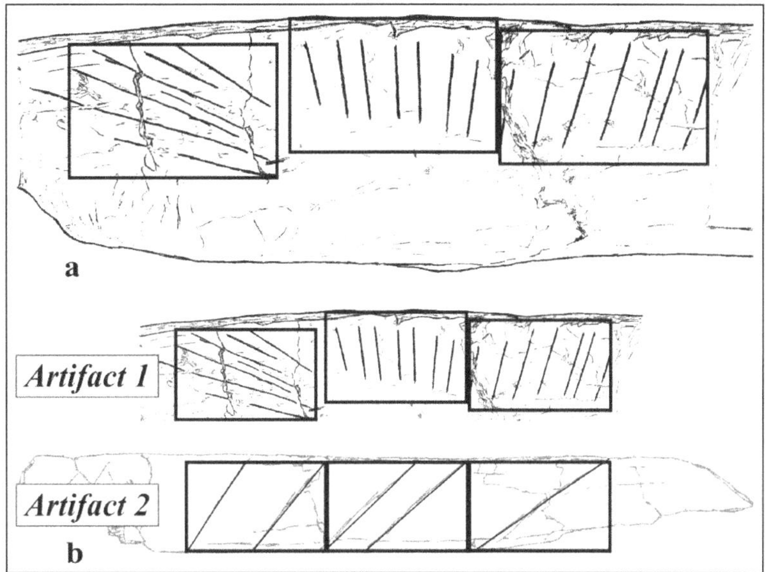

Figure 2.11. Further evidence suggesting a grasp of ratio as it relates to Phi. (a) 3 groups of 7: Golden rectangles superimposed over Artifact 1. While not as perfect a fit as the Artifact 2 "golden groups," this study suggests a definite unity of style between Artifacts 1 and 2. (b) Artifacts 1 and 2 compared. Both the motifs and rectangles are at the exact same scale, further supporting the idea of "phi-based conceptual units." Combined length lower rectangles=160mm. Artifact 1 is the tibia bone of a straight-tusked elephant. Drawing after photograph by R. Bednarik 1997. Artifact 2 after Mania and Mania 1988.

netic waves, photons, neutrinos, etc., could not be used to tell us anything at all regarding the chemical composition or age of distant stars. Everything we know about quasars and galaxies, even the Big Bang, is all derived by inference. From this perspective, therefore, I suggest that cognitive archaeology may just as appropriately infer past thought via artifacts and other items with which early peoples came into contact, since this may be regarded as evidence of equal veracity to that used in astronomy. In other words, our evidence is much closer to us in both space and time than nearly all of the evidence used in astronomy. We are able to make "direct" contact with the artifacts and even the find horizons. The only major problem, and it is substantial, is that the evidence used in cognitive archaeology is infinitely less abundant.

"Phi-based conceptual units," Part 4: Consistency of phi enclosures between two artifacts (Figure 2.11)

In the *Graphics* paper, I demonstrated that the same motif had been duplicated on two separate artifacts. The reason this was an important step is because duplicated motifs are the very hallmark of human language. A single motif can represent anything from a letter in an alphabet to the most complex multi-level construct anyone has ever imagined. And if a culture also understands variation, association, fractals, or any other concepts at all, then this very same motif can represent any number of different ideas variable by orientation, time, accompanied behavior, etc. A single motif, in other words is as versatile in the realm of communication as the Acheulian handaxe is if limited to only its utilitarian potentials. Comparing a visual motif with a single spoken word automatically takes the motif into infinitely different dimensions. With variations of inflection, repetition, etc., that one word can communicate a thousand subtle ideas.

With that background regarding the infinite potentials contained within a single motif, it is obvious how this can be expanded logarithmically when several already "loaded" motifs are used in combination with other motifs. This, of course, is nothing whatsoever new in linguistic study (see Chomsky 1972, Pinker 1994); the only thing that is new is that we are now talking this level of sophistication in regards to Lower Palaeolithic hominids.

"Phi-based conceptual units," Part 5: Fractal associations within Artifact 6 (Figure 2.12)

"Phi-based conceptual units," Part 6: Fractal associations between engravings and microliths (Figure 2.13)

The earliest "graphic" dividing line: Decimal theories 1 & 2 (Figures 2.14 & 2.15)

The earliest "graphic" dividing line: Mirror theory (Figure 2.16)

14 instances of phi in a seven-line motif (Figure 2.17)

Although evidence such as that presented in Fig. 2.17 may seem remarkable, this is only because we have been so long inundated with the idea of *Homo erectus* and other early hominins as "ape-men." If we considered such an engraving as having been created instead by the likes

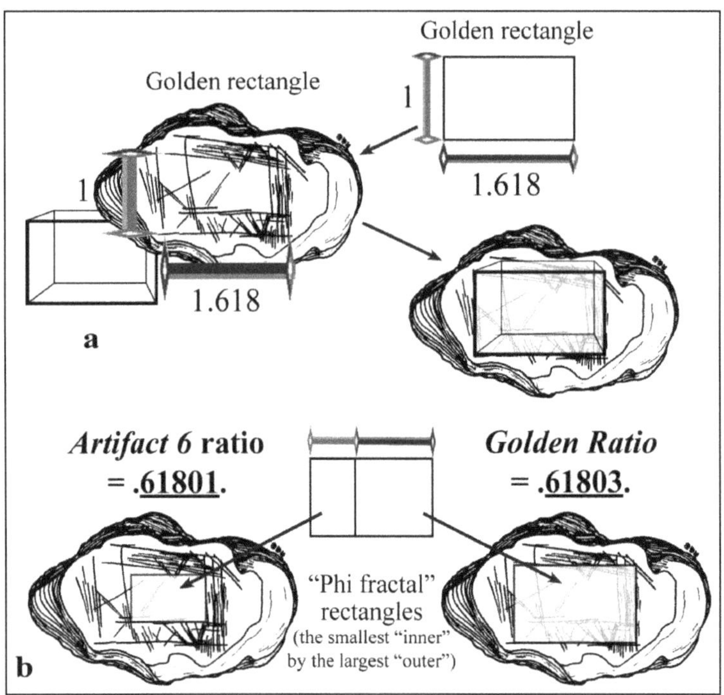

Figure 2.12. Confirmation of Phi awareness via deliberately engraved golden rectangles. (a) Artifact 6 golden rectangle and depth representation. (b) Artifact 6 fractal rectangles with phi carried out to five decimal points, supporting the idea of "phi-based conceptual units." Artifact 6 is the tarsal joint bone of a straight-tusked elephant, and measures 170mm in length. Bilzingsleben Artifact 6 drawing from Bednarik 1995. Used with permission. EXACT MEASUREMENTS for Figure 12b: The smaller Golden Rectangle (implied by its lower right 90°∠) is 48.351mm x 29.939mm. The larger Golden Rectangle (implied by its lower left 90°∠) is 78.236mm x 48.444mm. To figure the ratio between the two: 48.351 divided by 78.236% = 61.801% or .61801. The Golden Mean carried out to five decimal points is .61803. If the measures are correct it suggests either innate or deliberate Phi awareness to within 2 hundred-thousanths accuracy.

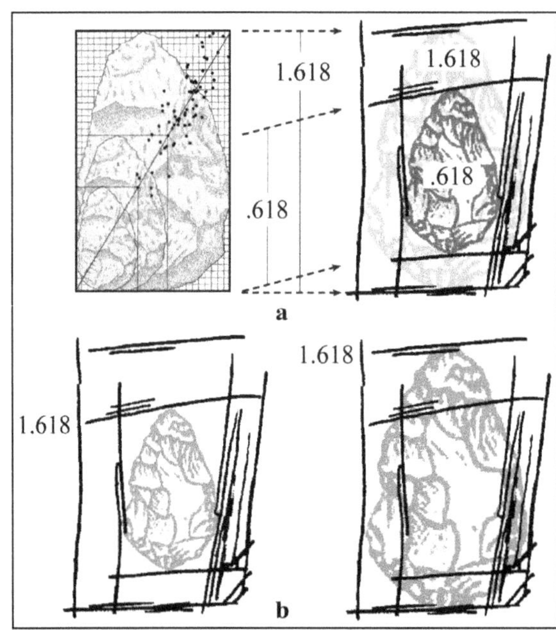

Figure 2.13. Artifact 6 golden rectangles match both the long-established Acheulian ratio standard and the layout choice for Gowlett's graph. (a) Proof that Gowlett's graph employs the exact same rectangle ratio as Artifact 6. Detail from graph by Gowlett 1993. Used with permission. Rectangles isolated from Bednarik 1995. Used with permission. Bilzingsleben microlith from Svoboda 1987. Used with permission. (b) The few parallel lines isolated from Artifact 6 reveals what may be evidence that the engraver was "tweaking" parameters–a basic technique of artists and technical designers alike. This too, supports the idea of "phi-based conceptual units."

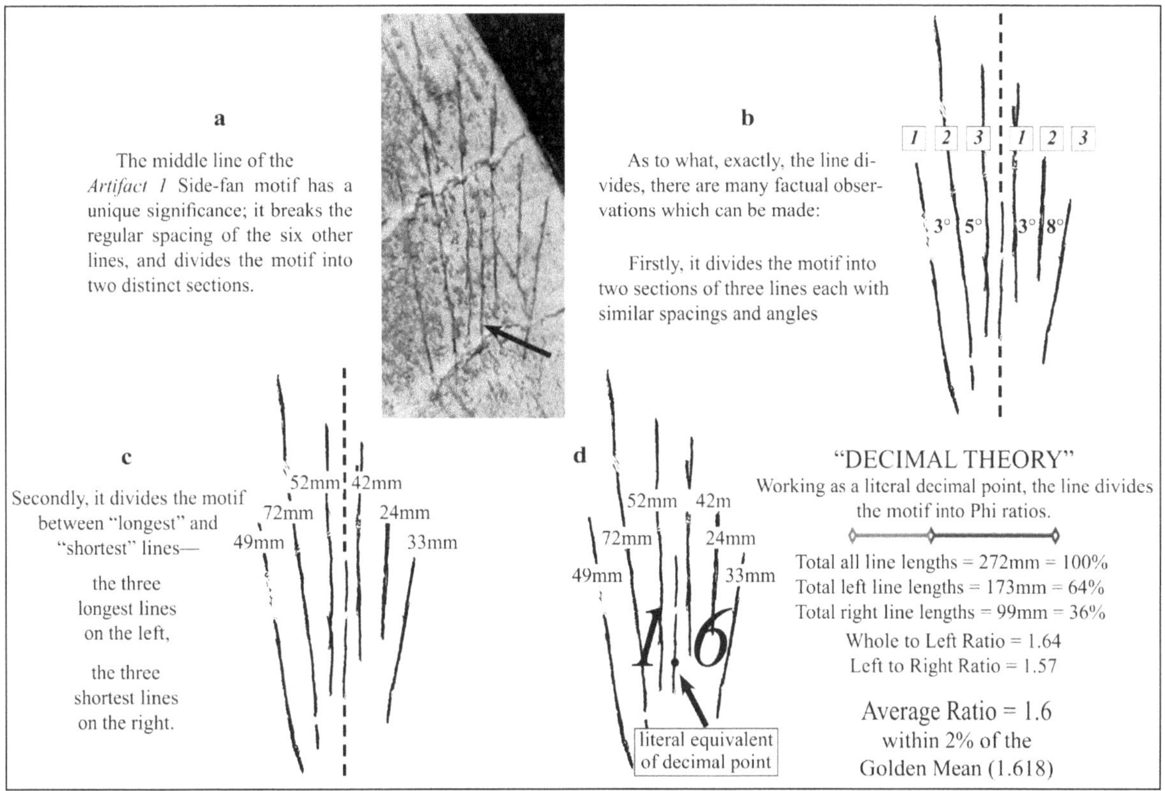

Figure 2.14. The earliest graphic dividing line (a–c) and "Decimal theory 1" (d): How the Phi ratio translates beyond three-dimensional geometry into mathematical abstraction. Artifact 1 detail from photograph by R. Bednarik 1997. Used with permission.

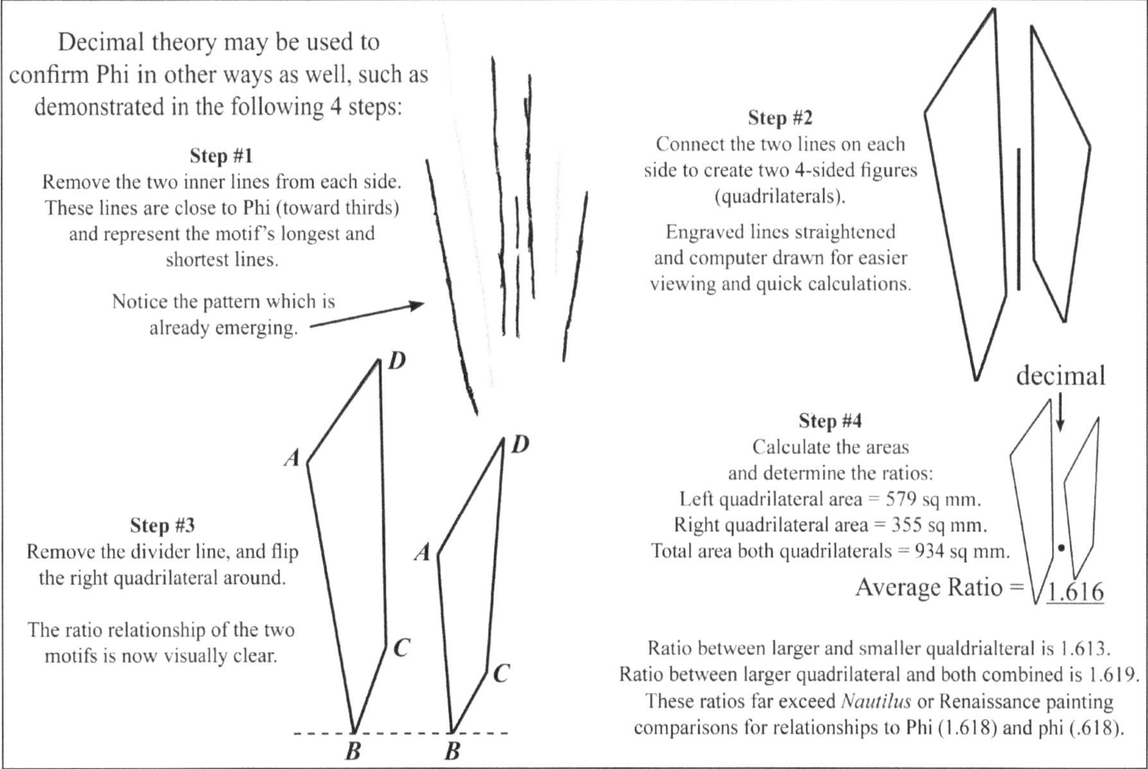

Figure 2.15. The earliest graphic dividing line: Decimal theory 2. Note the small inward curve at bottom left of the original motif. If this curve is left in (rather than straightened), it reduces the size of the left quadrilateral by 4–6 sq mm, bringing the ratio between left and right to perfect phi, and the ratio between larger and both combined to perfect phi. See Fig. 13 for more on tweaking and "phi-based conceptual units."

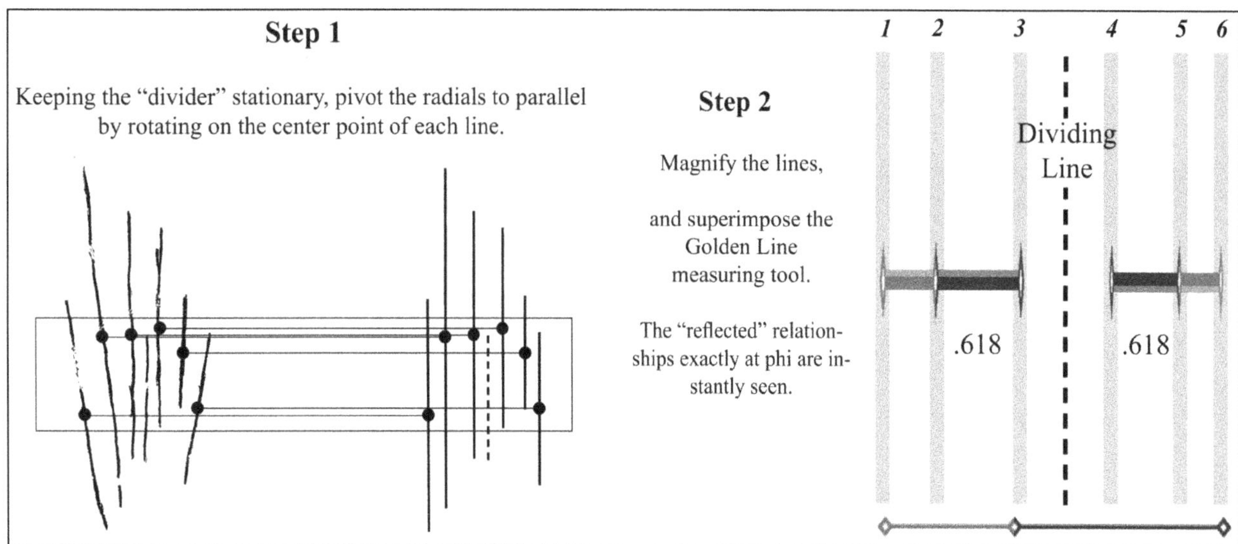

Figure 2.16. The earliest graphic dividing line: Mirror theory. Working as a "ratio mirror," the line divides each section into reflecting Phi planes. One measurement variable is removed by pivoting radials to parallel. Radials are pivoted on the center point of each line. Similar mirror effects were noted in the bilaterally-symmetric phi lines of Fig. 9 and the Hofstetter Construction, Fig. 10.

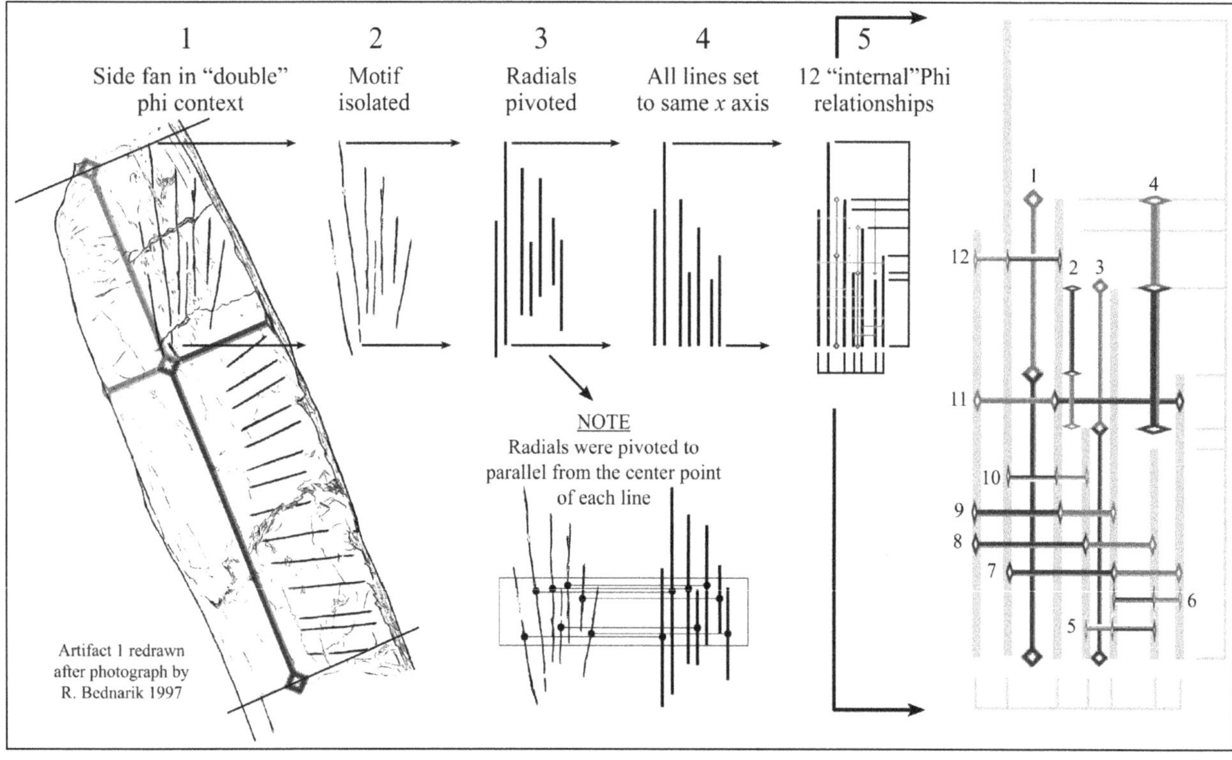

Figure 2.17. 14 instances of Phi in a 7-line motif. This study further demonstrates that Homo erectus and other hominids of Acheulian tradition had a profound sense of ratio and an ability to retain that sense across variables of line, shape, angle, and positioning. As in Fig. 16 one measurement variable was removed by setting all lines to parallel. A second variable was removed in Step 4 by setting all lines to the same x axis. (The zigzag effect of the line peaks created by the x-axis technique is known as a "compound line" in contrapuntal music terms, wherein one line of notes may be interpreted as two, and divided up between two players.)

of J. S. Bach, our preconceptions would result in immediate assumption of some underlying fugal theme. And yet, there are still many other instances of perfect phi in this very same motif. Complexities in every conceivable form are a natural part of human culture, and are comparable to the works of Bach, where, for instance, in a

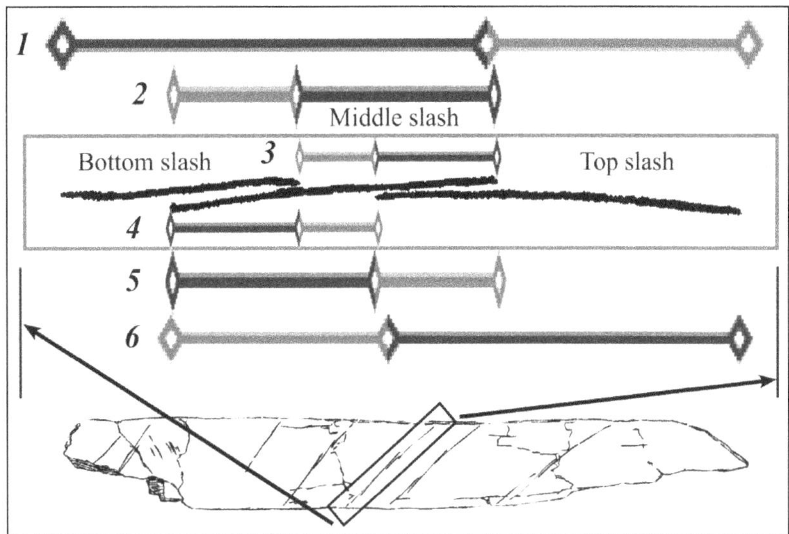

Figure 2.18. Fractals of Phi: Six instances of the golden ratio in a single 3-part motif. Artifact 2 after Mania and Mania 1988.

single fugue, the very same musical theme or motif is repeated in more varied ways (and even simultaneously) than any listener, even the most highly trained in the classical arts could ever keep up with. They include such as mentioned above (Figs. 2.8 & 2.9) and many more, including those that extend into symbolic fractal levels.

To expand on the analogy of comparing the Bilzingsleben engravings with the work of Bach, and to further demonstrate some of the interdisciplinary approaches I am using to study the Bilzingsleben artifacts, I will detail some of Bach's "non-musical" techniques of composition. Apart from traditional contrapuntal techniques, Bach was also known to deliberately employ long-established techniques of mysticism as passed down from the Pythagoreans, Plato, etc., such as number symbolism (turning words and names, etc., into musical melodies through the use of numerology), acrostichon (writing sentences, etc., in such a way as to convey a second message if certain letters from each word are singled out and then re-combined to form new words), chiasmatism (using the Greek letter *chi* in various creative ways; in musical symbolism *chi* is known as Plato's cross), and *Figurenlehre* (using sequences of musical notes to suggest specific human emotions, an idea inspired by techniques of rhetoric developed by Greek philosophers), as well as "puzzle canons" in which he presented one melody to be sung as a round with up to six separate voices, but withholding the critical information of exactly when the other voices were to enter (Feliks 1992, 1993, 1994). It must be noted that one of Bach's puzzle canons was not solved for over 100 years. Usually, these intricately-woven themes are only discovered by intensive study of the musical scores, with new aspects continuing to be discovered even today. It is with a similar enthusiasm that I believe the Bilzingsleben artifacts contain far more information than meets the eye. It is not the least bit difficult to accept these possibilities once we move past our antiquated views of early peoples.

Fractals of phi: Six instances of the golden ratio in a single three-part motif (Figure 2.18)

The type of extremely complex overlapping fractal structure suggested by this particular aspect of *Artifact 2* (detailed in Figs. 9–12 of the *Graphics* paper) is very common in the fugal work of Bach. (At this point it is an interesting aside to note that Bach lived within 20 km of Bilzingsleben.)

Crunching the numbers: Acheulian phi ratios as they rank with well-known natural and Renaissance art comparisons (Figure 2.19)

If the Bach examples seem too esoteric a comparison for Lower Palaeolithic peoples, here is a brief list of straightforward numerical values comparing the precision of Acheulian phi ratios with some of the classic examples from modern times, as further evidence that our species is not the pinnacle of humanity, but rather the inheritors of a fully developed cognitive tradition entirely laid out and set up for us in advance. The following ratios are part of a comparative list that can be expanded much further; for instance, even the famed Parthenon, often used as an example of the golden rectangle, does not present the same accuracies as nearly all of the Acheulian evidence presented in this paper.

Fractal location of the cerebellum: "Cross-dimensional fractals" and human indebtedness to phi (Figures 2.20-2.23)

Up to this point, I have focused on how Phi has been expressed through the creative work of Lower Palaeolithic peoples. I will now explain how the ratio crossed over from its ubiquitous role in the natural world to become one of the first cognitive archetypes of the conscious human mind. This transition may have been inevitable, as Phi has been an innate part of human morphology from the very beginning.

Nautilus shell =	*1.33*	(Falbo 2005)
Duccio's *Rucellai Madonna* =	*1.55*	(Livio 2002)
Leonardo's *Madonna of the Rocks* (#2) =	*1.58*	(ibid.)
Giotto's *Ognissanti Madonna* =	*1.59*	(ibid.)
Kilombe handaxe average =	*1.615*	(Gowlett 1984)
Actual golden ratio =	***1.618***	
Artifact 1 ("14 *Phi* Relationships") =	*1.618*	(Feliks 2006)
"Chaos" maps artifacts and elephant tusks =	*1.618*	(ibid.)
20+ Bilzingsleben flint tools =	*1.618*	(ibid.)
Skull of Turkana Boy *Homo erectus* =	*1.618*	(ibid.)
Location of Turkana Boy cerebellum =	*1.618*	(ibid.)
Artifact 1 sidefan by quadrilaterals =	*1.619*	(ibid.)
Kilombe handaxe average, graphic =	*1.625*	(Gowlett 1993)
Leonardo's *Madonna of the Rocks* (#1) =	*1.64*	(Livio 2002)
Cimabue's *Santa Trinita Madonna* =	*1.73*	(ibid.)

Figure 2.19. Acheulian Phi ratios as they rank with well-known natural and Renaissance art comparisons. (Note: The Gowlett averages provided are quick estimates by the author, and not by Gowlett.)

Many modern theorists agree that human self-awareness, for instance, came into being through the co-evolution of hand, eye, and brain (see Tallis 2003, Feliks 2006). With this in mind, no one should question that early humans were cognitively influenced by the ratio 1.618 on a minute-to-minute daily basis for millions of years because the human hand itself is built entirely on phi. This is demonstrated by the fact that each consecutive finger joint to the next "is" the phi ratio. The same ratio represents the hand proper and forearm, and many other aspects of the human body. A visual sense of the phi ratio in "line" form, therefore, would have been naturally incorporated into the human psyche from the outside-in through constant use of the hand and arm.

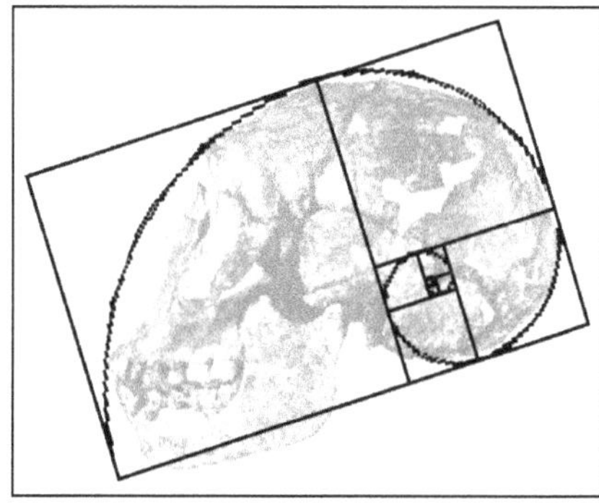

Figure 2.20. Type Homo erectus or ergaster skull (Turkana Boy) and perfect affiliation with the golden spiral. 1.6 million years old. From A. Walker and R. Leakey, "The Nariokotome Homo erectus Skeleton." Used with permission.

But less obvious are internal links to the hand and arm demonstrating a phi aspect of human morphology not hitherto observed, namely, that phi also serves as the very ratio in which the human mind resides, because phi is the fractal ratio of the human brain (Figures 2.20–2.23). While it will be obvious from Figure 2.21 that phi is the ratio for the overall structure of the brain, I would point out a deeper profundity, that phi is also the location of the cerebellum within the brain proper. Its being tucked away at the core of the brain's phi spiral (Figures 2.21–2.22) brings to mind the fractal growth pattern of the *Nautilus* shell. The cerebellum's location at phi is significant because the cerebellum just so happens to coordinate (among other things) complex movement of the hand and joints.

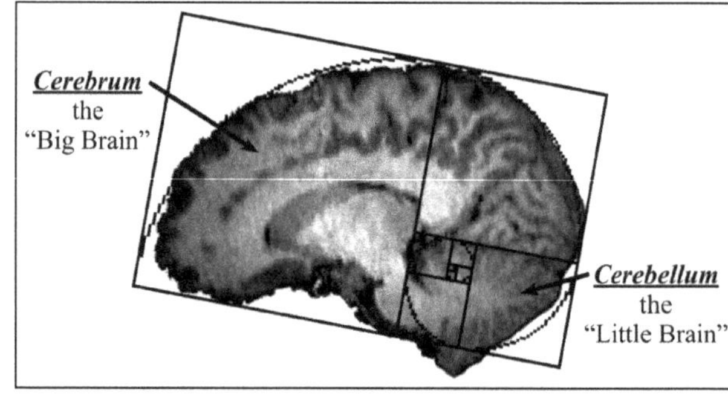

Figure 2.21. Fractal location of the cerebellum: The golden mean within the modern human brain. The cerebellum (along with the medulla and pons) represents the "oldest part" of the brain. Cerebellum location is the same for Homo erectus (see Bruner 2004, "Geometric morphometrics and paleoneurology: brain shape evolution in the genus Homo." (The MRI is public domain.)

Long thought responsible only for coordination and balance, cutting edge research is starting to reveal a cerebellum that is intimately involved in cognition, emotion, and even music (e.g., Gottwald *et al.* 2004, Schutter *et al.* 2005, Levitin 2006). The analogy of "big brain/little brain" (Fig. 2.21), therefore, is beginning to take on multilevel meaning beyond its use to describe mere morphology, in that the cerebrum may eventually be seen as a functional fractal expansion of the cerebellum. Since the cognitive skill of analogy is contained within the brain, it is crucial at such a research juncture to acknowledge the presence of phi so unambiguously represented in the physical brain. Also, the phi link between cerebrum and cerebellum and between brain and hand is

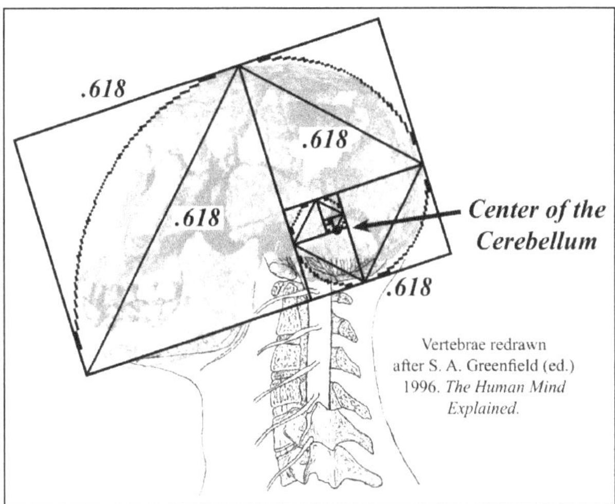

Figure 2.22. Fractal location of the cerebellum: The golden mean within the Homo erectus skull and brain. The cerebellum is the part of the brain that "understands" the positioning of the finger joints in space. Every movement of the fingers, therefore, is an internal confirmation of the phi ratio. The oldest part of the brain tucks away in the whirls of a golden spiral. This may be important, as the cerebellum is now understood to play a role in human thought processes, including emotion, in addition to its long-known roles in motor function, balance, etc. I.e. the cerebellum is an agent genuinely capable of linking the "internal golden mean" to actions in the physical world by way of cognition.

confirmed not only by way of the internal neural system, but also by way of the very same cross-dimensional fractal. The link between the cerebellum and the phi ratio joints of the fingers is that the cerebellum is the part of the brain that "understands" the positioning of the finger joints in space. Every movement of the fingers is an internal confirmation of the phi ratio. To instantly test the physical aspects of the cross-dimensional fractal, curl your left hand into a fist so that each joint creates a perfect perpendicular to the previous joint, and then hold your hand up to the image of Turkana Boy in Fig. 2.22. Skull, brain, and hand clearly adhere to the exact same ratio.

Inspired by Eglash *et al* (1998) Eglash (1999), Mikiten *et. al.* (2000), and others, I have done extensive work studying Palaeolithic fractals which retain their mathematical structure across different physical and non-physical mediums (similar to how phi can be expressed equally as a rectangle or as a non-repeating decimal). This is where fractal geometries in one medium are found to be exactly comparable to the fractal geometries in an entirely different medium even though there appears, otherwise, to be no association between them. Fractals of this nature are increasingly being discovered in archaeological contexts, including what appear at first to be "chaotic" contexts. (In my own work, I have produced more than 20 such studies regarding the distribution of artifacts at Bilzingsleben. But since cross-dimensional chaos and fractal theories are not yet commonly accepted in archaeology these "testable facts" will have to be published at a later date.) The idea of fractals that extend beyond scaled representations of each other in the same medium (i.e. "cross-dimensional" fractals) has profound implications not only for archaeology but for all of science, as it represents a potent unifying concept. As an earlier example of how this idea may be applied, Sacks made an observation regarding the identical similarity between fossils and phosphene forms in the human brain, namely, that even though the two exist in entirely different mediums, there may actually be similar restrictions that govern their shapes (Feliks 2003. See also Sacks 1999, 2002). Although the idea of similar restrictions (or "constraints") that appear to work equally whether regards fleeting patterns of light or the hard shells of sea creatures are not precisely the same as the concept of "archetypes," each need to be given special attention in the sciences as they support the increasingly important perspective that things are interconnected on integral levels (e.g., Capra 1982).

By old paradigm standards, it is inconceivable that Lower Palaeolithic peoples could have been aware of, let alone interested in, cross-dimensional fractals; but this may say more about our own limited scope than the capabilities of other cultures. Earlier, I offered ethnographic examples of how various cultures develop extremely sophisticated skills of subtlety and discernment which are not character-

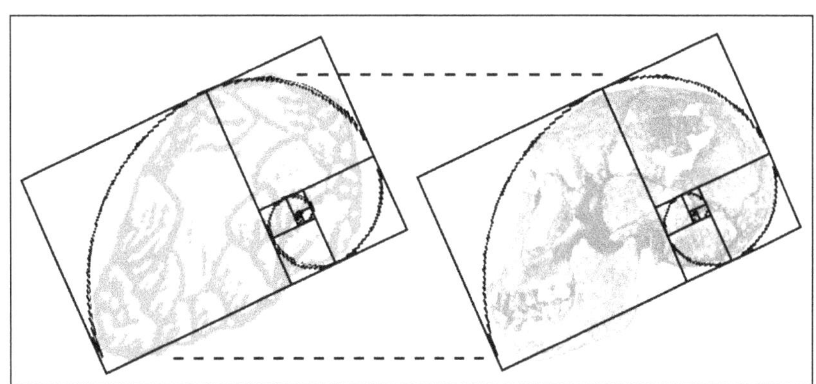

Figure 2.23. Two facts of Acheulian golden mean ubiquity. (Bilzingsleben microlith, Svoboda 1987. Used with permission. Turkana Boy skull, Walker and Leakey 1993. Used with permission.)

ristics of what we typically regard as "Western" culture. It should not be at all surprising, therefore, to find that people of other cultures are (or were) "better than us" at all kinds of different things, or who have "beat us" to skills or ideas we would like to take credit for ourselves. Eglash's recent discovery of fractal layouts in traditional African villages which have always been before our Western eyes proves this point. Again, just as our above-mentioned difficulties in seeing refinement as opposed to crudeness, our inability until recently to even see fractal layouts is due in part to our long preoccupation with the Cartesian grid system. This view of reality, predominant in Western science, attempts to organize everything according to arbitrarily-imposed equal increments, often reducing everything to "on-off" mechanics or "bits-and-pieces" rather than seeing everything as "interconnections" (perspective as per Capra [1982], Bohm and Peat [1987] etc.). Fractal values depend entirely upon interconnections. Fractal measurements can even reveal strong relationships between seemingly unrelated aspects of reality, effectively offering a science which is not incompatible with meaning. When Eglash first discovered fractals in African village layouts his initial scientific inclination was to see them as the result of unconscious organization; but his perspective changed after fieldwork, and he began to see intentional fractals as aspects of a knowledge system. Remarkably, the fractals were cross-dimensional; not only were they present in village layouts but also as miniature scale models of the villages within the village houses–components of religious altars–thus showing a direct fractal link between physical and spiritual worlds. Inspired, I followed a similar sequence and discovered that the Phi fractal extended well beyond the Acheulian handaxe to exactly matching fractals in the engraved artifacts. Since phi is the primary fractal of nature, this suggested that the people of Bilzingsleben had creative inclinations closely affiliated with the natural world. This led to discovery of the very same fractals in the human brain and skull of *Homo erectus*, linking brain and mind to physical evidence in the archaeological record, and indicating, what appeared to be an indebtedness to phi (Fig. 2.24).

The 1.618 ratio was a *"centralizing element"* in the culture of *Homo erectus* —therefore, a centralizing element in the developing human brain.

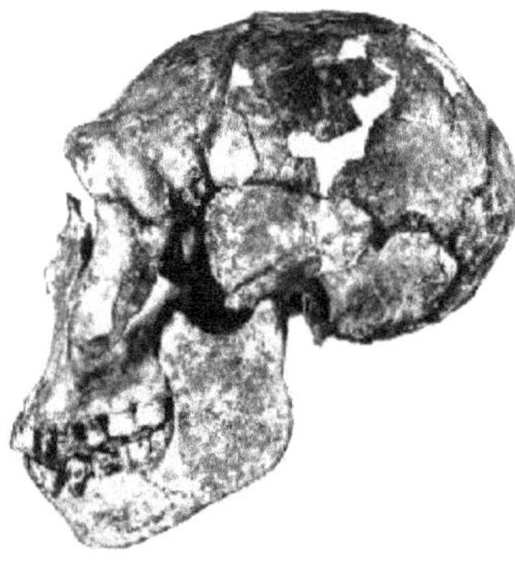

Figure 2.24. Cognitive implication of the ratio. "Turkana Boy" from Walker and Leakey 1993. Used with permission.

If there is a human indebtedness to phi, science should not be the last to recognize it. In this day and age, there is no reason for science to behave like a religion (as Bednarik often suggests that it does) and censor legitimate observations and measurements on the grounds that they may invite absurd deductions. Let scientists interpret as they see fit. If the math bears out, factual observations must be acknowledged regardless of where the newly discovered facts might lead. This is how science works–or, at least, how it should work.

Cognitive implication of the ratio (Figure 2.24)

CONCLUDING THOUGHTS

Whether by physical innateness or any other cause, phi represents the oldest abstract knowledge passed down "intact" by way of culture, and in more testable forms than any other humanly-grasped concept. That early peoples had a relationship with phi is beyond question, and it was likely a relationship little different than the same fascination phi receives from our own species in modern times.

Just as astronomy uses the ever-present cosmic microwave background radiation as a reference pointing backwards in time to the origin of the universe, phi may be traced backwards in time to the very origin of human cognition. To date, phi is the only physically confirmable and ubiquitous number preserved as archaeological evidence demonstrating how cultural ideas were able to cross millennia and even species. Its value, therefore, is immeasurable in the quest for universal meanings.

Regarding what the evidence says about the cognition of early humans, I suggest the following new perspective. We can no longer assume that the world of modern *Homo sapiens* reflects a higher average intelligence than that of *Homo erectus* or other early hominins, especially by the measure of phi or fractal comprehension. In evaluating the intelligence of other species, we must keep in mind the difference between intelligence and our "illusion" of intelligence created by easy access to culture-based knowledge, and the difference between the natural value systems of smaller communal populations and the increasingly unnatural systems developed by *Homo sapiens* often to resolve issues brought about by nothing more profound than overpopulation. Take our culture bank away and we would be hard-pressed to compete with *Homo erectus*. Certainly, the first *Homo erectus* to create a bifacial handaxe in the golden ratio was as capable as any modern engineer who now goes to a computer for quick specs.

The idea that increasing technological change is a sign of high intelligence while less change with a successful track record of millions of years is a sign of low intelligence is an antiquated idea that needs to be completely discarded if we are to understand our early ancestors. This is especially important when we study a period in which phi was so prevalent. The ancient Greeks themselves regarded phi in high esteem, perhaps best summed up by Plato's famous accolade in which he refers to the golden section as nothing less than the "key to the physics of the cosmos" (Timaeus). If we discover the use of phi, therefore, to have been common during Lower Palaeolithic times, we, as scientists, need to look at the implications very closely. Our own preoccupations with technology aside, in all likelihood *Homo erectus/ergaster*, Neanderthals, and *heidelbergensis* were the species that invented virtually everything that cognitively defines humanity.

Once the fractal human mind was switched on perhaps two million years ago, the whole range of emotions, language, and philosophy were instantly available. Clearly, there is a much longer history opening up, indicating that the cognitive richness of early peoples is not at all accurately reflected in our past interpretations of their stone tool technologies. I have provided openly testable archaeological evidence that the earliest cognitive abilities appear directly related to ratio and analogy, each of which are accessible through the phi fractal. In fact, it may well be that all human morphology and cognition is based on fractals and the phi fractal in particular. It seems that by looking anew at phi we will begin to understand an essential and fundamental aspect of human nature.

Acknowledgments

I would like to thank the following scholars for encouragement and/or contributions to my work during the past few years. In alphabetical order: Robert Bednarik, David Brill, Noam Chomsky, Ellen Dissanayake, Ekkehart Malotki, Adrienne Mayor, Steven Pinker, Oliver Sacks, Raymond Tallis, and Randy White. In addition, I wish to thank my family and friends, and others who have offered support and inspiration; but I wish especially to thank the eleven sponsors who made my presentations in Lisbon possible.

Publication note

Phi in the Acheulian was presented in Lisbon instead of the program, *Legends of the Sea*. However, it was not listed in the *UISPP Book of Abstracts*. Ironically, the "*Legends of the Sea*" abstract was only a rough draft not intended for publication. Since the abstract was published, it is important to the author that one critical fact be clarified; *Legends of the Sea* is an opera inspired by the bamboo raft archaeology of Robert Bednarik replete with all manner of human relationships, aspirations, tragedies, and achievements. Since none of this explanatory information was included, readers had no idea as to why the abstract referred so much to emotional content, and thus misunderstood the author's intentions.

References

BEDNARIK, R.G. 1995. Concept-mediated marking in the Lower Palaeolithic. *Current Anthropology* 36: 605–34.

BEDNARIK, R.G. 1997. The origins of navigation and language. *The Artefact* 20:16–56.

BEDNARIK, R.G. 2003. The earliest evidence of palaeoart. *Rock Art Research* 20: 89–135.

BOHM, D. and F. PEAT. 1987. *Science, order, and creativity: A dramatic look at the roots of science and life*. Bantam Books, New York.

BRUNER, E. 2004. Geometric morphometrics and paleoneurology: brain shape evolution in the genus *Homo*. *Journal of Human Evolution* 47: 279–303.

CAPRA, F. 1982. *The turning point: Science, society, and the rising culture*. Simon and Schuster, New York.

CHOMSKY, N. 1972. *Language and mind*. Enlarged Edition. Harcourt Brace Jovanovich, Inc. New York.

CORMAC, E.M. and M.I. STAMENOV (Eds.). 1996. *Fractals of brain, fractals of mind: In search of a symmetry bond*. Amsterdam, Philadelphia, John Benjamins Publishing Co.

DISSANAYAKE, E. 1989. *What is Art For?* Seattle and London: University of Washington Press.

DONALD, M. 1991. *Origins of the modern mind: three stages in the evolution of culture and cognition*. Cambridge: Harvard University Press.

EGLASH, R., C. S. DIATTA and N. BADIANE 1998. Fractal structure in Jola material culture. Paper presented at the *Congrès "Développement insulaire durable et rôles de la recherche et de la formation."* Rhodes, Greece. 277–83.

EGLASH, R. 1999. *African fractals: Modern computing and indigenous design*. Rutgers University Press, New Jersey.

FALBO, C. 2005. The golden ratio–a contrary viewpoint. *The College Mathematics Journal*, 36(2): 123–134.

FELIKS, J. 1992, 1993, 1994. *The Tao of Bach: J.S. Bach, mysticism, and ancient Chinese philosophy*. Pp. 1–53. Widely circulated unpublished thesis.

FELIKS, J. 1997a, 1997b. *The impact of fossils*. Preliminary drafts submitted for publication and widely circulated. [1995 version, while not specifically cited here, was also submitted for publication in the field, and widely circulated.]

FELIKS, J. 1998a. The impact of fossils on the development of visual representation. *Rock Art Research* 15: 109–34. (1995–97 versions submitted for publication and widely circulated).

FELIKS, J. 1998b. The value of interpretive approaches in archaeology. *Rock Art Research* 15: 128–29.

FELIKS, J. 2000. Iconic interface between the worlds. Comment on D. Hodgson, "Art, perception, and information processing: an evolutionary perspective." *Rock Art Research* 17: 23–25.

FELIKS, J. 2003. Toward a comprehensive paradigm. Comment on Robert G. Bednarik, "The earliest evidence of palaeoart." *Rock Art Research* 20: 111–14.

FELIKS, J. 2006a (submitted and circulated 2004–5). Musings on the Palaeolithic fan motif. In P. Chenna Reddy (ed.), *Exploring the mind of ancient man: Festschrift to Robert G. Bednarik*, 249–66. Research India Press, New Delhi.

FELIKS, J. 2006b. The Graphics of Bilzingsleben: Sophistication and subtlety in the mind of *Homo erectus*. Visual thesis presented in *The Pleistocene palaeoart of the world* session, Chaired by Robert Bednarik and Derek Hodgson. XVth UISPP Congress, Lisbon, September 7, 2006.

GOTTWALD, B., B WILDE, Z MIHAJLOVIC and H.M MEHDORN. 2004. Evidence for distinct cognitive deficits after focal cerebellar lesions. *Journal of Neurology, Neurosurgery and Psychiatry* 75:1524-31.

GOWLETT, J.A.J. 1984 Mental Abilities of Early Man: A Look at Some Hard Evidence, in *Hominid Evolution and Community Ecology: prehistoric human adaptation in biological perspective.* Edited by Robert Foley. London: Academic Press.

GOWLETT, J.A.J. 1993. *Ascent to civilization: The archaeology of early humans.* 2nd Edition. The McGraw-Hill companies.

GREENE, B. 1999. *The elegant universe: superstrings, hidden dimensions, and the quest for the ultimate theory.* First Vintage Books Edition, New York.

HARROD, J.B. 2003. Lower Palaeolithic palaeoart, religion and protolanguage. Comment on "The earliest evidence of palaeoart" by Robert G. Bednarik. *Rock Art Research* 20:115–16.

HOFSTETTER, K. 2002. A simple construction of the golden section. *Forum Geometricorum* (2): 65–6.

HREBÍCEK, L. 1994. Fractals in language. *Journal of Quantitative Linguistics* 1(1): 82–6.

KÖHLER, R. 1997. Are there fractal structures in language? Units of measurement and dimension in linguistics. *Journal of Quantitative Linguistics* 4(1-3): 122–125.

LEOPOLD, E. 2001. Fractal structures in language: The question of the imbedding space. In L. Uhlirova, G. Gejza, G. Altmann, R. Köhler (eds.), *Text as a linguistic paradigm: Level, constituents, constructs. Festschrift in honour of Ludek Hrebícek.* pp. 163-76. Wissenschaftlicher Berlag Trier.

LEROI-GOURHAN, A. 1961. Les Fouilles d'Arcy-Sur-Cure (Yonne). *Gallia Prehistoire* 4:3–16.

LEROI-GOURHAN, A. 1964. *Les Religions de la Préhistoire (Paléolithique).* Paris: Presses Universitaires de France.

LEVITIN, D. 2006. *This is your brain on music: The science of a human obsession.* Dutton, New York.

LIVIO, M. 2002. *The golden ratio: The story of phi, the world's most astonishing number.* Random House, New York.

MANDELBROT, B. 1982. *The Fractal Geometry of Nature.* W. H. Freeman & Co.

MANIA, D. and U. MANIA 1988. Deliberate engravings on bone artefacts of *Homo erectus. Rock Art Research* 5: 91–107.

MANIA, D. and U. MANIA 2003. Bilzingsleben - *Homo erectus*, his culture and his environment. The most important results of research. In J. M. Burdukiewicz and A. Ronen (eds.), *Lower Palaeolithic small tools in Europe and The Levant.* BAR S1115, pp. 29–48.

MANIA, D. and U. MANIA 2005. The natural and sociocultural environment of *Homo erectus* at Bilzingsleben, Germany. In C. Gamble and M. Porr (eds.), *The Hominid Individual in Context: Archaeological investigations of Lower and Middle Palaeolithic landscapes, locales and artifacts,* 98–114. Routledge, New York.

MARSHACK, A. 1977. The meander as a system: the analysis and recognition of iconographic units in Upper Paleolithic compositions. In *Form in Indigenous Art, Prehistory and Material Culture Series*, No. 13, ed. P. J. Ucko (Canberra: Australian Institute of Aboriginal Studies), pp. 286–317.

MARSHACK, A. 1990. Early hominid symbol and evolution of the human capacity. In P. Mellars (ed.), *The emergence of modern humans: an archaeological perspective,* pp. 457–98. Cornell University Press, Ithaca, N.Y.

MAYOR, A. 2005. *Fossil Legends of the First Americans.* Princeton University Press, Princeton.

MIKITEN, T.M., N.A. SALINGAROS, and H-S YU. 2000. Pavements as embodiments of meaning for a fractal mind. *Nexus Network Journal* 2: 63–74. http://www.nexusjournal.com/Miki-Sali-Yu.html. (To appear in *A Theory of Architecture* by Nikos A. Salingaros. Umbau-Verlag, Solingen).

MITHEN, S. 2003. Handaxes: the first aesthetic artefacts. In V. Eckhart and K. Grammer (eds.), *Evolutionary Aesthetics,* pp. 261–275. Springer Berlin, New York.

OAKLEY, K.P. 1973. Fossil shell observed by Acheulian man. *Antiquity* 47: 59–60.

OAKLEY, K.P. 1981. Emergence of higher thought, 3.0–0.2 Ma B.P. *Philolosophical Transactions of the Royal Society of London* B 292: 205–11.

PEAT, F.D. 1990. Mathematics and the language of nature. In R. E. Mickens ed.), *Mathematics and sciences.* Word Scientific. http://www.fdavidpeet.com /bibliography /essays/text/maths.

PINKER, S. 1994. The language instinct: How the mind creates language. William Morrow and Company, Inc., New York.

SACKS, O. 1999. *Migraine*. Revised and expanded edition. First Vintage Books Edition, Random House, New York.

SACKS, O. 2002. *Oaxaca journal*. National Geographic Society, New York.

SCHUTTER, DENNIS J.L.G. and JACK VAN HONK. 2005. The cerebellum on the rise in human emotion. *The Cerebellum* 4: 190–94.

SVOBODA, J. 1987. Lithic industries of the Arago, Vértesszöllös, and Bilzingsleben hominids: Comparison and evolutionary interpretation. *Current Anthropology* 28(2): 219–27.

TALLIS, R. 2003. *The hand: a philosophical inquiry into human being*. Edinburgh University Press, Edinburgh.

WALKER. A. and R. LEAKEY. 1993. *The Nariokotome* Homo erectus *skeleton*. Harvard University Press, Cambridge.

WHITE, R. 1989*a* "Toward a Conceptual Understanding of the Earliest Body Ornaments," in *The Emergence of Modern Humans: Biocultural adaptations in the later Peistocene.* Edited by Erik Trinkaus, pp. 211–31. Cambridge University Press.

WHITE, R. 1993 The Dawn of Adornment. *Natural History* 102:60–7.

WYNN, T. 2002. Archaeology and cognitive evolution. *Behavioral and Brain Sciences* 25: 389–438.

WYNN, T. 2003. The constraint of minimum necessary competence. Comment on Robert G. Bednarik, "The earliest evidence of palaeoart." *Rock Art Research* 20: 120–21.

THE LOWER PALAEOLITHIC ROCK ART OF INDIA

Robert G. BEDNARIK
International Federation of Rock Art Organisations, P.O. Box 216, Caulfield South, VIC 3162, Australia, auraweb@hotmail.com

Giriraj KUMAR
Faculty of Arts, Dayalbagh Educational Institute, Dayalbagh, Agra 282 005, India, girirajrasi@yahoo.com

***Abstract**: Petroglyphs of Lower Palaeolithic age have been discovered in central India since 1990, when two motifs were found that had been covered by Acheulian strata in Auditorium Cave, Bhimbetka site complex. Nine cupules occurring above ground in the same cave have been suggested to be of similar antiquity. A large corpus of cupules located in another quartzite cave, Daraki-Chattan, appeared to be of the same tradition. The presence of extensive exfoliation scars at the entrance to this site suggested that cupule-bearing wall fragments might occur within its floor sediments. Excavation of Daraki-Chattan since 2002 has yielded twenty-eight cupules on exfoliated slabs, and one more cupule made in situ, all of which occurred either within or below the substantial Acheulian deposits. In addition, three engraved grooves were also found in this deposit.*
***Keywords**: Lower Palaeolithic, Petroglyph, Cupule, Quartzite cave, India*

***Résumé**: Pétroglyphe datés du Paléolithique inférieur ont été découverts dans le centre de l'Inde depuis 1990. Deux motifs ont été trouvés lors de l'excavation d'un niveau Acheuléen dans la grotte de l'Auditorium. Cette grotte fait partie d'un système karstique comprenant une variété de sites connue sous le nom de Bhimbekta. Il a été suggérer que neuf cupules, situées au-dessus du sol dans la grotte de l'Auditorium, seraient des manifestations de l'Acheuléen. Un large corpus de cupules situées dans une autre grotte quartzitique et nommée Daraki-Chattan, seraient apparemment de la même période. La présence de vastes traces d'exfoliation à l'entrée du site pourraient signifier la présence de fragments de la parois associées à des cupules dans les sols sédimentaires sous-jacents. Depuis 2002, des campagnes d'excavations a Daraki-Chattan ont produit vingt-huit cupules sur des plaquettes exfoliées, et une autre cupule fabriquée in situ sur la paroi.*

Ces vingt-neuf cupules sont toutes associées à un niveau Acheuléen, situées soit a l'intérieur ou au-dessous. Finalement, il faut noter trois rainures gravées associées à ce même niveau Acheuléen.
***Mots clés**: Paléolithique inférieur, pétroglyphe, cupule, grotte quartzitique, Inde*

The defining characteristics of humans and their evolution have largely been disregarded in pursuing the two main preoccupations of palaeoanthropology, hominin origins and the emergence of modern humans. There is, contrary to much writing on these subjects, not one iota of evidence that the appearance of what is often described as 'modern human behaviour' appeared together with physical traits perceived as 'modern'. On the contrary, these two features are almost certainly unconnected and appeared separately.

Much of non-physical human evolution may have occurred outside of Africa, and in particular southern Asia is a region in need of special attention in that context. For instance, it was apparently here that *H. erectus* took to the sea around a million years ago, perhaps first in what today is Indonesia (Bednarik 1995a, 1997, 1999). The almost complete absence, east of Wallace's Line, of land-bound eutherians larger than rodents indicates, as Wallace (1890) correctly deduced, that there was never a land-bridge to the geologically very young islands of Nusa Tenggara (Lesser Sunda Islands). Proboscideans and hominins are the notable exceptions, and in the case of the former we know that they can swim more than twice the distance any other land mammal can (Bednarik and Kuckenburg 1999). Early seafaring, however, is far from being the only evidence suggesting that southern Asia could have been a hub of cognitive development in hominins. For instance, some of the earliest recorded use of pigment and presumed collection of crystal prisms comes from India (Bednarik 1990a; d'Errico *et al.* 1989). This implies a rudimentary appreciation of 'special qualities', or discrimination of ordinary from exotic objects, and the use of haematite and ochre pigments implies symbol use (Bednarik 1990b). These and other aspects suggest southern Asia, a geographically central region, was where much of cognitive human evolution occurred (Bednarik 1995b: 628).

The discovery of the oldest known rock art in the world in India adds yet another intriguing dimension. But it also highlights the neglect of Palaeolithic studies in the subcontinent, and the need for a greatly improved effort in exploring the Pleistocene history of that region. Unless *Homo habilis* or *ergaster* hominins reached eastern Asia via Siberia, which is very unlikely, we have no choice but to accept that they colonised southern Asia before reaching Java and northern China. On the basis of the fossil record as it stands, essentially erectoid hominins seem to appear in Africa as well as eastern Asia at the very same time, during the Plio-Pleistocene (Swisher *et al.* 1994). In whichever direction these presumed migrations took place, we should assume that India was greatly involved, and that India has been occupied by humans at least since the first appearance of *Homo erectus*, if not earlier.

On present indications only a faint outline of the Lower Palaeolithic of India can be offered (Bednarik *et al.* 2005: 149–151). The subcontinent is rich in Acheulian industries (Petraglia 1998; Korisettar 2002) but there is limited dating information available about them (Misra 1989; Raghvan *et al.* 1989; Szabo *et al.* 1990; Chesner *et al.* 1991; Mishra 1992; Acharyya and Basu 1993; Bednarik 1996; Korisettar 2002; Bednarik *et al.* 2005). Some commentators exclude a great antiquity for the early Acheulian, others suggest an age of up to 1.4 million years for the earliest phase (Misra and Rajaguru 1994; Badam and Rajaguru 1994). The preceding cobble tools of India, first reported stratigraphically by Wakankar (1975) at Bhimbetka, are practically unexplored. Since it is logical to expect human occupation evidence in India for at least 1.8 million years, it is to be expected that cobble tools should precede the bifaces of the Acheulian.

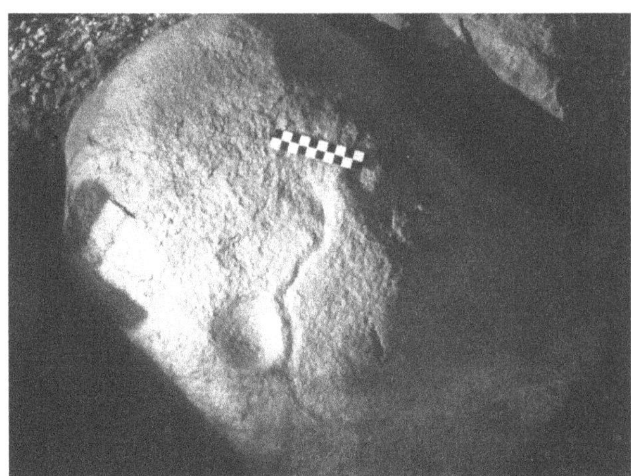

Figure 3.1. Lower Palaeolithic petroglyphs in trench II, Auditorium Cave.

In central India, no petroglyphs were reported until quite recently (Bednarik *et al.* 1991). Eleven petroglyphs were observed in Auditorium Cave, the natural focus of the large rock art complex of Bhimbetka, which otherwise consists entirely of rock paintings. Two of the petroglyphs, a cupule and a meandering line, occur in an excavation (Wakankar 1975) in an Acheulian occupation deposit directly covering them (Bednarik 1993, 1994, 2001a, 2003; Chakravarty and Bednarik 1997: 58–9). They were probably not seen by Wakankar, but became exposed by subsequent trampling and artefact collecting. The cup mark is well-shaped and circular, over 1.5 m below the sediment surface, on the sloping surface of the excavated boulder facing east. The line approaches the large cupule from above, then follows part of its circumference, running parallel to it but maintaining some millimetres distance from its periphery, and veers off to the right. It is not a natural marking of the rock, nor is the cupule (Fig. 3.1). The surface of the quartzite is quite weathered, including in the petroglyphs, as is the nearby bedrock. In view of the excellent recorded stratigraphy at the site it is possible to consider the cultural provenience of these petroglyphs. An important stratigraphic marker of the Pleistocene at the Bhimbetka site complex is a pisolitic layer, 60 cm thick at site III A-29 (Wakankar 1975). At that site, its upper part is looser and finer than the more compact, coarser lower part, and while the upper half contains an Acheulian, the lower half provides a heavily weathered cobble tool industry of choppers and scrapers. The pisolitic stratum occurs also at III A-30 and III F-24 (Auditorium Cave), and in trenches 1–7, Choti Jamun Jhiri Nala. V. N. Misra's (1978) excavation in III F-23 did not reach beyond the Acheulian, so here it was not encountered. The facies can be found widely throughout the Vindhyan Hills, it is often exposed at lower elevations where it contains early Acheulian tools and Levallois cores.

The Middle Palaeolithic stratum overlying the Acheulian in Auditorium Cave is so solidly cemented by calcite deposition that the possibility of post-depositional disturbance can be ignored. It has been proposed that the remaining nine motifs (all cupules), although found above ground, are almost certainly of similar age (Bednarik 1996). They are located on the vertical panel of a huge boulder on the floor of the cave, called Chief's Rock. The petroglyphs occur on heavily metamorphosed, extremely hard quartzite, which was extensively quarried for stone tool material in the Lower Palaeolithic. The Acheulian handaxes and cleavers at the site, and elsewhere in the Bhimbetka site complex, were made from it. The petroglyphs occur in the central part of the cave, well protected from weather, yet they are extremely corroded due to their extraordinary antiquity. An antiquity well in excess of 100,000 years is confirmed by an attempt to analyse the microerosion of one of the Auditorium Cave cupules (Bednarik 1993, 1994, 1996).

Kumar (1996) has since reported other cupule sites in central India that appear to be of great age. Daraki-Chattan is a small and narrow quartzite cave at the foot of a prominent escarpment. Apparent Acheulian and Middle Palaeolithic tools occur on the surface of its floor deposit. The two walls of the cave bear more than 500 cupules and Kumar recognised that there was a realistic possibility that their age might be similar to that of the Auditorium Cave petroglyphs. Since then, several more Indian cupule sites have been proposed to be of great antiquity.

These data reported from India contradict a great deal of the current model of Pleistocene archaeology. The establishment of a major research project focusing on the examination of these Indian data and of an international scientific commission to compile a comprehensive dossier on these extraordinary claims were initiated by the authors. Called the Early Indian Petroglyphs (EIP) Project it was established in 1999 (Bednarik 2001b). The Commission is to investigate all matters concerning the very early rock art of India thoroughly, using methods such as carbon isotope analysis, optically stimulated luminescence dating, microerosion analysis, uranium-thorium analysis and archaeological excavation. It consists of geologists, archaeologists, rock art scientists

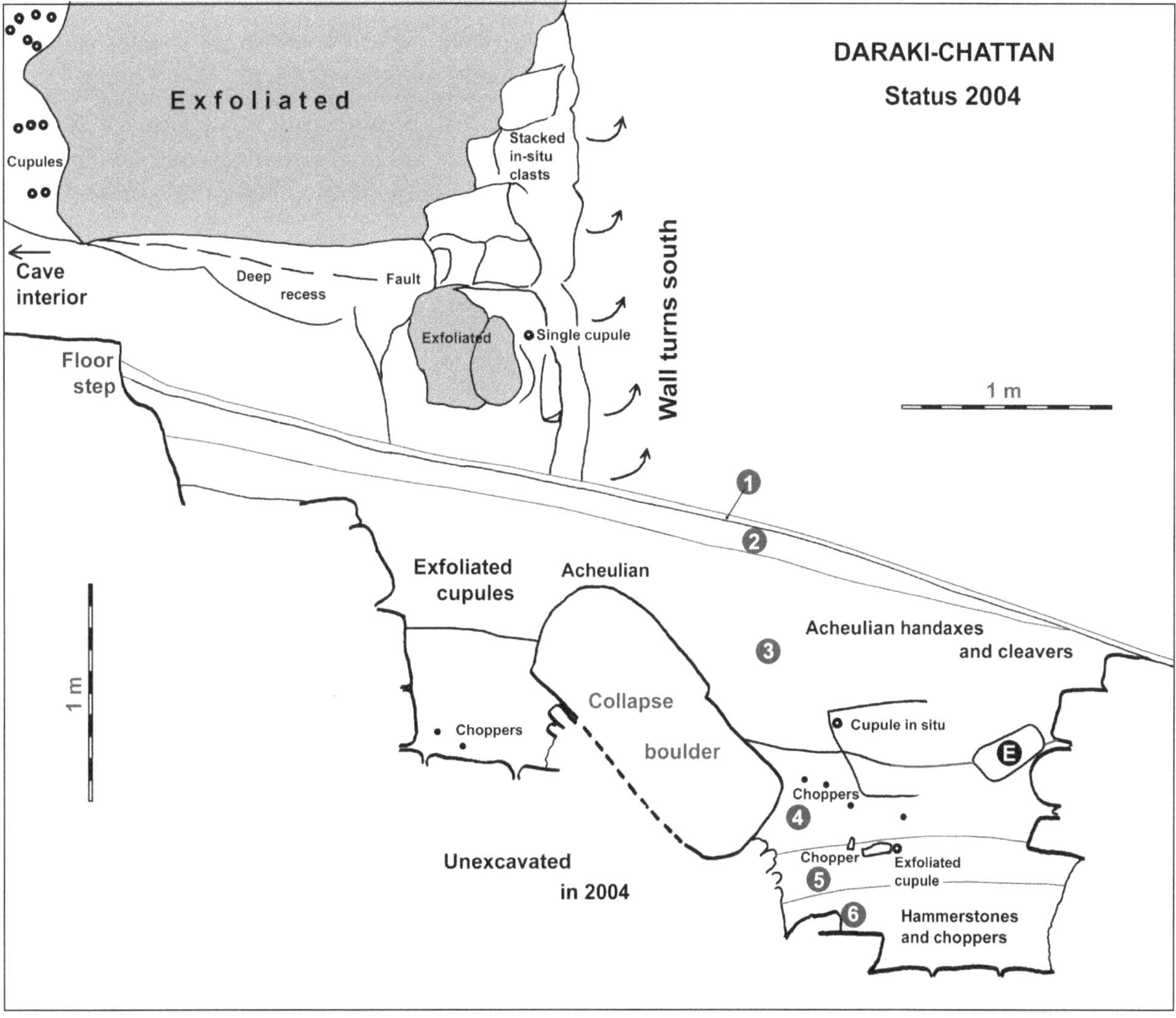

Figure 3.2. Generalised section view the entrance of Daraki-Chattan, looking south, with important features projected into the section. The spatial relationships of the exfoliated areas on the south wall, the outermost cupules on that wall, the general sediment layers, exfoliated slabs, engraved boulder 'E', and the excavated in-situ cupule are shown. Status November 2004.

and archaeometrists from India and Australia. In the course of its work so far, members of this Commission have already conducted research at almost twenty cupule sites in Madhya Pradesh and Rajasthan, as well as at numerous other, more recent rock art sites. The excavations of the EIP Project were commenced mid-2001 by Kumar and several colleagues, and peaked in 2002 with an intensive campaign involving several specialists (Kumar *et al.* 2002).

The quartzite cave Daraki-Chattan consists of a single passage, quite narrow and high, with a bare rock floor. It widens at the entrance where a substantial deposit of floor sediment has accumulated. The two vertical walls are covered by cupules up to a height of 4.02 m above the floor, indicating that the cupule makers sometimes climbed to that height. The cupules located furthest from the entrance have only 40–41 cm clear working space. Most of the cupules relate in their height to the present floor level, which was probably no higher at any time. The spatial distribution of the over 500 cupules densely covering much of both walls of the passage suggests that their makers averaged a body height in the order of 1.7 m to m 1.8 m, in terms of the maximum reach in positions from which it is possible to work most easily. Many of the cupules appear to be grouped in some form (Kumar 1996: Figs 5 and 6), but the degree of intentionality involved in their patterned placing needs to be questioned. Most groupings are perhaps a result of convenience, of subconscious reactions, or of conscious choices not corresponding to modern constructs of spatiality. A few occur on a rock ledge forming the southern margin of the cave floor, and two more were placed on the actual rock floor of the passage. One solitary cupule occurs on the southern wall of the entrance area, just above the excavation, where it managed to survive the extensive exfoliation that occurred in that area (Fig. 3.2). Another was found nearly 170 cm above the floor where the southern wall turns south. Apart from these two exceptions, there are no surviving cupules outside the distinct floor step at the cave entrance, which separates the entrance area or vestibule from the interior of the cave. Finally, there is a boulder measuring about one metre, some eight metres from the cave on the slope below the entrance, which bears several apparent cupules that are so weathered that they are almost beyond visual detection.

The almost complete absence of cupules on the walls of the entrance part of the cave is due to extensive mass exfoliation by insolation spalling. Because this occurred since the cupules were produced, it provides a prominent *terminus ante quem* for the cupules. Since the exfoliated slabs are likely to have been deposited in the floor sediment, we resolved to excavate the entrance of the cave, to establish the vertical extent of such fragments as well as that of the human occupation of the site. The stratigraphical position of exfoliated slabs, some hopefully bearing further cupules, would only provide minimum ages, but we also sought to recover any hammerstones that had been used in producing the rock art. In view of the large number of cupules it was very likely that many of these tools would be recovered.

The excavation yielded not only hundreds of stone artefacts, but also a large number of exfoliated slab fragments, many of which still bore cupules on their outer surfaces. These cupule-bearing slab fragments were vertically distributed through most of the sediment, almost down to bedrock, which indicates that the exfoliation process was very slow and gradual, rather than occurring over just a limited time period. Several of the slab fragments were refitted (Fig. 3.3)

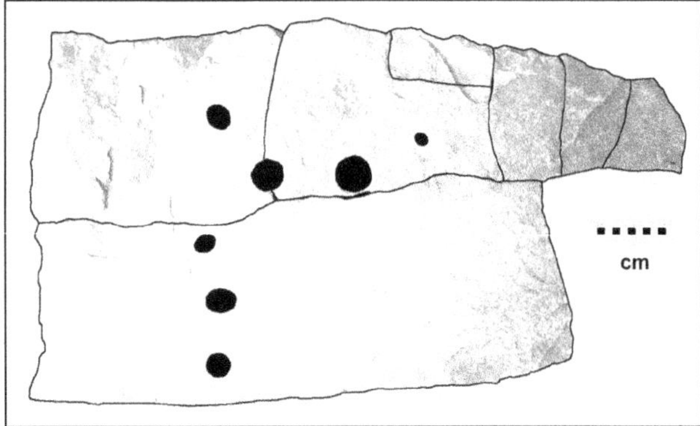

Figure 3.3. Refitted cupule-bearing slabs, Daraki-Chattan, Lower Palaeolithic.

Twenty-eight cupules and one doubtful specimen have now been recovered in the excavation, at varying depths throughout much of the Lower Palaeolithic deposit (Fig. 3.2). One more cupule was found in situ in the excavation, placed on the edge of a huge angular boulder. The trench also yielded three engraved grooves, two of them on one boulder and ranging in depth from 2.0 to 6.9 mm (Bednarik *et al.* 2005: Figs 36–38). All of the cupules on the walls appear to derive from a single period of cupule production. There are no obvious indications of greatly varying ages or differences in weathering. If this is the case, then the cupule production phase must correspond to the lowest sediment deposit, and exfoliation has occurred at various times over the duration of much of the site's sedimentary history. In the event that cupules were made over a much greater time span, the first to exfoliate and become buried must still be of an antiquity corresponding to the lowest sediment deposit, but others could have been made much later. However, the concentration of hammerstones of the type used to make petroglyphs (Bednarik 1998) just above and below the 'pavement floor' (see below) renders the first possibility more likely. In either case, the lowest occurrence of exfoliated slab fragments with cupules coincides with the earliest evidence of human occupation at Daraki-Chattan.

The substantial stone artefact assemblage from the excavation comprises two distinctive main groupings, leaving aside Holocene material trampled in from the top. The upper sediment units exhibit neither clear Acheulian nor typical Middle Palaeolithic features, being a rather indistinctive 'intermediate' industry. The absence of points and the presence of at least two Micoquian-type bifaces are perhaps diagnostic features. Overall there are few handaxes present but one or perhaps two rough awls or borers occur. Acheulian handaxes and cleavers occur with few large Levallois flakes featuring broad striking platforms and typical tortoise-pattern flaking indicative of core preparation. A specific type of flake tool is a very broad, Clactonian-type flake. The lower strata present a very different industry and sedimentary conditions. The implements are reminiscent of chopping-tool industries with cobble tools. This industry appears to be related to the lowest assemblages Wakankar has reported from three sites at Bhimbetka (III F-24, III A-29 and III A-30), and which have also been reported elsewhere in India (Ansari 1970; Armand 1980). This possibility is reinforced by the presence at Daraki-Chattan of laterite, occurring also at Bhimbetka, perhaps referring to distinctive environmental conditions. Moreover, like the chopping-tools at Bhimbetka, those at Daraki-Chattan are also deeply corroded or saprolithic. The most distinctive typological elements in the chopper industry at Daraki-Chattan are a few very thick bifacial chopping tools. They have a flat base opposite a distinctive, zigzagging convex working edge that was created by the removal of deeply conchoidal flakes, alternatively from each side. The geometrical regularity of this coarse retouch and consistent morphology suggest that this is not a by-product, a core, but that the removed flakes were the by-product. Another feature of this industry is the occasional occurrence of polyhedrons. This assemblage needs to be closely compared with similar stratified finds elsewhere in India, and the chronology of the Middle Pleistocene laterisation events in central India needs to be resolved. For the moment it will suffice to make one categorical observation: the period of cupule manufacture at Daraki-Chattan, or at least its earliest phase (if it should have continued later on, for which we lack evidence), coincides with this chopping tool industry with occasional coarse handaxes. The archaeology has shown this unambiguously, through the occurrence of exfoliated, cupule-bearing slabs down to the lower levels, as well as through the occurrence of definite petroglyph-making tools. At least ten of these hammerstones have been recovered from the excavation (Bednarik *et al.* 2005: 166–7).

We have also examined some cupule sites on the plateau of Indragarh Hill, i.e. above Daraki-Chattan, and some more in the wider vicinity of that key site. There are several cupule rocks at scattered locations on this plateau. There is no indication that these are of an antiquity comparable to that of the cupules in Daraki-Chattan as they are fully exposed to weathering processes and are relatively well preserved.

Almost 20 km south-west of Bhanpura, close to the shore of the Gandhi Sagar reservoir lake and near the village Hanumankheda is a prominent remnant of a quartzite formation, Pola Bata. Its huge, up to about 12-m-high weathered boulders form cavities that have for hundreds of millennia provided shelter to humans, as indicated by numerous Lower Palaeolithic surface artefacts. There are several concentrations of cupules among the rocks, especially on the wall of the main tunnel. Numerous largely faded red pictograms occur also in this cave-like space. The cupules are often unusually deep and large, and although there are many deeply weathered examples, others bear distinctively recent damage (Fig. 3.4). Indeed, some of the site's several dozen cupules are still being used, including at least three lithophones or 'rock gongs'.

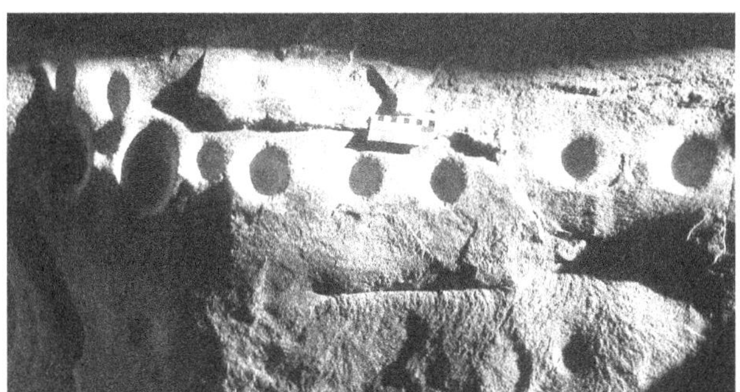

Figure 3.4. Cupules at Pola Bata, Gandhi Sagar dam, of unknown age.

About 3 km west of Pola Bata lies the small hamlet Amyabhau. Nearby is another of the quartzite stacks commonly observed in this otherwise fairly flat terrain, called Teej-kā-Pānā. The site, elevated about 15 m, consists of the flat top of the steep-sided outcrop. It features several groupings of cupules and abraded grooves. Some of these petroglyphs form an extensive geometric arrangement, now partly exfoliated, and most cupules are arranged in rows. Some of the abraded grooves resemble axe grinding grooves, and it is possible that these are Neolithic.

Hathikheda is an outer suburb of greater Ajmer, Rajasthan. A series of rock outcrops, spaced about one kilometre apart, extends to the west of the built-up area, forming a roughly discernible alignment along an east-west line (Bednarik and Kumar 2002). They rise between 8 m and 20 m above the alluvium and consist essentially of white quartz monoliths. They appear to mark the remains of an unusually broad quartz dyke that extends over a number of kilometres. The first outcrop occurs within the housing area and bears a small temple. The second is called Moda Bhata ('Big Rock') and is located immediately north of a usually dry watercourse, on the present periphery of Hathikheda. Moda Bhata is about 8 m high on its northern approach, and 15 m on its much steeper south side, which has given rise to a shallow rockshelter. The upper platform bears twenty distinct cupules as well as several faint cupules or worked surfaces bearing traces of impact, plus one very large cupule. Most occur in small groups and there is a preference in their positioning on slight rises of the rock platform. In addition there are four vertical cupules in the shelter below. We have applied microerosion analysis to one of the cupules on the plateau, noting two distinctive peaks in the micro-wane widths: one corresponds to an antiquity of about E2000 years BP, the other to roughly E9000 years BP. This clear separation cannot reasonably be accounted for by sampling inadequacies or imprecision, it is far too pronounced and we interpret it as unambiguous evidence that the older cupule surface was reworked at a much more recent time.

About one kilometre to the south-south-west of Moda Bhata lies a very similar formation, named Koteshwar Mahadev Bhata after a deity. Its dimensions and morphology are much like those of Moda Bhata, with steep sides and a horizontal platform with similar cupules. A line of such further quartz hills extending west were examined in 2003 and 2006 (Kumar and Prajapati 2005), and explored as far as Nankya Talav, about 2 km west of Moda Bhata. Koteshwar Mahadev Bhata is an elongated flat hill followed by smaller outcrops named Hills 3 and 4. The latter has a big rockshelter bearing large and small cupules. Opposite to them, nearly 500 m to the north, are rock outcrops numbered Hills 5 and 6 (Kannodia-ki-Pahadi). About 1 km west of this group occur Hills 7 and 8. The latter, Nankya Talav-ki-Pahadi, contains two big shelters facing north-west. Opposite them are two rocks named Hills 9 and 10. The nature, technique of execution, patination and state of preservation of the cupules found on all these ten quartz hills resemble those found on Pola Bhata.

Morajhari is located about 20 km east of Nasaribad, near Ajmer, Rajasthan, extending over almost 200 m near a shallow *nala* (Kumar 1998). There are several hundred gneissic boulders strewn over the flat alluvial plain, many of which bear cupules. The focal point of the site is a lithophonic rock resting on top of another boulder, immediately next to a much larger boulder that forms one of the highest of the site (Fig. 3.5). The lithophonic rock is of roughly discoid shape and bears numerous cupules on both sides. This means that only those on its upper surface can now be effectively worked, because those on the lower surface, although mostly visible, are too close to the support boulder to be struck effectively. Therefore the rock, which might weigh around 400 kg, must have been turned at some time. This event effectively provides a *terminus ante quem* for the cupules on the underside, which also cannot bear any recent reworking.

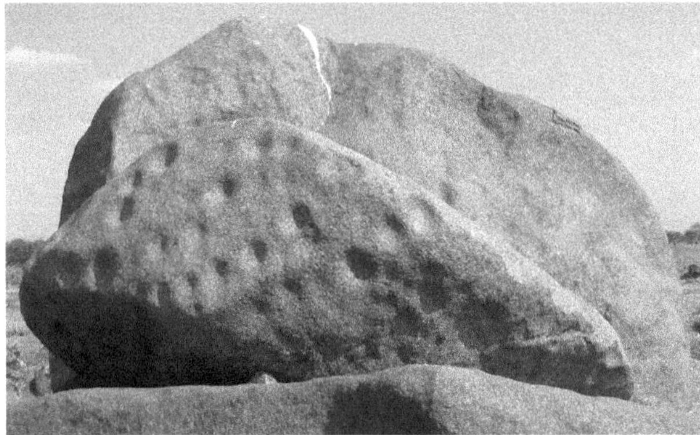

Figure 3.5. Cupule boulder at Morajhari, Rajasthan, of the Holocene.

Microerosion analysis of three cupules on the Morajhari ('Feathers of the Peacock') lithophone suggests that the groupings of the wane widths of one on the upper side indicates re-working at about E2600 years BP, E1750 years BP and E800 years BP. The results from one cupule on the underside substantiate the assumption that the petroglyphs on the rock's underside are older, with a mean age estimate of about E5000 years. The data derived from the third cupule is very compact, by contrast, favouring an age of about E1900 years, i.e. falling within the range of the events expressed in the results from the first cupule.

Another candidate for Palaeolithic-age cupules is Bajanibhat ('Rock that gives sound'; i.e. lithophone). The site is located about 24 km east of Kotputli (Sharma *et al.* 1992; Kumar and Sharma 1995). Near the foot of the mountain range Kalaphad is a prominent shallow shelter, 8 m wide and 5.5 m high. It features a corpus of sixty-seven cupules on its vertical wall, which vary greatly in both their sizes and ages. We consider that there were initially a few cupules, which prompted similar behaviour at much later times, and the practice was continued in many of the cupules until historical times. The latter bear still relatively fresh bruising evidence. One of the younger cupules yields a microerosion age in the order of 6000 years. Lower Palaeolithic tool types occur in profusion at the site, and in its vicinity for hundreds of metres. These include very finely worked, typical ovoid Acheulian handaxes in considerable quantity, rougher bifaces, cleavers, hammerstones and thick Levallois flake tools.

While we have huge numbers worldwide of Middle Palaeolithic rock art motifs, mostly from Australia, the incidence of Lower Palaeolithic examples remains very rare, and confirmed cases remain limited to India. There are specific common characteristics emerging, but because this subject has been so severely neglected until very recently it might be premature to elaborate on possible universal variables within these very early traditions, or the significance they might seem to have shared over immense spatial and temporal distances. The EIP Project (Bednarik 2001b; Kumar 2000–01; Kumar *et al.* 2002) is endeavouring to secure the first data of Lower Palaeolithic petroglyphs. It provides unambiguous evidence of such rock art from archaeological occupation strata at two sites, Auditorium Cave and Daraki-Chattan.

References

ACHARYYA, S.K.; BASU P.K. (1993) – Toba ash on the Indian subcontinent and its implications for the correlation of Late Pleistocene alluvium. *Quaternary Research* 40, p. 10–19.

ANSARI, Z.D. (1970) – Pebble tools from Nittur. In S. B. Deo & M. K. Dhavalikar (eds.): *Indian antiquary 4: Professor H. D. Sankalia felicitation volume*, p. 1–7. Bombay: Popular Prakashan.

ARMAND, J. (1980) – The Middle Pleistocene pebble tool site of Durkadi in central India. *Palaeorient* 5, p. 105–144.

BADAM, G.L.; RAJAGURU, S.N. (1994) – Comment on 'Toba ash on the Indian subcontinent and its implications for the correlation of Late Pleistocene alluvium' by S.K. Acharyya & P.K. Basu. *Quaternary Research* 41, p. 398–399.

BEDNARIK, R.G. (1990a) – An Acheulian haematite pebble with striations. *Rock Art Research*. Melbourne. 7, p. 75.

BEDNARIK, R.G. (1990b) – On the cognitive development of hominids. *Man and Environment*. Puna. 15, p. 1–7.

BEDNARIK, R.G. (1993) – Palaeolithic art in India. *Man and Environment*. Puna. 18/2, p. 33–40.

BEDNARIK, R.G. (1994) – The Pleistocene art of Asia. *Journal of World Prehistory* 8/4, p. 351–375.

BEDNARIK, R.G. (1995a) – Wallace's barrier and the language barrier in archaeology. *Bulletin of the Archaeological and Anthropological Society of Victoria*. Melbourne. 1995/3, p. 6–9.

BEDNARIK, R.G. (1995b) – Concept-mediated marking in the Lower Palaeolithic. *Current Anthropology* 36, p. 605–634.

BEDNARIK, R.G. (1996) – The cupules on Chief's Rock, Auditorium Cave, Bhimbetka. *The Artefact*. Melbourne. 19, p. 63–72.

BEDNARIK, R.G. (1997) – The origins of navigation and language. *The Artefact*. Melbourne. 20, p. 16–56.

BEDNARIK, R.G. (1998) – The technology of petroglyphs. *Rock Art Research*.Melbourne. 15, p. 23–35.

BEDNARIK, R.G. (1999) – Maritime navigation in the Lower and Middle Palaeolithic. *Comptes Rendus de l'Académie des Sciences Paris*. Parsi. 328, p. 559–563.

BEDNARIK, R.G. (2001a) – Cupules: the oldest surviving rock art. *International Newsletter on Rock Art*. Foix. 30, p. 18–23.

BEDNARIK, R.G. (2001b) – The Early Indian Petroglyphs Project (EIP). *Rock Art Research*. Melbourne. 18, p. 72.

BEDNARIK, R.G. (2003) – The earliest evidence of palaeoart. *Rock Art Research*. Melbourne. 20, p. 89–135.

BEDNARIK, R.G.; KUCKENBURG, M. (1999) – *Nale Tasih: Eine Floßfahrt in die Steinzeit*. Stuttgart: Thorbecke.

BEDNARIK, R.G.; KUMAR, G. (2002) – The quartz cupules of Ajmer, Rajasthan. *Purakala*. Agra. 13: 1–2, p. 45–50.

BEDNARIK, R.G.; KUMAR, G.; WATCHMAN, A.; ROBERTS, R.G. (2005) – Preliminary results of the EIP Project. *Rock Art Research*. Melbourne. 22, p. 147–197.

BEDNARIK, R.G.; KUMAR, G.; TYAGI, G.S. (1991) – Petroglyphs from central India. *Rock Art Research*. Melbourne. 8, p. 33–35.

CHAKRAVARTY, K.K.; BEDNARIK, R.G. (1997) – *Indian rock art and its global context*. Delhi: Motilal Banarsidass.

CHESNER, C.A.; ROSE, W.I.; DRAKE, A.D.R.; WESTGATE, J.A. (1991) – Eruptive history of earth's largest Quaternary caldera (Toba, Indonesia) clarified. *Geology* 19, p. 200–203.

D'ERRICO, F.; GAILLARD, C.; MISRA, V.N. (1989) – Collection of non-utilitarian objects by *Homo erectus* in India. *Hominidae. Proceedings of the 2nd International Congress of Human Paleontology*, p. 237–239. Milan: Editoriale Jaca Book.

KORISETTAR, R. (2002) – The archaeology of the south Asian Lower Palaeolithic: history and current studies. In S. Settar & R. Korisettar (eds.): *Prehistory. Archaeology of south Asia*, p. 1–65. Indian Archaeology in Retrospect, Volume 1, Manohar: Indian Council of Historical Research.

KUMAR, G. (1996) – Daraki-Chattan: a Palaeolithic cupule site in India. *Rock Art Research*. Melbourne. 13, p. 38–46.

KUMAR, G. (1998) – Morajhari: a unique cupule site in Ajmer District, Rajasthan. *Purakala*. Agra. 9, p. 61–64.

KUMAR, G. (2000–01) – Early Indian Petroglyphs: scientific investigations and dating by international commission, April 2001 to March 2004. *Purakala*. Agra. 11/12, p. 49–68.

KUMAR, G.; BEDNARIK, R.G.; WATCHMAN, A.; ROBERTS, R.G.; LAWSON, E.; PATTERSON, C. (2002) – 2002 progress report of the EIP Project. *Rock Art Research*. Melbourne. 20, p. 70–71.

KUMAR, G.; SHARMA, M. (1995) – Petroglyph sites in Kalapahad and Ganesh Hill: documentation and observations. *Purakala*. Melbourne. 6, p. 56–59.

KUMAR, G.; PRAJAPATI, S. (2005) – Petroglyphs discovered in Ajmer, Rajasthan. *Purakala*. Agra. 14–15, p. 116–117.

MISHRA, S. (1992) – The age of the Acheulian in India: new evidence. *Current Anthropology* 33, p. 325–328.

MISRA, S.; RAJAGURU, S.N. (1994) – Comment on 'Toba ash on the Indian subcontinent and its implications for the correlation of Late Pleistocene alluvium' by S.K. Acharyya and P.K. Basu. *Quaternary Research* 41, p. 396–397.

MISRA, V.N. (1978) – The Acheulian industry of rock shelter IIIF-23 at Bhimbetka, central India – a preliminary report. *Australian Archaeology*. Canberra. 8, p. 63–106.

MISRA, V.N. (1989) – Stone Age India: an ecological perspective. *Man and Environment*. Puna. 14, p. 17–64.

PETRAGLIA, M.D. (1998) – The Lower Palaeolithic of India and its bearing on the Asian record. In M. D. Petraglia & R. Korisettar (eds.): *Early human behaviour in global context: the rise and diversity of the Lower Palaeolithic record*, p. 343–390. London: Routledge.

RAGHVAN, H.; RAJAGURU, S.N.; MISRA, V.N. (1989) – Radiometric dating of a Quaternary dune section, Didwana, Rajasthan. *Man and Environment*, Puna. 13, p. 19–22.

SHARMA, M.L.; KUMAR, V.; SHARMA, P.T. (1992) – New rock art sites discovered in Sahibi valley, Rajasthan. *Purakala*. Agra. 3, p. 84.

SWISHER, C.C.; CURTIS, G.H.; JACOB, T.; GETTY, A.G.; SUPRIJO, A.; WIDIASMORO (1994) – The age of the earliest hominids in Indonesia. *Science* 263, p. 1118–1121.

SZABO, B.J., MCKINNEY, C.; DALBEY, T.S.; PADDAYYA, K. (1990) – On the age of the Acheulian culture of the Hunsgi-Baichbal valleys, peninsular India. *Bulletin of the Deccan College Postgraduate and Research Institute*. Puna. 50, p. 317–321.

WALLACE, A.R. (1890) – *The Malay Archipelago*. London: Macmillan.

WAKANKAR, V.S. (1975) – Bhimbetka – the prehistoric paradise. *Prachya Pratibha* 3/2, p. 7–29.

THE ORIGINS OF 'MODERN HUMANS' AND PALAEOART RECONSIDERED

Robert G. BEDNARIK

Convener, IFRAO, P.O. Box 216, Caulfield South, VIC 3162, Australia, auraweb@hotmail.com

***Abstract**: There is a widespread belief in archaeology that what are defined as modern humans and the cognition that led to palaeoart arose together about 35,000 years* BP. *This paper reviews the basis of this belief and examines both gracile human origins and the early evidence for symboling. It is shown that the favoured explanation of the rise of 'modern humans' is without adequate basis, that there is no evidence for a intrusive replacement of robust Homo sapiens in Europe or anywhere else, and that the development of human cognition is essentially not connected to skeletal evolution. Palaeoart was in widespread use by traditions of Middle and even Lower Palaeolithic technologies, in Australia, Asia, Africa and even in Europe.*
***Keywords**: Palaeoanthropology, Robusticity, Modernity, Grazilisation, Palaeoart, Europe*

***Résumé**: Il y a une opinion très répandue dans les milieux archéologiques qui définie l'émergence de l'homme anatomiquement moderne et de l'art paléolithique il y a approximativement 35,000 ans. Dans cet article, l'auteur interroge les bases de cette conviction et examine l'origine des humains de type gracile ainsi que les premiers témoignages de comportements symbolique. L'auteur établit le fait que les explications en cours sur l'émergence de l'homme anatomiquement moderne sont basées sur des convictions inadéquates et qu'il n'y a pas d'évidences qui soutiennent le remplacement importun de l'Homo sapiens de type robuste en Europe ou ailleurs. Il est démontré que le développement du système cognitif humain ne va pas forcément de pairs avec l'évolution ostéologique du squelette humain. L'art paléolithique était déjà très répandu dans les cultures du Paléolithique moyen et inférieur en Australie, en Asie, en Afrique et même en Europe.*
***Mots clés**: Paléoanthropologie, robuste, gracile, modernité, Europe*

The conceptually most complex portable and parietal art of the Upper Palaeolithic is not of the late phase of that period, but of the Aurignacian, at its beginning (Bednarik 1995a). It includes the two therianthropes from Swabia (Hohlenstein-Stadel, Schmid 1989; and Hohle Fels, Conard *et al.* 2003), numerous further portable items from other caves in the Swabian Alb, the anthropomorph from Galgenberg (Bednarik 1989), the small corpus of rock art of l'Aldène (created before the decorated passage became closed 30,260 ± 220 BP; Ambert *et al.* 2005: 276–7; Ambert and Guendon 2005); the early phase of the rock art in Baume Latrone (Bégouën 1941; Drouot 1953; Bednarik 1986); and most particularly the early phase in Chauvet Cave (Chauvet *et al.* 1995; Clottes 2001; Clottes *et al.* 1995; Valladas *et al.* 2004), a site that probably became sealed about 24 ka (thousand years) ago (Bednarik 2004). 'Aurignacians' seem to have been especially interested in 'dangerous animals', and one of the most interesting cultural markers of 'Aurignacoid' traditions is the evidence of intentionally deposited remains of cave bears, notably their skulls and long-bones (Fig. 4.1). Such deposition evidence occurs in Chauvet. Yet the dating endeavours by Clottes and colleagues at that site have attracted more sustained criticism than any of the other attempts to date European Pleistocene cave art (Zuechner 1996; Pettitt and Bahn 2003). Nevertheless, the site's rock art is the best-dated of the Palaeolithic sites so far subjected to any form of scientific dating. The reason for this disagreement is that the Chauvet results were the first to severely challenge the traditional stylistic chronology of Upper Palaeolithic rock art (Bednarik 1995a). Some authors define Chauvet as blending in well with aspects of style and content of secure Aurignacian art, such as the series of portable objects from south-western Germany, while others reject the Aurignacian antiquity of Chauvet on the basis of their individual stylistic constructs, and favour its placement in the Magdalenian.

The real problems with Chauvet are not even considered by the critics of the dating attempts, who seem only concerned with salvaging a stylistic chronology. Two issues are of paramount importance: all carbon isotope determinations of the *European Late Pleistocene Shift* in southern Europe need to be considered sceptically, because of the effects of the Campanian Ignimbrite event and the cosmogenic radionuclide peak about a millennium earlier (Fedele *et al.* 2002). The best available ^{14}C determinations for the CI eruption place it between 35,600 ± 150 and 33,200 ± 600 carbon-years BP (Deino *et al.* 1994), but the age of the event derived from a large series (36 determinations from 18 samples) of high-precision single-crystal $^{40}Ar/^{39}Ar$ measurements is 39,280 ± 110 BP (De Vivo *et al.* 2001). Fedele and Giaccio (2007) have proposed that a significant volcanogenic sulfate signal in the GISP2 ice core, occurring precisely 40,012 BP, represents the Campanian eruption. Therefore, in southern France, carbon isotope dates only marginally lower than the carbon age of the CI event may well be several millennia too low, and the true age of the early Chauvet phase could easily be as high as 36 to 38 ka.

More than ten years ago I pointed out that we have no evidence whatsoever that the Early Aurignacian is the work of 'moderns' (Bednarik 1995a), to which I can now add that we have no proof of an 'anatomically modern' ethnicity of the makers of *any tool tradition of the entire first half of the so-called Upper Palaeolithic* – including the entire Aurignacian. The search for physical modernity is itself misguided (Tobias 1995); modernity is indicated by cognition and culture, and more specifically by the

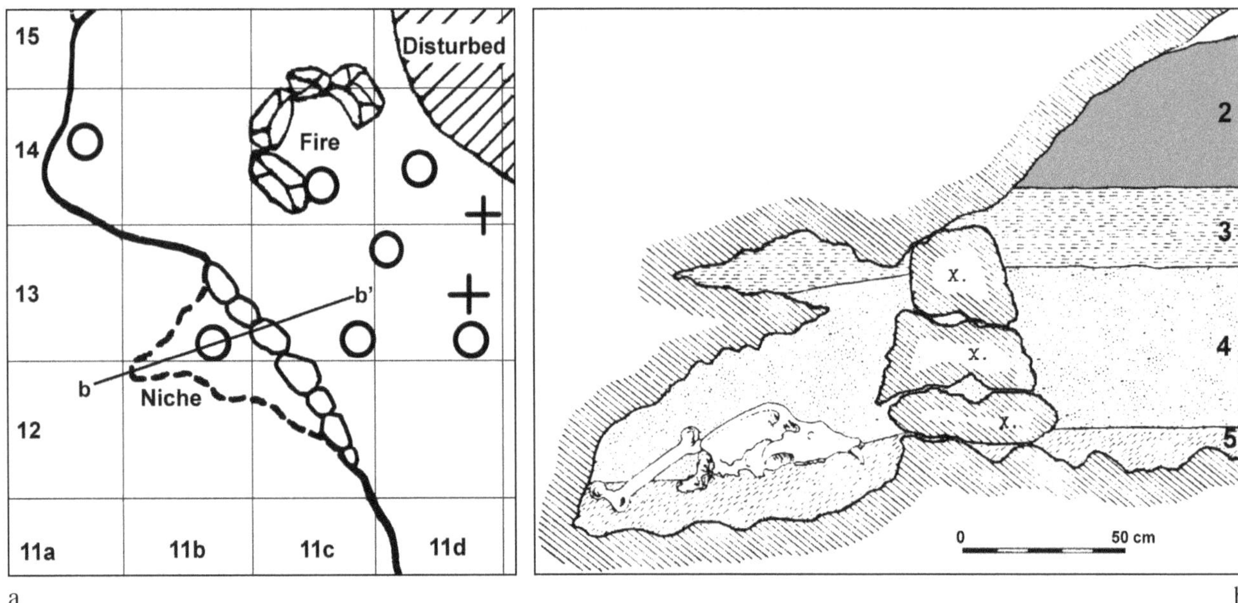

Figure 4.1. Plan view (a) and section (b) of the western niche in Veternica Cave, Croatia, indicating the artificial masonry wall and other elements of the Final Mousterian. The circles indicate cave bear skulls, the crosses represent human skulls (after Malez 1959).

external storage of cultural information (Donald 1993). The present archaeological and palaeoanthropological evidence suggests that we have Neanderthaloid remains from the time interval in question, and we have no securely provenanced 'moderns'. European Pleistocene archaeologists are obliged to consider the possibility that the Aurignacian is the work either of 'Neanderthals' or of their descendants who experienced genetic drift rather than 'replacement'. Science works by falsification, and the proposition to be tested now is that Aurignacian 'art', like Châtelperronian 'art', *was created not by 'moderns'*.

Contrary to Churchill and Smith (2000), the Stetten specimens tell us nothing about the skeletal anatomy of the 'Aurignacians' (Czarnetzki 1983: 231; Gieseler 1974). The putative age of the Stetten specimens, 32 ka, now stands refuted by their direct dating to the late Neolithic period (Conard *et al.* 2004), confirming the obvious: that they are intrusive burials. Direct carbon isotope determinations, of samples taken from the mandible of Stetten 1 (Fig. 4.2), the cranium of Stetten 2, a humerus of Stetten 3 and a vertebra of Stetten 4 all agree, falling between 3980 ± 35 BP and 4995 ± 35 BP.

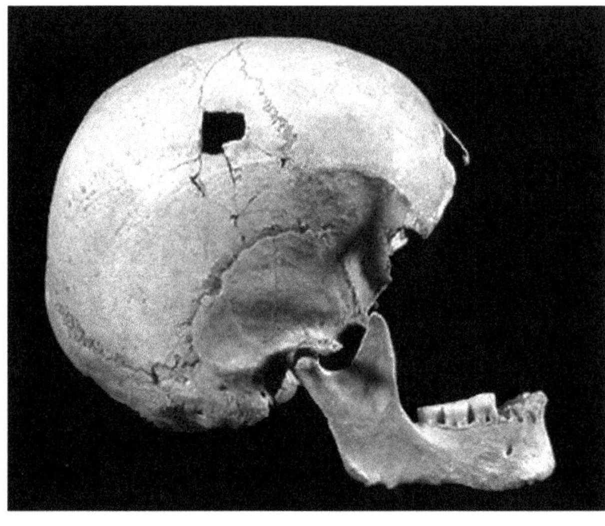

Figure 4.2. The skull and mandible of Stetten 1, long claimed to be of the Aurignacian, is actually of the late Neolithic.

The Hahnöfersand calvarium, described as so robust that it was judged to show typical Neanderthal features (Bräuer 1980), was initially dated to the earliest 'Upper Palaeolithic' (Fra-24: 36,300 ± 600 BP; UCLA-2363: 35,000 ± 2000 BP, or 33,200 ± 2990 BP; Bräuer 1980). These results conflict sharply with those secured by Terberger and Street (2003): P-11493: 7470 ± 100 BP; OxA-10306: 7500 ± 55 BP. The re-dating of the skull fragment from Paderborn-Sande yielded even more dramatic differences. Originally dated at 27,400 ± 600 BP (Fra-15; Henke and Protsch 1978), Terberger and Street (2003) report an age of only 238 ± 39 BP (OxA-9879). Then there is the cranial fragment of Binshof near Speyer, dated by R. Protsch in the 1970s as Fra-40 to 21,300 ± 320 BP. According to Terberger and Street it is only 3090 ± 45 carbon years old (OxA-9880). These authors also analysed two specimens from the Urdhöhle near Döbritz, which had been attributed to the Upper Palaeolithic, and found them both to be about 8400 years old. The skull from Kelsterbach had been dated to 31,200 ± 1600 BP (Fra-5) (Protsch und Semmel 1978; Henke und Rothe 1994), but has mysteriously disappeared. It is now also believed to be of the Holocene, perhaps the Metal Ages (Terberger and Street 2003). Indeed, of all the German

'Upper Palaeolithic' specimens, only one remains safely dated to earlier than 13,000 BP, from Mittlere Klause in Bavaria. A carbon isotope date of 18,200 ± 200 BP (UCLA-1869) from a tibia fragment (Protsch and Glowatzki 1974) has been confirmed by Terberger and Street's date from a vertebra, of 18,590 ± 260 BP (OxA-9856). It has therefore become clear that there are currently no 'modern' remains from the first two thirds of the west-central European Upper Palaeolithic.

Similarly, the sample from Crô-Magnon, traditionally regarded as typical representatives of invading 'moderns' in Europe, has been falsely attributed. Sonneville-Bordes (1959) placed the four adults and four juveniles in the late Aurignacian, Movius (1969) suggested an age of about 30 ka BP and preferred an attribution to the Aurignacian 2. The recent re-dating to about 27,760 carbon years BP (Henry-Gambier 2002) renders previous opinions invalid, and the remains are probably of the Gravettian. Moreover, the very pronounced supraorbital torus, projecting occipital bone and other features of cranium 3 are Neanderthaloid rather than gracile. This and other aspects of the partially robust Crô-Magnon series question the full 'modernity' of the group – but irrespective of this, it tells us also nothing about the anatomy of the 'Aurignacians'.

The identical claims for the Mladeč specimens from the Czech Republic are just as tenuous. It is uncertain that the cave was even accessible to Upper Palaeolithic humans (Jelínek 1987). Recent attempts to provide direct dates from some of the human remains (Wild *et al.* 2005) yielded five results ranging from about 26,330 to 31,500 BP. The fossils are therefore at best from the latest part of the Aurignacian period (45 ka to 30 ka BP), but also point to a possible Gravettian age. Moreover, there is considerable evidence that the Mladeč humans were far from fully 'modern' (Smith 1982, 1985; Frayer 1986; Trinkaus and Le May 1982). Sexual dimorphism is pronounced, with male crania being very robust. The material from Pavlov Hill is among the most robust available from the European Upper Palaeolithic, sharing its age of between 26 and 27 ka with yet another Moravian site of the Gravettian, Předmostí. The more gracile finds from Dolní Vestonice are around 25 ka old and still feature some archaic characteristics (particularly the Neanderthaloid specimen DV16). Morphologically similar specimens also come from Cioclovina (Romania), Bacho Kiro levels 6/7 (Bulgaria) and Miesslingtal (Austria), so this is unlikely to be a local phenomenon.

Other specimens that have been considered as very early European Moderns include the calotte from Podbaba, near Prague, variously described as sapienoid and Neanderthaloid, but undated. Then there are the robust but 'modern' hominin remains of the EUP (early 'Upper Palaeolithic') at Velika Pećina, Croatia, close to the Neanderthal site Vindija. This specimen is now considered to be only 5045 ± 40 carbon years old (OxA-8294; Smith *et al.* 1999).

The loss of the only relevant Spanish remains, from El Castillo and apparently of the very early Aurignacian, renders it impossible to determine their anatomy. French contenders for EUP age present a mosaic of unreliable provenience or uncertain age, and direct dating is mostly not available. Like the Vogelherd and other specimens, those from Roche-Courbon (Geay 1957) and Combe-Capelle (originally attributed to the Châtelperronian levels; Klaatsch and Hauser 1910) are thought to be of Holocene burials (Perpère 1971; Asmus 1964), and the former is now apparently lost. Similar considerations apply to the partial skeleton from Les Cottés, whose stratigraphical position could not be ascertained (Perpère 1973). Finds from La Quina, La Chaise de Vouthon and Les Roches are too fragmentary to provide diagnostic details. The *os frontale* and fragmentary right maxilla with four teeth from La Crouzade, the mandible fragment from Isturitz and the two juvenile mandibles from Les Rois range from robust to very robust. Just as the Crô-Magnon human remains now appear to be of the Gravettian rather than the Aurignacian, so do those from La Rochette. The Fontéchevade parietal bone does lack prominent tori but the site's juvenile mandibular fragment is robust. The currently earliest 'intermediate' finds in Europe, the Peştera cu Oase mandible and face from south-western Romania (Trinkaus *et al.* 2003), are perhaps about 35,000 carbon years old, but are without an archaeological context. Although in some aspects 'modern', their 'derived Neanderthal features' identify them as a Post-Neanderthal rather than a gracile 'modern'. Soficaru *et al.* (2006) have reported six human bones from another Romanian cave, Peştera Muierii, which are also intermediate between robust and gracile Europeans (~30,000 BP).

This pattern of features intermediate between what palaeoanthropologists regard as Neanderthals and moderns is found in literally hundreds of specimens apparently in the order of 45 to 25 ka old. Grazilisation is a universal process in all world regions then occupied by humans, from Portugal to Australia. Intermediate forms between archaic *Homo sapiens* forms and *Homo sapiens sapiens* include examples, some of them much older, from right across the breadth of Eurasia, such as those from Largo Velho, Crete, Starosel'e, Rozhok, Akhshtyr', Romankovo, Samara, Sungir', Podkumok, Khvalynsk, Skhodnya, Narmada, as well as Chinese remains such as those from Jinniushan. The model of the replacement protagonists cannot tolerate such intermediate forms, nor can it allow hybrids, yet in Europe there is a clear continuation of some Neanderthaloid features right up to and into the Holocene. This is demonstrated not only by the Hahnöfersand specimen, but also by many others, such as the equally robust Mesolithic skull fragment from Drigge, about 6250 years old (Terberger 1998). The process of gracilisation has in fact continued to the present time, with notable changes continuing in the Final Pleistocene and the Holocene. The humans at the beginning of the Holocene were about 10% more robust than modern Europeans, those of the Solutrean were more robust again, as were those of the Gravettian. The latter in fact show very distinctive sexual dimorphism, with the males being almost as robust as 'Neanderthals', the females far more gracile, but still more robust than Holocene males. EUP hominins, including those of the Aurignacian and Châtelperronian, are more robust again, and from all available evidence should be considered Neanderthal. Therefore the most distinctive aspect of human evolution over the past 45 ka is a continuous trend of gracilisation.

There are now almost no supposedly modern specimens left as possible contenders for attribution to EUP or Aurignacoid industries. The maxilla from Kent's Cavern, United Kingdom (c. 31 ^{14}C ka BP), and the Pestera Cioclovina remains (~29 ^{14}C ka BP) lack secure and diagnostic archaeological association. There are, however, numerous 'Neanderthal' remains to fill this void. Of particular interest are the most recent, those from Saint Césaire (Châtelperronian, c. 36 ka), Arcy-sur-Cure (Châtelperronian, c. 34 ka), Trou de l'Abîme (Aurignacian), Vindija Cave (Olschewian, c. 28 and 29 ka) and Máriaremete Upper Cave (Jankovichian, c. 38 ka). Arcy-sur-Cure yielded numerous ornaments and portable art objects, which prompted various convoluted explanations of how these pendants could have possibly found their way into a 'Neanderthal' assemblage (e.g. White 1993; Hublin *et al.* 1996; a similar accommodative argument was used by Karavanic and Smith 1998 in explaining the UP bone points of Neanderthals in Vindija layer G1). The Vindija late Neanderthals used EUP tools and technology (Ahern *et al.* 2004) and are more gracile than Neanderthals of earlier periods, and they are considered to be transitional (Smith and Raynard 1980; Wolpoff *et al.* 1981; Frayer *et al.* 1993; Wolpoff 1999). Vindija Vi-207 is a mandible of 29,080 ± 400 carbon years BP (OxA-8296), Vindija Vi-208 is a parietal of 28,020 ± 360 carbon years BP (OxA-8295) (Smith *et al.* 1999).

Therefore all the evidence from the crucial period of 45 to 25 ka indicates in Europe a mosaic of robust and intermediate human anatomy, and one of gradual gracilisation. It is incredible that this trend has attracted almost no detailed attention, despite obviously being repeated in the three other continents then occupied. For instance in Australia there are distinctive gracile specimens, well over 30 ka old and, some would say, even twice that age, while in the same geographical region, near the Murray River, robusticity is well represented as recently as 10 ka BP. Just as in Europe, the two morphological types share technologies and even palaeoart traditions. Just as in Europe, cultures and physical traits are clearly unrelated, but in Australia no archaeologist has ever suggested that one group 'scavenged' palaeoart objects from the other. By explaining away the incredible reduction of brain size, bone robustness and musculature as being attributable to mass migration and replacement, if not genocide, European researchers have replaced search for evidence with dogmatic belief. There is, after all, not one iota of evidence of an Upper Palaeolithic tradition passing through northern Africa or the Levant before such tools appear in Siberia and Europe. Nor is there any evidence along such potential migration routes of figurative art traditions, all the evidence indicates that these evolved in situ, in such places as south-western Germany and southern France. So did the EUP tool traditions, commencing in various centres from Spain to the Far East, and so also did human anatomy, in all regions of the world then occupied by humans.

The EUP tool, rock art and portable art traditions of Europe can be either the work of 'Neanderthals', or of the descendents of Neanderthals, or of invading 'moderns'. There is currently no evidence for the third possibility. Consequently we need to assume that the Aurignacian was a technological and cultural tradition of robust, Neanderthal-like people. This brings us back to Chauvet Cave, where we began these considerations. On the basis of current evidence, the strongest hypothesis is that the rock art in that cave was made by 'Neanderthal' people.

Of particular interest in that context are the very numerous human footprints in Chauvet Cave (in Salle des Bauges, Salle du Crâne and Galerie des Croisillions). The superbly preserved human tracks I have examined in the cave are, in my view, more likely to be of Neanderthaloids than of 'Moderns', for a number of reasons. In most if not all 'Neanderthal' skeletal remains it appears that the big toe is shorter than the second toe, whereas the converse applies to the known 'Crô-Magnon' remains as well as footprints. This may of course be coincidence, both versions can be found among modern Europeans. However, in the case of the supposedly 8 to 10-year-old child that strode through Chauvet Cave, the second toe is not only longer, it is offset above its two neighbours (Fig. 4.3). In a child not used to wearing tight footwear, this might be a diagnostic feature. Moreover, the Chauvet tracks also show other characteristics that differ from most modern human tracks. The ratio of the widths across heel and front of foot is markedly greater, and more pressure has been applied to the outside margin, which is perfectly straight (Clottes 2001: Fig. 28). This suggests a somewhat bow-legged gait, which may be consistent with 'Neanderthals'.

Finally, there is the fallacious argument that 'art' began with the mythical intrusive 'modern' people in Europe. We have long known that art-like productions precede the Upper Palaeolithic by hundreds of millennia (Bednarik 1992, 1995b). Even figurative art did not commence with Chauvet, the earliest currently known example is one of three engravings from Oldisleben (Fig. 4.4), being of the Micoquian (Bednarik 2006). Now that we assume that even the palaeoart of the Châtelperronian, the Bachokirian and the Aurignacian is the creation of robust, Neanderthal-like people, we lack any good reason to doubt that robust humans of the Middle and even of the Lower Palaeolithic lacked the capacity of symbolism and palaeoart production. We have long known about

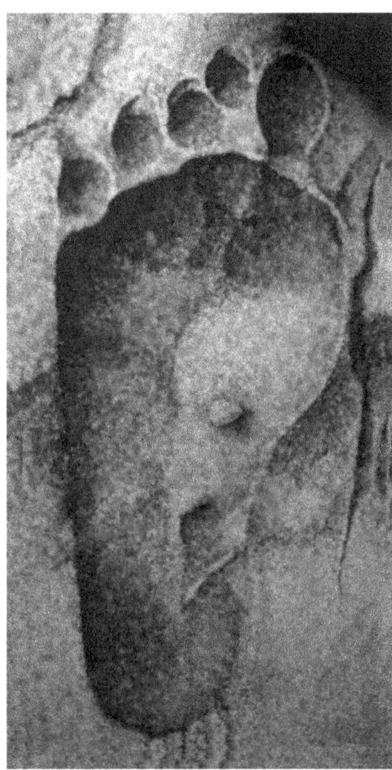

Figure 4.3. Footprint of a Neanderthaloid child on the floor of Chauvet Cave, France.

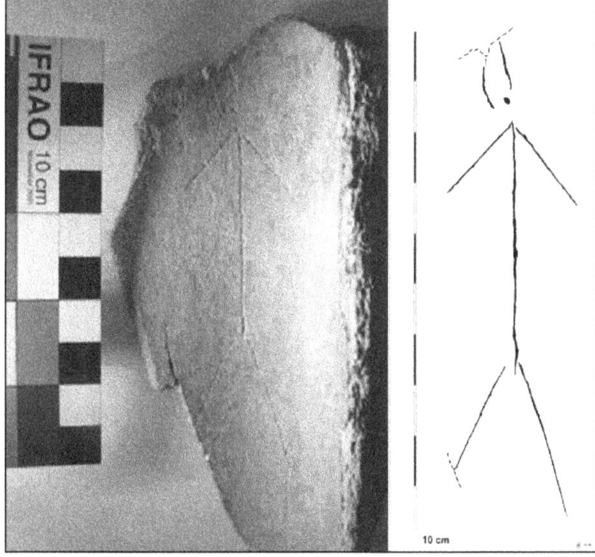

Figure 4.4. Engraving on a shoulder blade from Oldisleben, Germany, apparently figurative, of the Micoquian.

thousands of such productions, which include stone beads (Fig. 4.5) (Bednarik 2005) and proto-sculptures (Fig. 4.6) of the Acheulian (Bednarik 2003), and petroglyphs even from a cultural layer predating Acheulian occupation (Fig. 4.7) (Bednarik *et al.* 2005).

In summary, we have no evidence that the Aurignacian, Châtelperronian, Uluzzian, Uluzzo-Aurignacian, Proto-Aurignacian, Olschewian, Bachokirian, Bohunician, Spit-

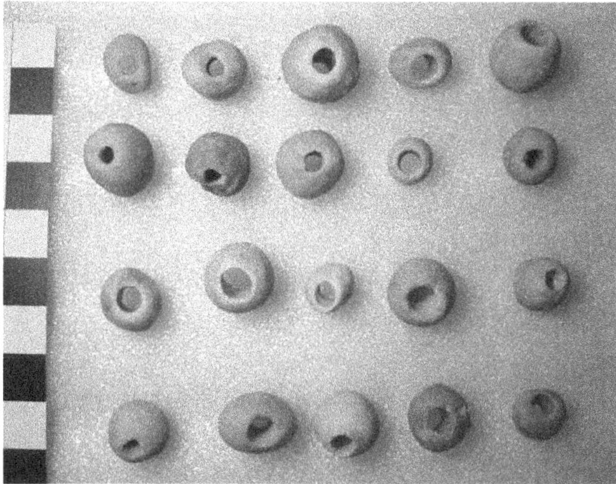

Figure 4.5. Acheulian stone beads from Bedford, England.

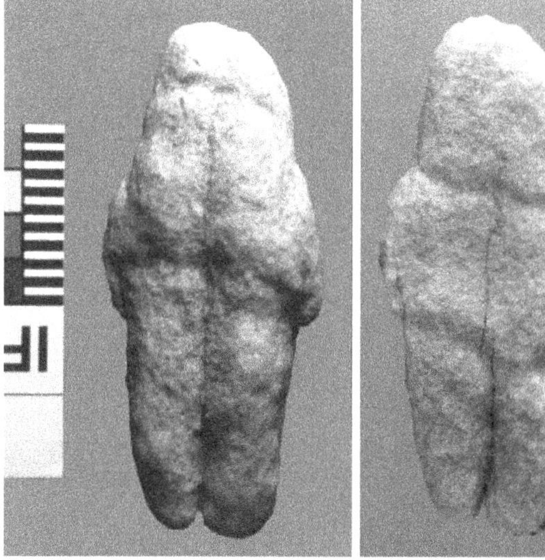

Figure 4.6. Proto-sculpture of the Middle Acheulian, from Tan-Tan, southern Morocco, naturally shaped quartzite with artificial grooves and microscopic traces of former haematite coating.

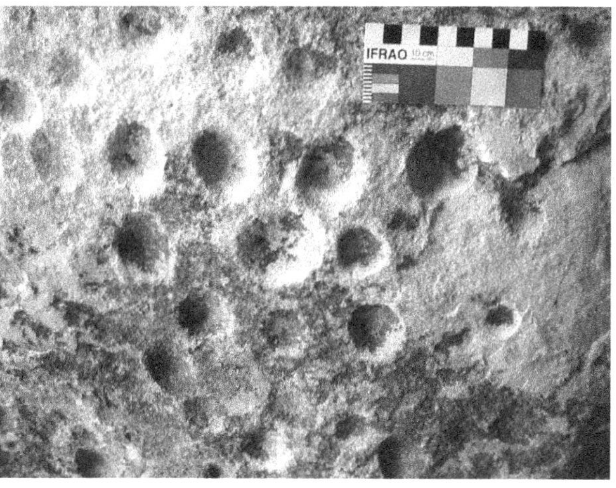

Figure 4.7. Cupules dated to the Lower Palaeolithic period, Daraki-Chattan, India.

syn culture, Szeletian, Jankovichian, Streletsian, Altmühlian, Lincombian or Jerzmanovician (all of which seem to have developed in situ) are the work of physically modern people. We have evidence that at least some of them are of 'Neanderthals' or 'Post-Neanderthals', and quite probably this applies to all pre-Gravettian traditions in Europe. By the time of the Gravettian, the rate of grazilisation of humans suggests culturally moderated breeding: robust characteristics were selected against by culturally determined preferences. Grazilisation is a global phenomenon of the Final Pleistocene and Holocene, and it has been completely neglected until now that its great evolutionary cost (reduced muscle bulk and brain size, more delicate bone architecture) suggests natural selection was replaced by unintended 'self-domestication'.

References

AHERN, J.C.M.; KARAVANIC, I.; PAUNOVIĆ, M.; JANKOVIĆ, I.; SMITH, F.H. (2004) – New discoveries and interpretations of fossil hominids and artifacts from Vindija Cave, Croatia. *Journal of Human Evolution* 46, p. 25–65.

AMBERT, P.; GUENDON, J.-L.; GALANT, P.; QUINIF, Y.; GRUNESEIN, A.; COLOMER, A.; DAINAT, D.; BEAUMES, B.; REQUIRAND, C. (2005) – Attribution des gravures paléolithiques de la grotte d'Aldène (Cesseras, Hérault) à l'Aurignacien par la datation des remplissages géologiques. *Comptes Rendus Palevol,* Elsevier, Paris 4, p. 275–284.

AMBERT, P.; GUENDON, J.-L. (2005) – AMS estimates of the age of parietal art and human footprints in the grotte d'Aldène (southern France). *International Newsletter on Rock Art*. Foix. 43, p. 6–7.

ASMUS, G. (1964) – Kritische Bemerkungen und neue Gesichtspunkte zur jungpaläolithischen Bestattung von Combe-Capelle, Périgord. *Eiszeitalter und Gegenwart* 15, p. 181–186.

BEDNARIK, R.G. (1986) – Parietal finger markings in Europe and Australia. *Rock Art Research*. Merlbourne. 3, p. 30–61, 159–170.

BEDNARIK, R.G. (1989) – The Galgenberg figurine from Krems, Austria. *Rock Art Research*. Melbourne. 8, p. 118–125.

BEDNARIK, R.G. (1992) – Palaeoart and archaeological myths. *Cambridge Archaeological Journal*. Cambridge. 2, p 27–43.

BEDNARIK, R.G. (1995a) – Refutation of stylistic constructs in Palaeolithic rock art. *Comptes Rendus de L'Académie de Sciences Paris*. Paris. 321 (série IIa, No. 9), p. 817–821.

BEDNARIK, R.G. (1995b) – Concept-mediated marking in the Lower Palaeolithic. *Current Anthropology* 36/4, p. 605–634.

BEDNARIK, R.G. (2003) – A figurine from the African Acheulian. *Current Anthropology* 44/3, p. 405–413.

BEDNARIK, R.G. (2004) – The cave bear in Chauvet Cave. *Cave Art Research*. Melbourne. 4, p. 1–12.

BEDNARIK, R.G. (2005) – Middle Pleistocene beads and symbolism. *Anthropos*. St Augustin. 100/2, p. 537–552.

BEDNARIK, R.G. (2006) – The Middle Palaeolithic engravings from Oldisleben, Germany. *Anthropologie*. Brno. 44/1, p. 113–121.

BEDNARIK, R.G.; KUMAR, G.; WATCHMAN, A.; ROBERTS, R.G. (2005) – Preliminary results of the EIP Project. *Rock Art Research*. Melbourne. 22, p. 147–197.

BEGOUËN, H. (1941) – La Grotte de Baume-Latrone á Russan (Sainte-Anastasie), *Mémoires de la Société Archéologie du Midi de la France* 20, p. 101–130.

BRÄUER, G. (1980) – Die morphologischen Affinitäten des jungpleistozänen Stirnbeins aus dem Elbmündungsgebiet bei Hahnöfersand. *Zeitschrift für Morphologie und Anthropologie* 71, p. 1–42.

CHURCHILL, S.E.; SMITH, F.H. (2000) – A modern human humerus from the early Aurignacian of Vogelherdhöhle (Stetten, Germany). *American Journal of Physical Anthropology* 112, p. 251–273

CHAUVET, J.-M.; BRUNEL-DESCHAMPS, E.; HILLAIRE, C. (1995) – *La Grotte Chauvet à Vallon-Pont-d'Arc*. Paris: Seuil.

CLOTTES, J. (ed.) (2001) – *La Grotte Chauvet: l'art des origines*. Paris: Seuil.

CLOTTES J.; CHAUVET, J.-M.; BRUNEL-DESCHAMPS, E.; HILLAIRE, C.; DAUGAS, J.-P.; ARNOLD, M.; CACHIER, H.; EVIN, J.; FORTIN, P.; OBERLIN, C.; TISNERAT, N.; VALLADAS, H. (1995) – Les peintures paléolithiques de la Grotte Chauvet-Pont d'Arc, à Vallon-Pont-d'Arc (Ardèche, France): datations directes et indirectes par la méthode du radiocarbone. *Comptes Rendus de l'Académie des Sciences de Paris*. Paris. 320, Ser. II, p. 1133–1140.

CONARD, N.J.; GROOTES, P.M.; SMITH, F.H. (2004) – Unexpectedly recent dates for human remains from Vogelherd. *Nature*. London. 430, p. 198–201.

CONARD, N.; LANGGUTH, K.; UERPMANN, H.-P. (2003) – Einmalige Funde aus dem Aurignacien und erste Belege für ein Mittelpaläolithikum im Hohle Fels bei Schelklingen, Alb-Donau-Kreis, in *Archäologische Ausgrabungen in Baden-Württemberg 2002*, p. 21–27. Stuttgart: Konrad Theiss.

CZARNETZKI, A. (1983) – Zur Entwicklung des Menschen in Südwestdeutschland. In: H. Müller Beck (ed.): *Urgeschichte in Baden-Württemberg*, p. 217–240. Stuttgart: Konrad Theiss.

DEINO, A.L.; SOUTHON, J.; TERRASI, F.; CAMPATOLA, L.; ORSI, G. (1994) – ^{14}C and ^{40}Ar/^{39}Ar dating of the Campanian Ignimbrite, Phlegrean Fields, Italy. In *Abstracts, ICOG 1994*, Berkeley, CA.

DE VIVO, B.; ROLANDI, G.; GANS, P.B.; CALVERT, A.; BOHRSON, W.A.; SPERA, F.J.; BELKIN, H.E. (2001) – New constraints on the pyroclastic eruptive history of the Campanian volcanic Plain (Italy). *Mineralogical Petrology* 73, p. 47–65.

DONALD, M. (1993) – Précis of the origins of the modern mind. Three stages in the evolution of culture and cognition. *Behavioral and Brain Sciences* 16, p. 737–791.

DROUOT, E. (1953) – L'art paléolithique á La Baume-Latrone, *Cahiers ligures de préhistoire et d'archéologie*, Pt 1, p. 13–46.

FEDELE, F.G.; GIACCIO, B. (2007) – Paleolithic cultural change in western Eurasia across the 40,000 BP timeline: continuities and environmental forcing. In: P. Chenna Reddy (ed.): *Exploring the mind of ancient man. Festschrift to Robert G. Bednarik*, p. 292–316. New Delhi: Research India Press.

FEDELE, F.G.; GIACCIO, B.; ISAIA, R.; ORSI, G. (2002) – Ecosystem impact of the Campanian Ignimbrite eruption in Late Pleistocene Europe. *Quaternary Research* 57, p. 420–424.

FRAYER, D.W. (1986) – Cranial variation at Mladeč and the relationship between Mousterian and Upper Palaeolithic hominids. *Anthropologie*. Brno. 23, p. 243–256.

FRAYER, D.W.; WOLPOFF, M.H.; SMITH, F.H.; THORNE, A.G.; POPE, G.G. (1993) – The fossil evidence for modern human origins. *American Anthropology* 95, p. 14–50.

GEAY, P. (1957) – Sur la découverte d'un squelette aurignacien? en Charente-Maritime. *Bulletin de la Société Préhistoroque Française* 54, p. 193–197.

GIESELER, W. (1974) – *Die Fossilgeschichte des Menschen*. Stuttgart: Konrad Theiss.

HENKE, W.; PROTSCH, R. (1978) – Die Paderborner Calvaria – ein diluvialer *Homo sapiens*. *Anthropologischer Anzeiger* 36, p. 85–108.

HENKE, W.; ROTHE, H. (1994) – *Paläoanthropologie*. Berlin.

HENRY-GAMBIER, D. (2002) – Les fossiles de Cro-Magnon (Les-Eyzies-de-Tayac, Dordogne): Nouvelles données sur leur position chronologique et leur attribution culturelle. *Bulletin et Mémoires de la Société d'Anthropologie de Paris* 14/1-2, p. 89–112.

HUBLIN, J.-J.; SPOOR, F.; BRAUN, M.; ZONNEVELD, F.; CONDEMI, S. (1996) – A late Neanderthal associated with Upper Palaeolithic artefacts. *Nature*. London. 381, p. 224–226.

JELÍNEK, J. (1987) – Historie, identifikace a význam mladečských antropologických nálezů z počátku mladého paleolitu. *Anthropologie*. Brno. 25, p. 51–69.

KARAVANIC, I.; SMITH, H. (1998) – The Middle/Upper Palaeolithic interface and the relationship of Neanderthals and early modern humans in the Hrvatsko Zagorje, Croatia. *Journal of Human Evolution* 34, p. 223–248.

KLAATSCH, H.; HAUSER, O. (1910) – *Homo Aurignaciensis Hauseri*. *Prähistorische Zeitschrift* 1, p. 273–338.

MOVIUS, H.L. (1969) – The Abri of Cro-Magnon, Les Eyzies (Dordogne) and the probable age of the contained burials on the basis of the nearby Abri Pataud. *Anuario de Estudio Atlanticos* 15, p. 323–344.

PERPÈRE, M. (1971) – *L'aurignacien en Poitou-Charentes (étude des collections d'industries lithiques)*. University of Paris, unpublished PhD thesis.

PERPERE, M. (1973) – Les grands gisements aurignaciens du Poitou. *L'Anthropologie* 77, p. 683–716.

PETTITT, P.; BAHN, P. (2003) – Current problems in dating Palaeolithic cave art: Candamo and Chauvet. *Antiquity*. Cambridge. 77, p. 134–141.

PROTSCH, R.; GLOWATZKI, H. (1974) – Das absolute Alter des paläolithischen Skeletts aus der Mittleren Klause bei Neuessing, Kreis Kelheim, Bayern. *Anthropologischer Anzeiger* 34, p. 140–144.

PROTSCH, R.; SEMMEL, A. (1978) – Zur Chronologie des Kelsterbach-Hominiden. *Eiszeitalter und Gegenwart* 28, p. 200–210.

SCHMID, E. (1989) – Die Elfenbeinstuatuette vom Hohlenstein-Stadel im Lonetal. *Fundberichte aus Baden-Württemberg* 14, p. 33–96.

SMITH, F.H. (1982) – Upper Pleistocene hominid evolution in south-central Europe: a review of the evidence and analysis of trends. *Current Anthropology* 23, p. 667–686.

SMITH, F.H. (1985) – Continuity and change in the origin of modern *Homo sapiens*. *Zeitschrift für Morphologie und Anthropologie* 75, p. 197–222.

SMITH, F.H.; RANYARD, G. (1980) – Evolution of the supraorbital region in Upper Pleistocene fossil hominids from south-central Europe. *American Journal of Physical Anthropology* 53, p. 589–610.

SMITH, F.H.; TRINKAUS, E.; PETTITT, P.B.; KARAVANIĆ, I.; PAUNOVIĆ, M. (1999) – Direct radiocarbon dates for Vindija G_1 and Velika Pećina Late Pleistocene hominid remains. *Proceedings of the National Academy of Sciences of the United States of America* 96/22, p. 12281–12286.

SOFICARU, A.; DOBOŞ, A.; TRINKAUS, E. (2006) – Early modern humans from the Peştera Muierii, Baia de Fier, Romania. *Proceedings of the National Academy of Sciences of the U.S.A.* 103/46, p. 17196–17201

SONNEVILLE-BORDES, D. DE (1959) – Position-stratigraphique et chronologique relative des restes humains du Palaéolithique supérieur entre Loire et Pyrénées. *Annales de Paléontologie* 45, p. 19–51.

TERBERGER, T. (1998) – Endmesolithische Funde von Drigge, Lkr. Rügen – Kannibalen auf Rügen? *Jahrbuch für Bodendenkmalpflege Mecklenburg-Vorpommern* 46, p. 7–44.

TERBERGER, T.; STREET, M. (2003) – Jungpaläolithische Menschenreste im westlichen Mitteleuropa und ihr Kontext. In J. M. Burdukiewicz, L. Fiedler, W.-D. Heinrich, A. Justus and E. Brühl (eds.): *Erkenntnisjäger: Kultur und Umwelt des frühen Menschen*, p. 579–591. Halle: Veröffentlichungen des Landesamtes für Archäologie Sachsen-Anhalt – Landesmuseum für Vorgeschichte, Vol. 57/2.

TOBIAS, P.V. (1995) – The bearing of fossils and mitochondrial DNA on the evolution of modern humans, with a critique of the 'mitochondrial Eve' hypothesis. *South African Archaeological Bulletin* 50, p. 155–167.

TRINKAUS, E.; Le MAY, M. (1982) – Occipital bunning among Later Pleistocene hominids. *American Journal of Physical Anthropology* 57, p. 27–35.

TRINKAUS, E.; MOLDOVAN, O.; MILOTA, Ş.; BÎLGAR, A.; SARCINA, L.; ATHREYA, S.; BAILEY, S.E.; RODRIGO, R.; MIRCEA, G.; HIGHAM, T.; BRONK RAMSEY, C.; van der PLICHT, J. (2003) – An early modern human from the Peştera cu Oase, Romania. *Proceedings of the National Academy of Sciences of the United States of America* 100/20, p. 11231–11236.

VALLADAS, H.; CLOTTES, J.; GENESTE, J.-M. (2004) – Chauvet, la grotte ornée la mieux datée du monde. *À l'Échelle du Millier d'Années* 42, p. 82–87.

WHITE, R. (1993) – Technological and social dimensions of Aurignacian-age body ornaments across Europe. In H. Knecht, A. Pike-Tay & R. White (eds.), *Before Lascaux: the complex record of the early Upper Palaeolithic*, p. 277–299. Boca Raton: CRC Press.

WILD, E.M.; TESCHLER-NICOLA, M.; KUTSCHERA, W.; STEIER, P.; TRINKAUS, E.; WANEK, W. (2005) – Direct dating of Early Upper Palaeolithic human remains from Mladeč. *Nature*. London. 435, p. 332–335.

WOLPOFF, M. (1999) – *Paleoanthropology*, second edn. New York: McGraw-Hill.

WOLPOFF, M.; SMITH, F.H.; MALEZ, M.; RADOVČIĆ, J.; RUKAVINA, D. (1981) – Upper Pleistocene hominid remains from Vindija Cave, Croatia, Yugoslavia. *American Journal of Physical Anthropology* 54, p. 499–545.

ZUECHNER, C. (1996) – The Chauvet Cave: radiocarbon versus archaeology. *International Newsletter of Rock Art*. Foix. 13, p. 25–27.

NEUROVISUAL THEORY, THE VISUO-MOTOR SYSTEM AND PLEISTOCENE PALAEOART

Derek HODGSON

2 Belle Vue Street, York, North Yorks YO10 5AY, England, U.K., derekhodgson@hotmail.com

***Abstract**: The structure and function of the early visual cortex has been shown to be relevant to the understanding of Pleistocene palaeoart. In order to obtain a more complete appreciation of how brain function may be relevant to this issue, it is necessary to take account of how the hominin visual cortex may relate to the visuo-motor areas. The ability to translate the 'passively' experienced visual world into a visuo-motor frame of reference involving hand-eye co-ordination would have been vital before any purposely made Pleistocene palaeoart was possible. Delineating the probable course of this dynamic can provide clues as to the existence and timing of when particular kinds of palaeoart may have arisen and will constitute the main focus of this paper. There are three main topics relevant to this issue – the influence of the early visual cortex with regard to the making of geometric marks during the Lower to Middle Palaeolithic, the role of the visuo-motor cortex in relation to representation, and lastly how the visuo-spatial/motor regions of the brain dovetail with the visual pathway. Understanding how these areas interrelate will help to ascertain what skills early Pleistocene hominins were capable of and by implication whether this ability was sufficient to permit the making of early palaeoart.*

***Keywords**: neurovisual theory, visuo-motor system, palaeoart, evolution, brain*

***Résumé**: Il est constaté que la structure et la function du cortex oculaire premier sont liés à la compréhension du paléoart Pleistocene. Pour pouvoir apprécier de manière plus complète la façon dont la fonction cérébrale pourrait se lier à ce fait, il est nécéssaire de tenir compte de la manière dont le hominin visual cortex pourrait être lié aux zones moteur-visuels. La capacité de traduire le monde visuel 'passif' à une référence moteur-visuel, ayant la nécéssité d'une coordination main-oeuil, aurait été essentiel avant que la fabrication intentionel du paléoart Pleistocene soit possible. La délineation de la route probable de cette dynamique peut donner des indications sur l'existence de certains types de paléoart ainsi que l'époque à laquelle elles auraient surgi et constituera la matière principale de cet article. Trois sujets principaux sont liés à ce fait – l'influence du cortex oculaire premier, concernant la création de marques géométriques pendant le Paléolithique inférior et moyen, la fonction du cortex moteur-visuel en relation avec la représentation et, finalement, comment les régions du cerveau spatial/moteur- visuel concordent avec le chemain visuel. Comprendre comment ces zones sont interliées aiderait à établir quels techniques les hominins Pleistocene possédaient et, par implication, si cette habilité était suffisante pour permettre la création du paléoart premier.*

***Mots clés**: neurovisuel théorie, visuo-moteur systéme, paleoart, évolution, cerveau*

THE INFLUENCE OF VISUAL CORTEX ON THE MAKING OF EARLY GEOMETRIC MARKS

Figure 5.1 shows two cells in V2 of the early visual cortex of a macaque. This area is thought to encode simple shapes and receives incoming information that has undergone some initial processing in V1. There are two main points of interest. First, each of the two cells illustrated is concerned with encoding particular kinds of geometric form. The upper illustration indicates how one cell codes for angles and the lower one for concentric circles. Different cells in V2 encode for other types of geometric shape that are also illustrated in this figure. These examples show how the early visual cortex is especially tuned to encode certain basic forms. V1 and V2 are common to primates and quite ancient in evolutionary terms (Preuss 2005). The visual co-ordinates encoded at this level represent the first stages in the construction of the visual image that are fed-forward to the later stages of the visual hierarchy for further processing. Relative to the higher areas that encode actual objects these areas, in modern humans, appear to be reduced in size (Holloway *et al*. 2001; 2003). This is thought to be a consequence of the expansion of the visual association areas indicating that evolutionary pressure has favoured a more sophisticated level of processing for object recognition and visual memory in hominins. In this respect, the temporal cortex is believed to have expanded quite early in hominin evolution, perhaps as far back as *Homo habilis* or *Australopithecus* (Falk 2000; 2006). Moreover, the modern human temporal lobe is about 20–30% larger than what one would expect for an ape of a similar body size with an ability to process greater amounts of information as indicated by the existence of significantly more white matter (Rilling and Seligman 2002). An early expansion of the temporal lobe suggests that *Australopithecus* or an early species of *Homo* may well have been capable of a passive appreciation of natural occurring objects and might corroborate the authenticity of the almost 3 million-year-old Makapansgat manuport and Mary Leakey's 1.8 million-year-old baboon-like object. It also indicates that such objects may be more widespread than is implied by the archaeological record.

THE ROLE OF THE VISUO-MOTOR CORTEX

The crucial question arises, how did the capacity for enhanced but passive visual awareness come to be translated into a material form? We might obtain some idea of the difficulties involved by examining some recent research into the mark-making of chimps. To compensate for the difficulty apes have in manipulating drawing implements Iverson and Matsuzawa (1997) employed a

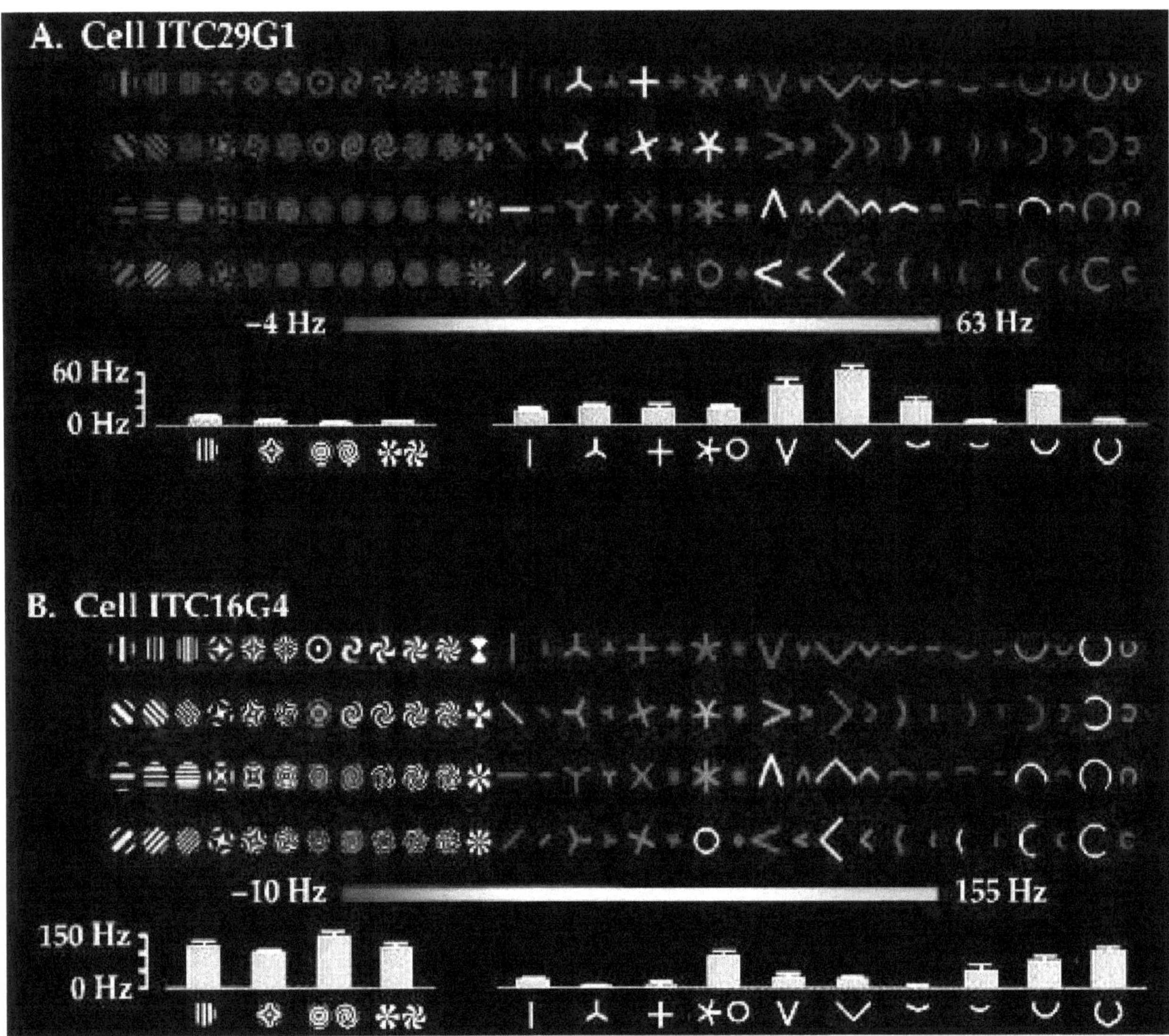

Figure 5.1. Showing how two separate neurons in V2 respond preferentially to particular kinds of geometric forms A. Right angles and B. Concentric circles (concentric circles are often mistaken for spirals and vice versa). The red (positive) through to blue (negative) colour scale indicates extent of preference. Note that the tuning of these cells is graded in the sense that they also fire with stimuli that are close to their best option. This may be a means whereby the overlapping tuning curves of each neuron serves as an efficient way of encoding a broad range of shape with a limited number of cells. The bar charts present the same information in a different format (Hegdé, J. and Van Essen, D. C. Selectivity for Complex Shapes in PrimateVisual Area V2. *The Journal of Neuroscience*. 20 [jNeurosci,2000, 0:RC(61)1-6].) Published online at http://www.jneurosci.com.org/.cgi/content/full/3976). (Reproduced with permission of authors and The Journal of Neuroscience ©).

finger-touch screen, of the type illustrated in Figure 5.2, that automatically registered any marks produced. This investigation found that, after a considerable training schedule involving a reinforcement regime, chimps were able to copy a previously made guide line – including horizontal, vertical, and diagonal lines, as Figure 5.3 illustrates. The results also indicated that, although chimps initially have difficulties comprehending what is required, they are eventually able to copy various lines but only after following a specific training schedule. In sum, chimps do not find the making of accurate straight lines of various orientations an easy task, which suggests a deficit in visuo-spatial motor co-ordination.

A corresponding study sheds further light on the chimps' ability to make marks, again by way of a touch screen, but this time in the absence of a training or reinforcement regime (Tanaka *et al.* 2003). Thirteen-month-old chimps were found to spontaneously produce a limited range of graphic motifs – dots, straight lines, curves and loops, as shown in Figure 5.4. Adult chimps, however, were capable of making much longer and smoother co-ordinated strokes, suggesting some limited development in visuo-motor control, yet the motifs remained basically the same as those produced by younger chimps. The chimpanzees were obviously interested in the various marks because, when these were rendered invisible,

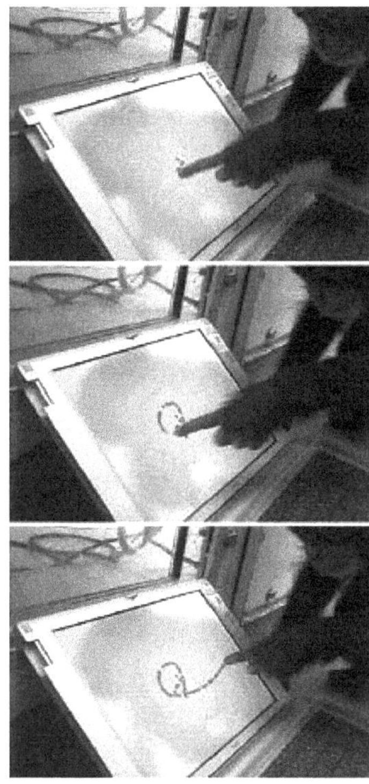

Figure 5.2. Showing chimp using touch Screen. (Figure 1 in, Tanaka, M., Tomonaga, M., Matsuzawa, T. 2003. Finger drawing by infant chimpanzees (*Pan troglodytes*). *Animal Cognition* (By permission of Blackwell publishers ©)

interest waned, indicating that perceptual factors were decisive to the task. Chimps, however, have never been observed making such marks other than in captivity. This study concluded that even at an early age chimps, given appropriate circumstances, are self-motivated to make marks and this ability improves with age. These findings support the previous research of Morris (1962) and others on ape graphic abilities who reported similar results – although a broader repertoire of marks were found in some of these studies, e.g. intersections.

The graphic marks made by chimps show a general concern for the difference between certain basic forms, namely the curve and straight line. The straight line, however, was found to be the more common motif with the closed loop being an occasional occurrence. The various straight and curved lines produced by chimps parallel the different classes of visual primitives to which neurones in early visual cortex are sensitive – as Figure 5.1 exemplifies. As both V1 and V2 in chimps are relatively large compared to foreward visual areas, and the straight and curved line are two perceptual primitives decisive for discrimination of the visual world, it is probable that these factors serve to guide the course of hand movements in the mark-making of chimps.

Iverson and Matsuzawa concluded that chimps possess the ability for perceptual-motor control for the visually-guided production of marks on a touch screen that is underpinned by an intrinsic motivation to draw. This is corroborated by the fact that chimps show a sensitivity to the balance and order of the marks produced (Morris 1962). Lenain (1995), however, advises caution by stating that chimp 'art' should be regarded as an immediate response to presiding circumstances rather than as an activity governed by a detached awareness of events. This reflexive response may be a function of what Donald terms episodic cognition based upon event perception.

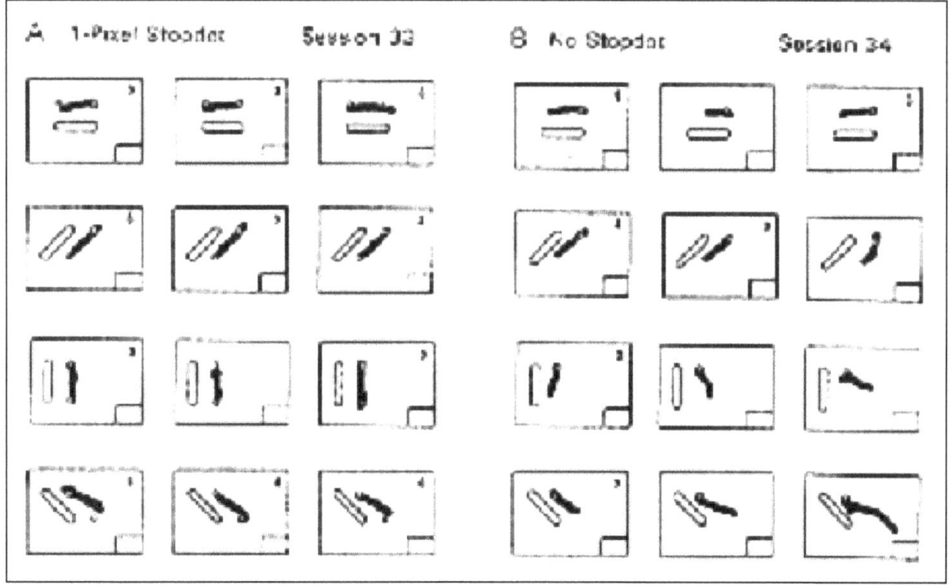

Figure 5.3. Showing the attempts of chimps at producing various oriented straight lines with and without guide dots (Figure 11 in, Iverson, I. H. and Matsuzawa, T. 1997. Model Guided Line Drawing in the Chimpanzee (*Pan troglodytes*). *Japanese Psychological Research*. 39 (3), 154-181. *Cognition*. 6, 245-251. (By permission of authors and Springer-Verlag ©)

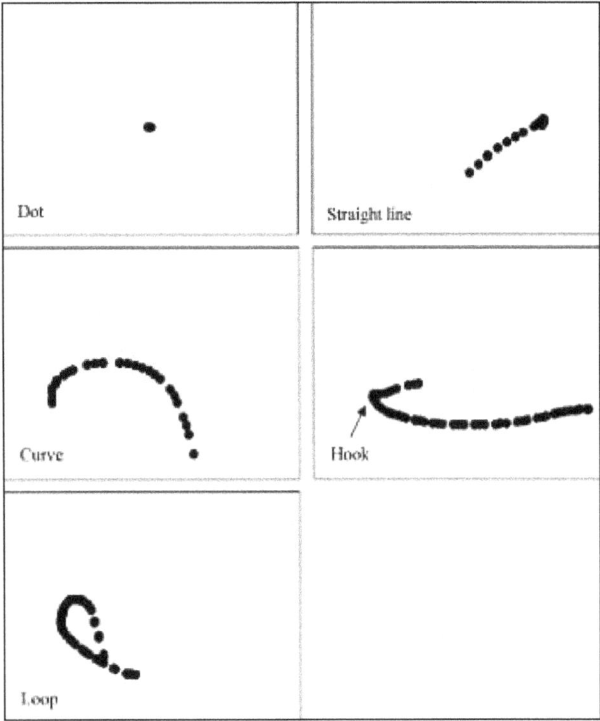

Figure 5.4. The basic marks made by chimps on a touch screen. (Figure 2 in, Tanaka, M., Tomonaga, M., Matsuzawa, T. 2003. Fingerdrawing by infant chimpanzees (*Pan troglodytes*). *Animal Cognition*. 6, 245-251. By permission of authors and Springer-Verlag ©)

As well as being able to produce a limited range of graphic primitives chimps are also able to recognise objects in photographs yet have more difficulty with less realistic pictures, such as outline forms for which a certain amount of training is required (Tanaka n.d.) – a finding that has been confirmed by neuroimaging studies of the monkey brain (Denys *et al.* 2004). None of the above studies, however, found any evidence of an ability to produce actual representational figures. Therefore, although chimps may be able to recognise objects in some kinds of pictures, at the same time they are unable to produce graphic equivalents – a case of understanding running ahead of production. This suggests that *Australopithecus* will have been cognisant of the fortuitous resemblance of a natural feature to an object such as a face or animal.

Infants, on first learning to draw, produce similar kinds of marks to chimps that rapidly become more complex beyond that of what apes are able to make – such as the closed circular form that becomes the basis for the human figure that Arnheim has termed the 'primordial circle' (Arnheim 1974). Arnheim regards the tendency for drawing to progress from simple lines and shapes to more complex forms as a 'law'. This is borne out in both picture-less and picture-informed communities where adults drawing for the first time begin with simple lines that subsequently gravitate towards more complex shapes (Cox 2005). Gibson (1979), one of the 20th centuries foremost perceptual psychologists, regards marks of this type as elemental invariants of the visual array to which the visual system, due to its evolutionary heritage, is particularly disposed. Thanks to modern neuroscience, we are now able to see such invariants in the early visual cortex of alert primates as Figure 5.1 demonstrates.

THE RELATIONSHIP OF VISUAL AREAS TO VISUO-MOTOR SKILLS

The limitations of chimp mark-making is underlined in Figure 5.5 when their graphic efforts are compared with those of some of the early marks from the Acheulean and Middle Palaeolithic made by hominins (the form primitives encoded by V2 in early visual cortex of non-human primates are also included for comparison). The question arises, what were the decisive factors that allowed hominins to proceed from the rudimentary marks of chimps to the first intentionally made motifs of *Homo heidelbergensis* – that is, from an immediate response to prevailing contingencies to what Ingold (1999) refers to as 'self conscious modification'. The tendency towards more regularly shaped stone tools before 500,000 BP may be significant in this regard in relation to an expansion of the superior parietal area in *Homo erectus* (Stout *et al.* 2000; Stout 2005) – an area where the 'blind' where/how pathway for on-line hand-eye control terminates (Goodale *et al.* 1991; Milner and Goodale 1995; Ungerleider and Mishkin 1982). The smaller superior parietal cortex in chimps may explain their inability to produce both shaped tools and complex marks. Crucially, the posterior parietal area, particularly the inferoparietal cortex, seems to have undergone significant expansion in archaic humans (Roland 1993). In this respect, the brain of *Homo heidelbergensis* also appears to have increased to around 1206 cc, beyond the 937 cc average of *Homo erectus* (Rightmire 2003).

The inferoparietal area is thought, in modern humans, to be involved in planning for action as part of a third stream (Glover 2004). In non-human primates, however, this pathway terminates in the superior temporal region. The human inferoparietal area appears to link on-line motor control with enhanced conscious awareness in relation to the ventral 'what' pathway in what has been termed a sensory-motor interface (Mattingly *et al.* 1998), as outlined in Figure 5.6. The expanded inferoparietal area in *Homo heidelbergensis* will therefore have promoted an assimilation of the 'blind' dorsal pathway with the more consciously predisposed 'what' ventral stream, thereby promoting more effective planned actions involving hand-eye co-ordinates. As the ventral pathway for the recognition of objects has a capacity for greater generalisation in modern humans than apes, i.e. is more cue invariant (Denys *et al.* 2004), the integration of these various streams at a higher level of functioning will have provided the essentials that can help explain the appearance of artefacts attributed to *Homo heidelbergensis*. The multiple cross-referencing of these areas will have im-

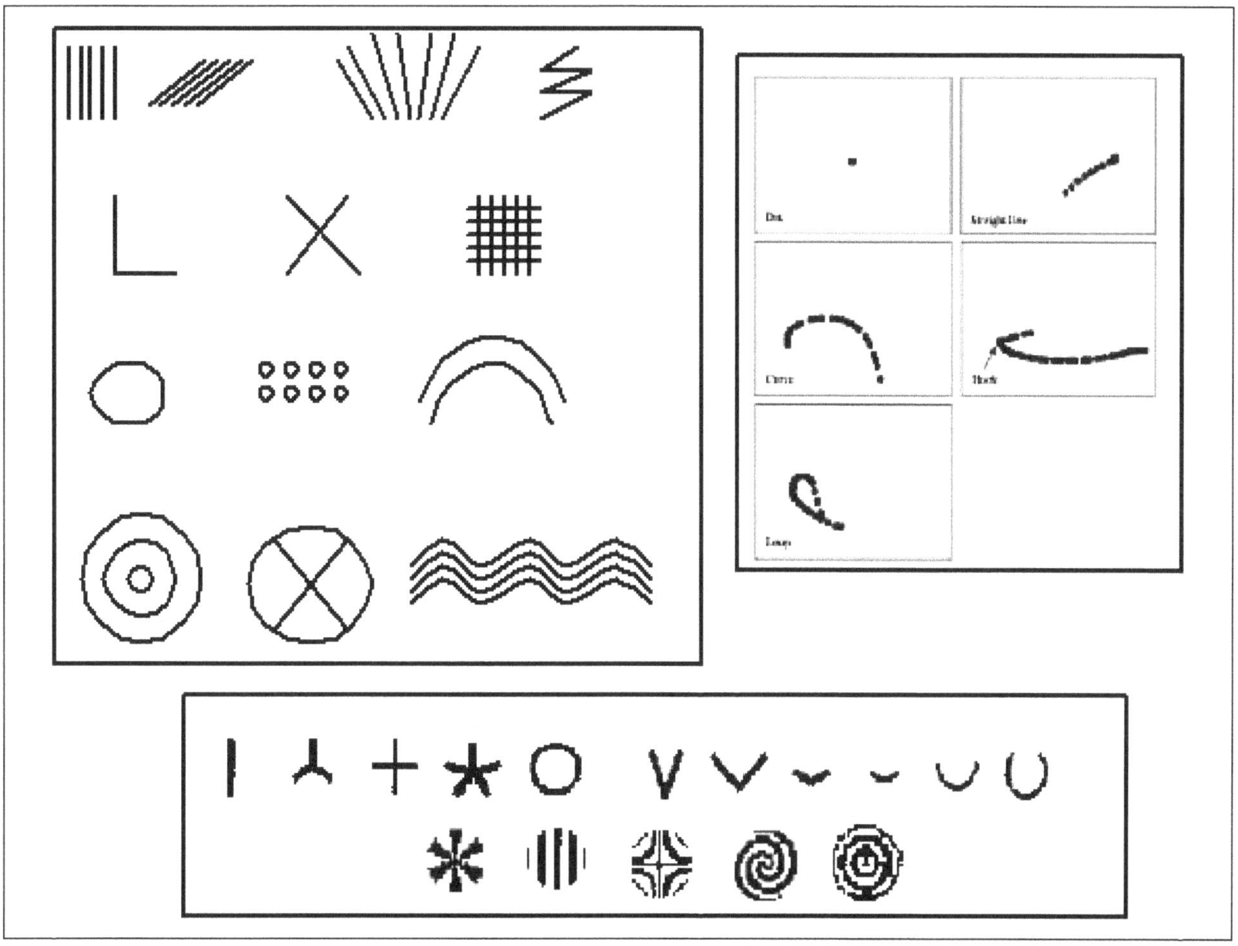

Figure 5.5. Comparison of Pleistocene and Middle Pal. marks with those of chimps and basic shapes encoded in early visual cortex (V2).

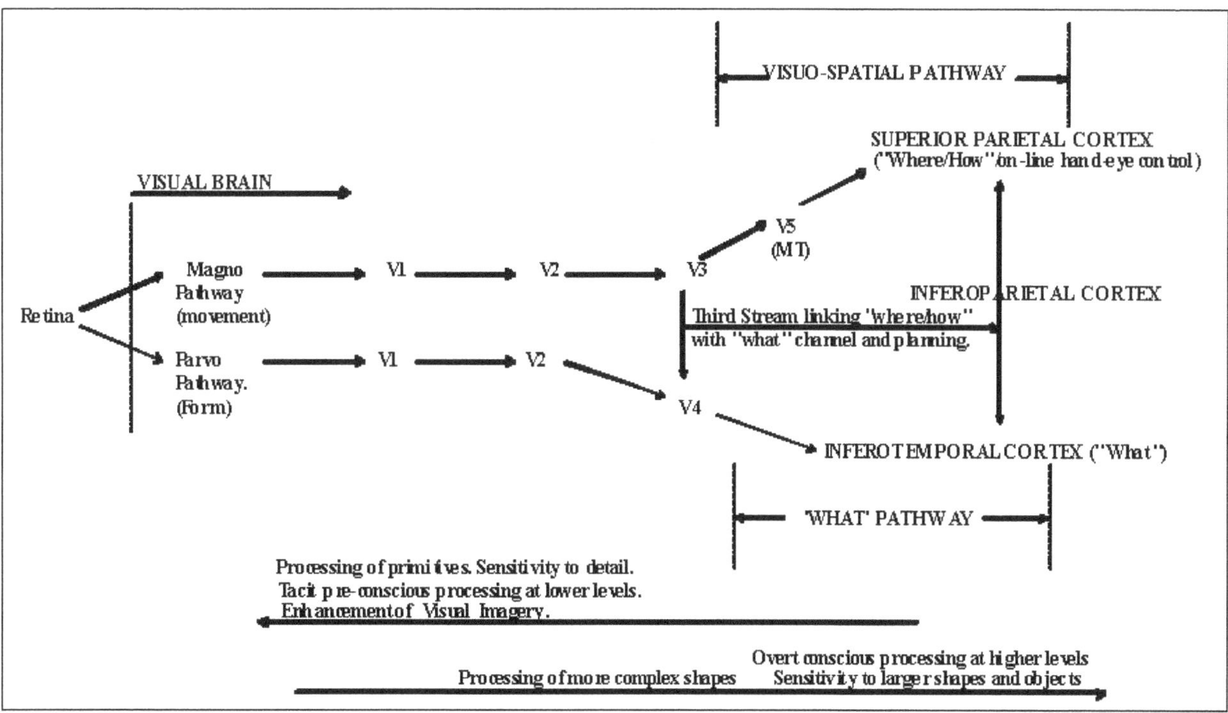

Fig. 5.6. Simplified illustration of the two main pathways of the visual brain and hypothesised third stream showing how more complex information is processed as incoming visual information flows through the system.

proved hand-eye co-ordination to the extent that planning routines became available for the conversion of passively received visual signals into materially embodied marks and artefacts in a way that was not entirely related to practical needs. This expansion would also have involved increased connections between parietal and frontal lobes (Bruner 2004; Van Essen *et al.* 2001) including mirror neurones (Buccino *et al.* 2001), crucial association areas in relation to visuo-motor skill for holding, biasing and generalising information for future use (Brass *et al.* 2005). The increased processing capacity of these areas occurred about the same time that the symmetries of Acheulean tools were becoming more complex, including three-dimensional symmetries (Wynn 2002) – the two phenomena may therefore be linked. The skill required to craft such tools is quite sophisticated and would have easily been transferable to the production of geometric marks as well as to the enhancement of naturally occurring iconic-like objects so as to accentuate the resemblance to a human figure, face or animal feature.

Although non-utilitarian marks appear in the archaeological record approximately 300,000 years ago, they were probably being produced at a much earlier period in a degradable form. It is likely that such geometric primitives were inspired by the accidental marks made in the making and using of tools. At Boxgrove in England, a *Homo heidelbergensis* site, animal bones have been found where, due to the systematic and planned cutting of flesh, accidentally-made but regularly spaced cut marks appear as a series parallel lines. In view of the cognitive abilities of archaic humans as described, it would not have gone unnoticed that such accidental lines might have been imbued with some non-utilitarian significance – a significance that probably arose out of a resonance with neurones in early visual cortex (Hodgson 2000a, 2000b, 2003, 2006). Correspondingly, Frolov (cited in Rudgley 1998) suggests that the straight line may have been abstracted from the uniform edges of symmetrically shaped tools, which thereby became a commodity able to be realised in other domains. Finally, with the appearance of modern humans, the reorganisation of the brain seems to have continued in the same direction (Bruner 2004) leading to even more complex artefacts than those typical of *Homo heidelbergensis*.

CONCLUSION

The foregoing analysis proposes that, given favourable circumstances, captive chimps are capable of spontaneously producing a limited number of graphic primitives but are unable to advance much beyond these. This limitation may be due to a less developed visual capacity, as indicated by a reduced temporal cortex compared to humans, as well as an inability to translate these contingencies into co-ordinated motor programs for the purpose of material realisation. The restricted set of marks produced by chimps – straight lines, curves and loops – may be a reflection of the relative dominance of V1 and V2 in non-human apes, a part of the brain especially devoted to processing such primitives. The increasing size and processing capacity of inferotemporal regions from *Australopithecus* through *Homo habilis* to *Homo erectus* suggests an incremental awareness as to the significance and representational potential of naturally occurring objects. By the time of *Homo heidelbergensis*, the temporal cortex had expanded to such an extent that an extensive visual memory capacity was possible. The parietal-frontal areas of the brain had also undergone enlargement and reorganisation in that passive visual co-ordinates were capable of being translated into an action plan that could be realised in a material form. This was promoted by integration of the blind 'where/how' pathway for manipulating objects with the consciously predisposed 'what' system for overt recognition in the form of a third pathway centred on an enlarged inferoparietal cortex that acted as a visuo/sensory-motor interface.

References

ARNHEIM, R. (1974) – *Art and visual perception.* Berkeley: University of California Press.

BRASS, M., ULLSPERGER, M., KNOESCHE, T. R., VON CRAMON, D.Y. and PHILLIPS, N. A. (2005) – Who comes first? The Role of the Prefrontal and Parietal Cortex in Cognitive Control. *Journal of Cognitive Neuroscience.* 17: 9, p. 1367-1375.

BRUNER, E. (2004) – Geometric morphometrics and paleoneurology: brain shape evolution in the genus Homo. *Journal of Human Evolution* 47: p. 279-303.

BUCCINO, G., BINKOFSKI, F., FINK, G.R., FADIGA, L., FOGASSI, L. GALLESE, V., SELTZ, J., ZILLES, K, RIZZOLATTI, G. and FREUND, H.-J. (2001) – Action observation activates premotor and parietal areas in a somatotopic manner: an fMRI study. *European Journal of Neuroscience.* 13, pp. 400-404.

COX, M. (2005) – *The Pictorial World of the Child.* Cambridge: Cambridge University Press.

DENYS, K., VANDUFFEL, W., FIZE, D., NELISSEN, K., PEUSKENS, H., VAN ESSEN, D. and ORBAN, G.A. (2004) – The Processing of Visual Shape in the Cerebral Cortex of Human and Nonhuman Primates: A Functional Magnetic Imaging Study. *The Journal of Neuroscience.* 24: 10, p. 2551-2565.

FALK, D., REDMOND, J.C., GUYER, J., CONROY, G.C., RECHEIS, W., WEBER, G.W. and SEIDLER, H. (2000) – Early hominid brain evolution: a new look at old endocasts. *Journal of Human Evolution* 38: p. 695–717.

FALK. D. (2006) – Evolution of the Primate Brain. In W. HENKE, H. ROTHE and I. TATTERSALL eds. *Handbook of Palaeoanthropology, Primate Evolution and Human Origins.* Vol. 2, Springer-Verlag,

GIBSON, J.J. (1979) – *The Ecological Approach to Visual Perception.* Boston: Houghton Mifflin.

GLOVER, S. (2004) – Separate visual representations in the planning and control system of action. *Behavioral and Brain Sciences*. 27: p. 3-78.

GOODALE, M.A., MILNER, D.A. JAKOBSON, A.D. and CAREY, D.P. (1991) – A neurological dissociation between perceiving objects and grasping them. *Nature*. 349: p. 154-156.

HODGSON, D. (2000a) – Art, Perception and Information Processing: An Evolutionary Perspective. *Rock Art Research* 17: 1, p. 3-34.

HODGSON, D. (2000b) Shamanism, Phosphenes, and Early Art: An Alternative Synthesis. *Current Anthropology*. 41: 5, p. 866-873.

HODGSON, D. (2003) – Primitives in palaeoart and the visual brain: the building-blocks of representation in art and perception. *Rock Art Research*. 20: 2, p. 116-117.

HODGSON, D. (2006) – Altered States of Consciousness and Palaeoart: an Alternative Neurovisual Explanation *Cambridge Archaeological Journal*. 16: 1, p. 27-37.

HOLLOWAY, R., BROADFIELD, D.C. and YUAN, M. S. (2001) – Revisiting australopithecine visual striate cortex; newer data from chimpanzee and human brains suggest it could have been reduced during australopithecine times. In D. FALK and K.R. GIBSON eds. *Evolutionary anatomy of the primate cerebral cortex*. Cambridge (MA): Cambridge University Press. p. 177–187

HOLLOWAY, R. BROADFIELD, D.C. and YUAN, M. S. (2003) – Morphology and histology of chimpanzee primary visual striate cortex indicate that brain reorganization predated brain expansion in early hominid evolution. *The Anatomical Record*, Part A, 273a: p. 594–602.

INGOLD, T. (1999) – Social relations, human ecology, and the evolution of culture: an exploration of concepts and definitions. In A. LOCK and C.R. PETERS eds. *Handbook of Human Symbolic Evolution*. Oxford: Blackwell. p. 178-203.

IVERSON, I.H. and MATSUZAWA, T. (1997) – Model Guided Line Drawing in the Chimpanzee (*Pan troglodytes*). *Japanese Psychological Research*. 39: 3, p.154-181.

LENAIN, T. (1995) – Ape-painting and the problem of the origin of art. *Human Evolution*. 10: 3, p. 205-215.

MATTINGLY, J.B., HUSSAIN, M., RORDEN, C., KENNARD, C. and DRIVER, J. (1998) – Motor role of human inferior parietal lobe revealed in unilateral neglect patients. *Nature*. 392: (March 12th) p. 179-182.

MILNER, A.D. and GOODALE, M.A. (1995) – *The visual brain in action*. Oxford: Oxford University Press

MORRIS, D. (1962) – *The Biology of Art*. London: Methuen.

PREUSS, T.M. (2005) – Evolutionary Specializations of Primate Brain Systems. In M. J. RAVOSO and M. DAGOSTO (eds). *Primate Origins and Adaptations*, New York: Kluwer Academic/Plenum Press.

RIGHTMIRE, G.P. (2003) – Brain size and encephalization in early to Mid-Pleistocene Homo. *American Journal of Physical Anthropology*. 124: 2, p. 109-123.

RILLING, J.K. and SELIGMAN, R. A. (2002) – A quantitative morphometric comparative analysis of the primate temporal lobe. *Journal of Human Evolution*. 42: p.505-533.

ROLAND, P.E. (1993) – *Brain Activation*. New York: Wiley-Liss

RUDGLEY, R. (1998) – *Lost Civilisations of the Stone Age*. London: Random House.

STOUT, D. TOTH, N. and SCHICK, K. (2000) – Stone Tool-Making and Brain Activation: Positron Emission Tomography (PET) Studies. *Journal of Archaeological Science*. 27: p. 1215-1223.

STOUT, D. (2005) – Neural Foundations of Perception and Action. In V. ROUX and B. BRIL. eds *Stone Knapping*. Cambridge: McDonald Institute for Archaeological Research. p, 273-286.

TANAKA, M. (n.d.) – Unpublished manuscript. Section of Language & Intelligence, Primate Research Institute, Kyoto University. Abstract available at: www.saga-jp.org/sccs/sccsoz/abstracts/tanaka.html

TANAKA, M., TOMONAGA, M. and MATSUZAWA, T. (2003) – Finger drawing by infant chimpanzees (*Pan troglodytes*). *Animal Cognition*. 6: p. 245-251.

UNGERLEIDER, L.G. and MISHKIN, M. (1982) - Two cortical visual systems. In D.J. INGLE, M.A. GOODALE and R.J.W. MANSFIELD eds. *Analysis of Visual Behavior*. Cambridge, MA: MIT Press. p.549-586.

VAN ESSEN, D.C., LEWIS, J.W., DRURY, H.A., HADJIKHANA, N., TOOTELL, R.B. H., BAKIRCIOGLU, M. and MILLER, M.I. (2001) – Mapping visual cortex in monkeys and humans using surface-based atlases. *Vision Research*. 41: p.1359-1378

WYNN, T. (2002) – Archaeology and cognitive evolution. *Behavioral and Brain Sciences*. 25: 3, p. 389-438.

THE ARCHAEOLOGY OF GRAPHIC SIGNS: EVOLUTIONARY AND SYSTEMIC APPROACHES 1

Paul BOUISSAC
University of Toronto, Victoria College

Abstract: *Current views of writing hold that scripts were devised in the Neolithic in order to perform some political and economic functions. Consequently, their history retraces their further transformations with changing linguistic and cultural needs. Inspired by the methods outlined by Edouard Piette (1827-1906) and William Flinders Petrie (1853-1942), this paper proposes heuristically to reverse the direction of the inquiry and to investigate backward the steps that may have lead to these systems. It relies on the methods of evolutionary logic applied to technological changes. It assumes that the earliest known systems of graphic signs, rather than being absolute beginnings, are the results of long evolutionary processes that can be traced back to symbolic representations in the palaeolithic archaeological record.*
Key words: *cultural evolution, palaeolithic, scripts, signs, symbolism*

Résumé: *L'origine de l'écriture est généralement attribuée à une invention du Néolithique répondant à des besoins économiques et politiques. Son histoire consiste à suivre ses évolutions multiples à partir de cette source selon les contextes linguistiques et culturels qui se sont formés par la suite. Cet article propose une démarche heuristique différente, inspirée par les travaux de deux pioniers, Edouard Piette (1827-1906) et William Flinders Petrie (1853-1942), qui se sont penchés sur ces problèmes il y a plus de cent ans. Leur approche consistait à remonter vers les antécédents morphologiques et fonctionels des premières écritures qui étaient alors conçues non comme des innovations absolues mais comme l'aboutissement d'un long processus de changements culturels soumis aux lois de l'évolution.*
Mots clés: *écriture, évolution culturelle, paléolithique, signes, symbolisme*

INTRODUCTION: THEORY BETWEEN COGNITION AND EMOTION

The extent to which expectations can bias perceptions has been well documented by psychologists (e.g., Hoffman 1998). The contemporary cognitive neurosciences have shown that there exist some templates in the brain that have been wired-in by evolution and make it prone to identify certain patterns that are particularly relevant to survival. But such specific sensitivity applies to any forms that broadly resemble the typical relations and proportions of these relevant patterns. There are numerous examples of this phenomenon that have been observed across all animal species. Human neonates, for instance, respond by a smile to a cardboard on which two darker patches have been drawn where the human eyes are located on a face (e.g., Goren *et al.* 1975). Sketchy visual information suffices to prime perception templates and trigger adaptive behaviors (e.g., Cox *et al.* 2004). But even in adults, when neuronal selective sensitivity and plasticity allow the brain to discriminate among a great variety of patterns in all the sensorial modalities, specialized neurons take shortcuts and constantly anticipate on the basis of limited information (e.g., Glimcher 2003, Gonzalez-Crussi 2006). The emerging science of neuro-economics that endeavors to find out how brains make decisions theorizes that adaptive behavior cannot wait for exhaustive analyses of incoming information before appropriate moves are made. We are constantly projecting meaningful percepts that usually, but not necessarily lead to correct interpretations of our environments (Guthrie 2006). The brain can be deceived by its own evolved functionality, a feature that can be (and often is) exploited by predators and deceivers (e.g., Piatelli-Palmarini 1994). Scientific methods consist precisely of devising ways of avoiding the traps of self-deception. These efforts, however, are constantly threatened by the power of our imagination, a form of perceptive projection, as well as by our emotions, which are an important source of perceptual biases (e.g., Pfaff 2005).

In prehistoric archaeology, the most general sources of expectations usually come from the representations of human origins that prevail in the imagination of the researcher as a member of a cultural community. The early "scientific" and popular iconography displayed in magazines, books, and museums, later amplified by films and other media, conveys powerful images and narratives. Hence the frequent reactions of "surprise", or denial, when new archaeological discoveries put into question established wisdom based on the common sense that has historically developed in archaeological disciplines. We tend to think that theories are rationally constructed on the basis of what we observe but what we perceive often is to a large extent biased by the set of expectations created by theories. As Paul Bahn points out in his review of Dale Guthrie's book on the nature of palaeolithic art: "People often see what they want to see in rock art." (Bahn 2006:575). This does not imply willful dishonesty – we actually do not see what we do not expect to see – but reflects a general condition of human inquiry and a consequence of the kind of brain that has evolved in the context of our immediate survival not in view of an ultimate rational capacity for science (Gigerenzer *et al.* 2001).

The rigorous heuristics and methodologies that have been painfully devised in very recent times (relatively to the time frame of evolution) are constantly challenged by the weight of the selective pressures which fine-tuned our perception apparatus with respect to a range of particular environments. It seems that we find it hard not to fall into the trap of a "good" pattern in any perceptual medium and that we cannot resist a "good" narrative, that is, the representation of a dramatized series of events whose conclusion is virtually rewarding in as much as it construes our ontological status as being the latest and highest of all organisms. Our cognition is attracted by such perceptual and cognitive constraints that seem to put nicely into order the diversity, and often the incoherence of the information our sensory apparatus captures. It is not so much that we do not want to take contrary evidence into consideration but simply that we do not see all that is here to be seen. All scientific observation must sort out what is relevant information from what is noise but what is noise for a theory may be crucial information for another. Moreover, the emotional relation of an individual to theories is not immune to the biases of ethnic and tribal thinking.

These preliminary reflections are in order when the vexed question of the origin of writing is raised. A powerful narrative is entrenched in our culture(s), and prehistoric archaeology has already a long disciplinary history that has "educated" our perception of rock art. Any "deviance" with respect to the mainstream interpretations of the day triggers fierce debates, as two pioneers, Edouard Piette and William Flinders Petrie, whose ideas (and evidence) were at odds with the accepted wisdom of their time, experienced about a century ago.

THE ARCHAEOLOGY OF WRITING. TWO PIONEERS: EDOUARD PIETTE AND WILLIAM FLINDERS PETRIE

The name of Edouard Piette (1827-1906) is usually associated in the contemporary literature (e.g., Delson *et al.* 2000) with the Azilian that is generally considered to be a culture that links, in the European context, the late Upper Palaeolithic and the Neolithic (ca. 11-9 Ka). Piette dubbed this period of time "Epipalaeolithic" or "Early Mesolithic". It is mainly based on the excavations he did in 1887, 1888, and 1889 at the Mas d'Azil cave on the left bank of the river Arise, which is located in Ariège, a French Pyrénées region. Piette was a lawyer and a judge by profession. He funded his own archaeological research which he completed during his free time between 1871 and 1889. Drawing from his knowledge of geology and stratigraphy, his relative dating of prehistoric artifacts was based on clearly marked strata which included a succession of cultural assemblages formed by stone and bone tools as well as evidence of climatic changes and subsequent variations of the *fauna* and *flora*. Some strata were neatly demarcated by period of flooding (Piette 1895). In addition to geology, he adduced to his rigorous reasoning reliable zoological, botanical and chemical knowledge. His most important results concerning the Mas d'Azil excavations were published between 1895 and 1905 in *L'Anthropologie* and the *Bulletins de la société d'anthropologie de Paris*. His collection was displayed at the International Exhibition of 1889 in Paris. The latter event was crucial in convincing other prehistorians of the validity of his claims concerning the importance of the Azilian culture.

This was indeed needed because he advocated a continuum in cultural evolution at a time when the dominant dogma was that there had been a gap between the Upper Palaeolithic and the Neolithic, an extended period of time when the previous populations and their cultures had become extinct. Neolithic technologies and art were viewed as an absolute beginning, the hallmarks of a new race, the humans proper. A debate was raging between those who attributed to an actual ontological and historical "hiatus" the absence of any transition in the archaeological record of the time (e.g., Emile Cartailhac 1845-1921), and those who thought that this was more likely due to a "lacuna" in the knowledge that had been acquired so far through a limited number of excavations (e.g., G. de Mortillet 1821-1898). Piette provided evidence that the apparent gap could be resolved but he was first confronted to an aggressive skepticism. Nowadays, a similar debate is being replayed regarding the earliest evidence of palaeoart with respect to the relationship between Neanderthals and anatomically modern humans (e.g., Bednarik 2003).

The particular relevance of Piette to the object of this paper is that he repeatedly argued that the numerous geometric patterns that were engraved or painted on bones, ivory and pebbles constituted an archaic script of which he described the elements that were variously combined on inscribed artifacts (Piette 1895, 1905). He related these patterns to both Palaeolithic iconic signs that preceded them and to the earliest forms of hieroglyphic and alphabetical writings that succeeded them along a chronological sequence of continuity and transformations. He did not make any attempt at deciphering these inscriptions but focused of their morphological characterristics. He tentatively analyzed some of them according to the contemporary theory of symbolism, for which he thought advice from Classic archaeologists such as Salomon Reinach (1858-1932). His approach was encapsulated in the word he chose to designate the Mesolithic: "L'âge glyptique", from the Greek word meaning "engraving", and by analogy with the term hieroglyphs (sacred engravings). This terminological choice made it clear that he saw the development of refined geometrical and figurative patterns not only as an art form but also as an important step toward symbolic, abstract representations that would soon lead to writing if it was not already a kind of archaic script.

In fact, one of his last essays was squarely entitled "Les écritures de l'âge glyptique" (1905). His claim is based on two kinds of artifacts: pebbles on which individual patterns are painted, and larger objects such as pieces of prepared bones, antlers or ivory on which sequences of distinctive signs have been engraved. Interestingly, he notes that the individual patterns visible on the pebbles appear to have been made without particular consideration for their aesthetic perfection but could rather be considered as implementations of algorithms such as the general specifications of how straight lines and curves should intersect so as to achieve distinctive figures. What appears to be relevant is indeed what makes each pattern an individually recognizable sign or, in other words, a token implementing a type. These signs are variously combined on the larger artifacts where they have been engraved with great care. It is the formal relationship between these two kinds of artifacts that constitutes the basis of his argument for the existence of a script. However, Piette repeatedly insists that he does not claim that this script is decipherable in view of the available data.

It is noteworthy that the dating propounded by Piette is not based on style but strictly on stratigraphy. Contrary to what is the case with cave paintings, artifacts are located within a natural time capsule that provides information about the contemporaneous climatic and environmental changes, and can yield reliable dating as long as a proper methodology is applied during the excavations. This latter aspect of archaeological research was scrupulously addressed by Piette who had scientific credentials in geology and palaeontology. Keenly aware of taphonomic logic, he emphasizes that the layers of sediments left by the periodic flooding of the banks of the river Arise and on the floor of the cave provide a reasonable ground for distinguishing the relative age of the cultural assemblages excavated at the Mas d'Azil.

William Flinders Petrie (1853-1942) was a British archaeologist and anthropologist who conducted extensive excavations in Egypt and in the Middle East from 1880 on. His career has been retraced in several accounts of his life (e.g., Drower 1985). He developed a rigorous methodology both in the way in which the sites were dug and managed, and in the interpretation of the archaeological record. He applied statistical analysis to artifacts' analysis, and formalized a systematic method called "seriation" in order to establish relative chronology, notably for the prehistoric potteries found in the cemeteries he discovered (e.g., Naqada). His findings and theoretical writings appeared in numerous publications (see Uphill 1872). Like Piette, with whom he corresponded, Petrie was impressed by some individual patterns he found painted and engraved on prehistoric pottery and other artifacts as they evoked familiar characteristics of the signs of ancient alphabets that appeared later. Petrie's particular relevance to the topic of this paper comes from *The Formation of the Alphabet,* a monograph he published in 1912.

Against the accepted theory that a systematic alphabet had been invented by a tribe or an individual in a developed civilization, Petrie contended that "a wide body of signs had been gradually brought into use in primitive times for various purposes" and that "they were interchanged by trade, and spread from land to land, until the less-known and less useful signs were ousted by those in more general acceptance" (Petrie 1912:3) Two original premises characterize Petrie's approach. Firstly, he dismisses the theory that abstract patterns originated in picture and pictographs that had been simplified, and claims that meaningful distinctive geometric forms are more primitive signs than pictures. He states for instance that "[s]igns rather than pictures are the primitive system." and that "[p]ictographs tend to wear down and be schematized but this is a secondary development, not a primitive one. [Long before the earliest hieroglyphs] there had existed, from the beginnings of the prehistoric ages, a totally different system of linear signs, full of variety and distinction" (Petrie 1912: 3). Secondly, he applies to the history of the changes that are observed over time in these multifarious "signaries" a Darwinian logic of natural selection in view of the cultural context, including the particular language, in which they came to be used. He thus interestingly anticipated, on the one hand, the discovery of the earliest forms of human markings such as the engraving of patterns on mineral supports that were discovered in the Blombos cave (e.g., Henshilwood 2006; Errico *et al*, 2001), and, on the other hand, the main tenets of memetics, an epistemological perspective that endeavors to apply evolutionary logic to cultural changes. As a consequence of these views, he considered that Egyptian hieroglyphs were a secondary development in the history of writing. Petrie's ideas did not take shape in a theoretical void but were informed by the relevant literature of his time which he questioned. He was familiar, for instance, with Isaac Taylor's *The Alphabet* (1883) and Philippe Berger's *Histoire de l'écriture dans l'antiquité* (1891) which expounded the state of the art toward the end of the century. He also sought advice from contemporary philologists such as Alan Gardiner, and was conversant with basic semiotic concept as he stated in a chapter entitled "The growth of signs": "Man is a sign-using animal" (Petrie 1912: 3), obviously meaning by "signs" the Saussurian notion of a conventional association between a signifier (in this case a geometric figure) and a signified (a meaning).

In view of his experience as a field archaeologist who had excavated prehistoric sites, he could not help questioning the accepted theory that writing had started rather suddenly. He had recorded indeed many prehistoric signs very similar to the ones that later formed historical syllabaries and alphabets. He had noted the greater diversity of the most ancients "signaries" (the word by which he refers to these sets of geometric signs in the prehistoric archaeological record), and he brought to the question a Darwinian perspective. First, one should look at what preceded a particular form rather than what followed it, going back step by step toward the most ancient one in the belief that there is no absolute beginnings. This was an approach that transferred the principles of biological evolution to the realm of technological (or cultural) evolution, a strategy that has been foregrounded in recent times (e.g., Basalla 1988). The relatively small number of signs in syllabaries, and the still smaller number in alphabets were interpreted by Petrie as the result of a kind of natural (cultural) selection. His theory was that the most ancient geometric signs referred to broad entities or behaviors and had been in use long before pictures appeared. First associated with ideas or categories of objects, these geometric patterns became more closely associated with the words that designated them, and eventually the forces of what could be called "semiotic economy" (not Petrie's term) tended to reduce the number of signs towards the smaller number of signs needed for syllabary, then for alphabetical coding. His approach does not lead to any pronouncement regarding either phonetic or semantic values. It consists of ordering on the time scale based on stratigraphy numerous sets of distinct patterns that have been engraved or painted, and making the assumption that each one is coming through imitation (teaching, copying, trading, stealing, etc.) from a previous one. The selection of forms over time (why some survived and other did not in rock art assemblages) is dictated by their functionality with respect to particular semiotic systems. Some contemporaries of Petrie criticized this view on the ground that such geometrical patterns were generated by universal properties of the human mind and did not need to be explained by vertical transmission, or population contacts and transversal imitation. This is a debate that is still raging in the context of memetics and the conceptualization of cultural evolution, not to mention controversies among mathematicians themselves.

ARCHAEOLOGY OF WRITING: QUESTIONS OF IDEOLOGY, THEORY, AND METHOD

The rationale for focusing on the century-old publications by Piette and Petrie is that these archaeologists have adumbrated a promising heuristic strategy that could be fruitful in view of today's expanded body of data and greatly improved technological means of investigation. Their contributions, however, have been forgotten as time passed. For a variety of reasons, the legacy of the mainstream prehistoric archaeology of their time, against which they developed their original arguments supported by reliable data, remained the dominant ideology and inspired interpretations based on different premises. Issues concerning the "invention" of writing loom large in the ideological agenda of philosophical and religious institutions. Indeed these issues ultimately pertain to the very definition of humanity, mind, progress, civilization, history, all being conceived on the discontinuous mode, a kind of "cultural creationism". The overall structure could be characterized as a "negative before" opposed to a "positive after". These "values" are neatly ordered in the fundamentally ideological narratives that describe the emergence of writing implemented by various theories. By contrast, Piette and Petrie advocated the continuous mode inspired by Darwinian thinking. They were applying to cultures a methodology that followed the principles of evolution through natural selection among variations that cannot be too discontinuous but only confer a slight advantage with respect to a particular environment, which may be, of course, a cultural environment. Any apparent gap in the genealogy of forms is circumstantial and can only come from our imperfect knowledge of the archaeological record, not from some kind of ontological hiatus. This approach evokes cladistics as a method of choice for ordering the data, a method that was adumbrated by Petrie "seriation."

Obviously, not everybody is equally eager to freely investigate possible earlier forms of writing that would be at odds with currently accepted theories that legitimate fundamental assumptions upon which full systems of meaning are based. The issue is not indifferent to religious establishments of whatever brand and has never been so. For instance, Piette lamented that the caves at Lourdes had been dug and emptied of large quantities of Azilian artifacts in order to make space for catholic religious shrines. Painted pebbles were found spread among the ballast on roads or in heaps of excavated dirt and rocks that had been downloaded away from the caves. Some archaeologists had no choice but collecting them among the detritus without having the benefit of stratigraphic information (Piette 1905: 6). He also mentioned that a complete collection of painted pebbles and other evidence had been stolen from his home (Piette 1905:7).

Both Piette and Petrie described the emergence of writing as an evolutionary process congruent with the evolution of any technology (e.g., Basalla 1988), which is based on constant modifications applied to existing artifacts which are improved in view of whatever functions they serve until, because of taphonomic logic, there appears to be a gap between a previous kind of artifacts and a novel technology. Engraved signs are such artifacts. Piette and Petrie focused on the morphology of the geometrical figures of rock art and ordered them in view of their stratigraphic locations along a genealogy of small modifications and selection. They cautiously proposed hypotheses regarding not so much the meanings of these signs as their potential functions in discriminating meanings. They described their continuity and changes, their successive co-occurrences in cultural assemblages. They speculated on their cognitive values mindful of the fact that only further discoveries could confirm or disprove their hypotheses.

Unlike most researchers, they focused their scientific attention on continuous lines of descent rather than on the sudden emergence of new technologies and new styles. Petrie advocated a sort of regressive method: Given an alphabet or syllabary character, one should look for patterns that preceded it in previous contexts, and progress back on the time scale as far as possible so as to establish a genealogy of forms as series of descent with modifications. Piette's starting point was a relatively well established chronological period from which he could proceed confidently both forward and backward in archaeological time. Petrie's reference point in time was prehistoric Egypt. Their method, however, were very similar and inspired by the same evolutionary epistemology. Their focus was on establishing successive repertories of signs through following genealogies, noting the "extinction" of some lineages. There have been, since them, many attempts at cataloguing and classifying signs, either on the ground of their topological properties (straight lines, curves, open or closed figures, etc.) or with reference to assumed sexual referents (one of the latest such repertories being Guthrie 2006).

The drawback of these repertories, however useful they may be, is that they focus on individual signs rather than on clusters or sequences of signs. Each identifiable geometric pattern is abstracted from its context and assigned to the type to which it appears to belong. Little effort is made to record the collocation of different signs, probably because the dominant theories exclude the possibility that such combinations could be pertinent. Each geometric pattern is perceived and interpreted in itself as the schematic representation of an iconic referent, let it be a phosphene, a weapon, a trap, a penis or a vulva depending on the interpretative matrix that guides the perception of the observer. The discipline has generated a set of descriptive terms that forms a heteroclite vocabulary in which words inspired by Euclidian geometric are mixed with a variety of trivial metaphors and neologisms. These terms constitute powerful perceptual filters that detract observers from paying attention to their mutual relations within a sequence or a cluster.

The script hypothesis is as worthy of attention as any others from a heuristic point of view, since there has not been any conclusive demonstration that the other extant hypotheses are more than tentative interpretations. This is why observational strategies should be devised to record and systematically compare clusters and sequences of geometric signs which appear to be formed of different types. Engraved bones, antlers, stones and other objects should be the starting point of such investigations as they offer better degrees of certainty concerning their intentionality and functionality. Piette and Petrie were mindful of such criteria as they called attention to items that exhibited the formal organization that would be expected from a script. Piette mentioned that some Azilian pebbles show sequences of aligned different signs, and also published samples of what he considered "glyptic writing" engraved on bones. He also often called attention to the fact that some of these individual geometric patterns were also found in much more ancient artifacts and cave walls.

It is certainly appropriate to recall, in concluding this paper, that André Leroi-Gourhan (1911-1986), who published in the form of tables several inventories of the types of Palaeolithic geometric signs (1958a, 1958b), remarked once that we could think that this would be a form of script if these populations had known writing. The circularity of the reasoning thus clearly exposes the biases that ideology imposes on cognition. Both perception itself in the recording of data and the methodology devised to interpret those data can be distorted by our ideological assumptions to an extent that is rarely recognized. At least, a keen awareness of these limits can alert us to the danger of some epistemological pitfalls.

Acknowledgments

I gratefully acknowledge the help of Dr. Stephen Quirke (Curator of the Petrie Museum of Egyptian Archaeology in London) and Dr. Laurent Olivier (Curator at the Musée d'archéologie national in Saint-Germain-en-Laye) in locating relevant sources concerning respectively William Flinders Petrie and Edouard Piette.

References

BAHN, P. (2006). Sex and violence in rock art: Are cave paintings really little more than the testosterone-fuelled scribbling of young men? Review of *The Nature of Paleolithic Art*. *Nature* vol. 441 (1 June 2006). p. 575-576.

BASALLA, G. (1988). *The Evolution of Technology*. Cambridge: Cambridge University Press.

BEDNARIK, R.G. (2003). The earliest evidence of palaeoart. *Rock Art Research*, vol. 20-2. p. 89-135.

BOUISSAC, P. (1997) New epistemological perspective for the archaeology of writing. In BLENCH, R.; SPRIGGS, N., eds. *Archaeology and Language, Vol. 1*. London: Routledge. p.3-62.

COX, D.; MEYERS, E.; SINHA, P. (2004). Contextually evoqued object-specific responses in human visual cortex. *Science*. Vol. 304. p.115-117.

DELSON, E.; TATTERSALL, I.; COUVERING van J.A.; BROOKS, A.S, eds. (2000). *Encyclopedia of Human Evolution and Prehistory, Second Edition*. NewYork: Garland.

DROWER, M.S. (1985). *Flinders Petrie: A Life in Archaeology*. London: Victor Gollancz.

ERRICO, F. d'; HENSHILWOOD, C.S.; NILSSEN, P. (2001). An engraved bone fragment from ca. 75 kyr Middle Stone Age levels at Blombos Cave, South Africa: implications for the origin of symbolism. *Antiquity*, 75. p. 309-318.

GIGERENZER, G.; SELTEN, R., eds. (2001). *Bounded Rationality: The Adaptive Toolbox*. Cambridge: MIT Press.

GLIMCHER, P.W. (2003). *Decisions, Uncertainty, and the Brain: The Science of Neuroeconomics*. Cambridge: MIT Press.

GONZALEZ-CRUSSI, F. (2006). *On Seeing: Things Seen, Unseen and Obscene*. New York: Duckworth.

GOREN, C.C.; SARTY, M.; WU, P.Y.K. (1975). Visual following and pattern discrimination of face-like stimuli by newborn infants. *Pediatrics* 56. p. 544-549.

GUTHRIE, R.D. (2006). *The Nature of Paleolithic Art*. Chicago: University of Chicago Press.

HENSHILWOOD, C.S. (2006). Modern humans and symbolic behavior: Evidence from Blombos Cave, South Africa. In BLUNDELL, G., ed., *Origins*. Cape Town: Double Storey. p. 78-83.

HOFFMAN, D.D. (1998). *Visual Intelligence: How We Create What We See*. New York: Norton.

LEROI-GOURHAN, A. (1958a). La fonction des signes dans les sanctuaires paléolithiques. *Bulletin de la Société Préhistorique Française*. Vol.55. p. 307-321

LEROI-GOURHAN, A. (1958b). Le symbolisme des grands signes dand l'art pariétal paléolithique. *Bulletin de la Société Préhistorique Française*. Vol. 55. p. 384-398.

PETRIE, W. M. F. (1912). *The Formation of the Alphabet. British School of* Archaeology *in Egypt Studies Series*. Vol. III. London: MacMillan

PFAFF, D. (2006). *Brain Arousal and Information Theory: Neural and Genetic Mechanisms*. Cambridge: Harvard University Press.

PIATELLI-PALMARINI, M. (1994). *Inevitable Illusions: How Mistakes of Reason Rule our Minds*. New York: John Wiley & Sons.

PIETTE, E. (1895). Hiatus et lacune. – Vestiges de la période de transition dans la grotte du Mas-d'Azil. *Bulletins de la Société d'Anthropologie de Paris*. Tome sixième (IVe série). Paris: Masson & Cie. p. 235-267.

PIETTE, E. (1905). Les écritures de l'âge glyptique. Etudes d'ethnographie préhistorique. *L'Anthropologie*. Tome seizième. p. 1-11.

UPHILL, E. P. (1972). A Bibliography of Sir William Matthew Flinders Petrie (1853-1942), *Journal of Near Eastern Studies* 31. p. 356-379.

LOWER PALAEOLITHIC PETROGLYPHS FROM EXCAVATIONS AT DARAKI-CHATTAN IN INDIA

Giriraj KUMAR

Rock Art Society of India, Faculty of Arts, Dayalbagh Educational Institute, Dayalbagh, Agra-282 005, Índia, girirajrasi@yahoo.com

Abstract: *Daraki-Chattan is a Palaeolithic cupule site in the Chambal basin near Bhanpura in Mandsaur district of Madhya Pradesh in India. It is a narrow cave in the quartzite buttresses on Indragarh Hill. To its north is a gorge, which is nearly 1.5 km wide. A perennial river, the Rewa, flows through it. The gorge opens into a nearly 3.5 to 4.0 km wide fertile valley in front of the cave. This valley and the hills on both its sides are very rich in Lower Palaeolithic artefacts. Daraki-Chattan Cave bears more than 500 cupules on both its vertical walls. They were claimed to belong either to the late phase of the Lower Palaeolithic or the transitional phase of the Lower Palaeolithic-Middle Palaeolithic, on the basis of archaeological remains obtained from surface of the cave. In order to test these bold claims the Rock Art Society of India (RASI) and the Australian Rock Art Research Association (AURA) ventured on a joint multidisciplinary project, 'Early Indian Petroglyphs: Scientific Investigations and Dating by International Commission', briefly called the EIP Project. This project has the backing and support of the Archaeological Survey of India (ASI), Indian Council of Historical Research (ICHR), Australia-India Council and the International Federation of Rock Art Organisations (IFRAO). Under the EIP Project, excavation has been conducted at Daraki-Chattan from 2002 to 2006 under the supervision and with the support of the ASI. The excavation yielded Lower Palaeolithic artefacts throughout its depth down to bedrock. It also yielded exfoliated pieces of stone slabs bearing 28 cupules, hammerstones used for their production and also a thick slab bearing two incised engraved lines. These evidences appear through the entire thickness of the exposed sediments, even from the lowest deposits near the bedrock.*
Keywords: *Lower Palaeolithic, Petroglyph, Cupule, Excavation, Daraki-Chattan, India*

Résumé: *Daraki-Chattan est un site rupestre (avec une large quantité de cupules) du paléolithique inférieur se trouvant dans un bassin nommé Chambal à proximité de Bhanpura dans le district de Mandsaur au Madhya Pradesh en Inde. C'est une grotte étroite dans un contrefort quartzitique sur la plaine d'Indragarh. Au nord de la grotte se trouve une gorge qui fait approximativement 1.5 kilomètre de large et parcourue par une rivière saisonnière, la Rewa. La gorge s'ouvre sur une vallée fertile de 3.5 à 4 kilomètres de large dominée par la grotte. Cette vallée et les collines adjacentes sont toutes très riche en matériels archéologiques datées du Paléolithique inférieur. On compte plus de 500 cupules sur les murs verticaux de la grotte de Daraki-Chattan. Ces cupules ont été attribuées parfois à la phase terminale du Paléolithique inférieur ou parfois à l'époque transitoire entre le Paléolithique inférieur et le Paléolithique moyen. Ces dates ont été établies sur la base de vestiges archéologiques trouvés en surface sur le sol de la grotte. Afin de tester la plausibilité de ces dates, le Rock Art Society of India (RASI) et l'Australian Rock Art Research Association (AURA) se sont associés pour former une cellule pluridisciplinaire et aujourd'hui reconnue sous l'éponyme EIP (Early Indian Petroglyphs : investigation et datation scientifique sous la tutelle d'une commission internationale). Ce projet reçoit le support financier et technique de l'Archaeological Survey of India (ASI), Indian Council of Historical Research (ICHR), Australia-India Council et l'International Federation of Rock Art Organisations (IFRAO). Sous la tutelle d'EPI une excavation de longue durée a été menée à Daraki-Chattan entre 2002 et 2006 en collaboration et avec le support et la supervision d'ASI. Cette campagne archéologique a produit une variété d'artefacts du Paléolithique inférieur dans la totalité du sol de la grotte et ce jusqu'au niveau du soubassement. Il a aussi été trouvé 28 cupules sur des morceaux quartzitique exfoliés provenant de la paroi. Il faut aussi noter la présence de pierres de percussion [mur-e] utilisées pour la fabrication des cupules ainsi que la présence d'une large plaque rocheuse comportant deux lignes incisées. Toutes ces objets archéologiques se trouvent repartis sur toute la profondeur du sol, y compris certains associés au soubassement.*
Mots clés: *Paléolithique inférieur, pétroglyphes, cupules, excavation, Daraki-Chattan, Inde*

INTRODUCTION

For the first time in the history of world archaeology excavations at Daraki-Chattan Cave in India from 2002 to 2006 have produced confirmed evidence of petroglyphs and hammerstones used for their production in Lower Palaeolithic period (Kumar *et al.* 2005). It also endorsed the occurrence of Lower Palaeolithic petroglyphs from an excavation carried out in the Auditorium Cave, Bhimbetka, by V. S. Wakankar in 1970s, that were recognised later on by Robert G. Bednarik, in 1990 (Bednarik 1993a). It shattered the biased conception of the Eurocentric origin of art and culture in Upper Palaeolithic period. It strongly supported the view that rock art is a global phenomenon and non-iconic rock art precedes the iconic art in the Pleistocene period. In Australia hundreds of thousands of petroglyph motifs are considered to be of Middle Palaeolithic age on technological grounds (cf. Foley and Lahr 1997). Even in Europe itself, we have at least one instance of Middle Palaeolithic rock art, in the form of eighteen cupules executed on the underside of a large limestone slab placed on top of La Ferrassie burial No. 6, the grave of a Neanderthal infant (Peyrony 1934). This, however, is an isolated case, whereas in other continents, pre-Upper Palaeolithic rock art and portable palaeoart are much more common (Bednarik 1992, 1993a, 1994, 2001a, 2002a, 2003). While we have huge numbers of Middle Palaeolithic rock art motifs, mostly from Australia, the incidence of Lower Palaeolithic cases remains very rare, and confirmed cases are limited to India.

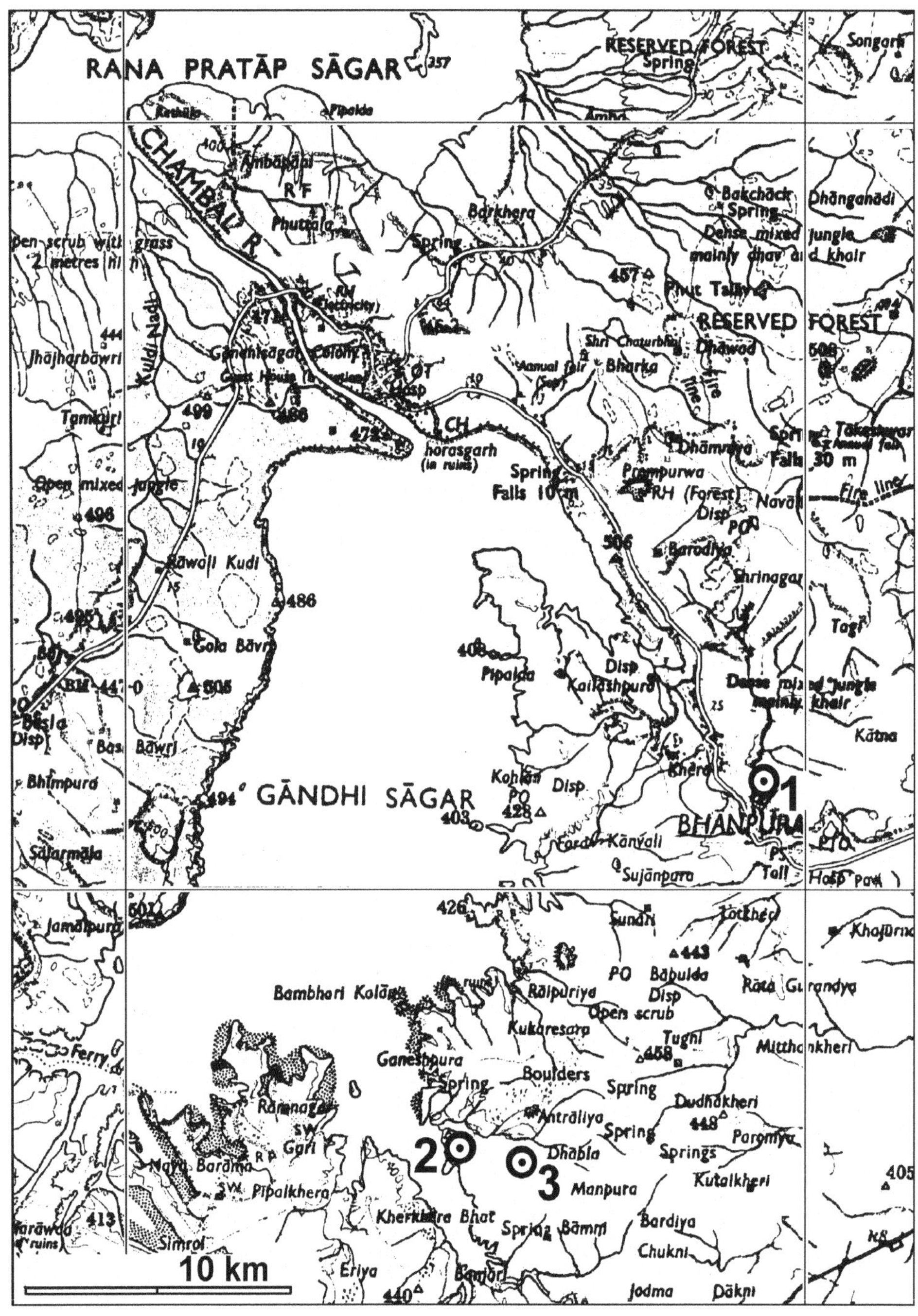

Figure 7.1. Map of the Bhanpura area, central India, showing the locations of Daraki-Chattan (1), Pola Bata (2) and Arnyabhan (3).

DARAKI-CHATTAN

Daraki-Chattan, with more than 500 cupules on both of its vertical walls, is an extraordinary Palaeolithic cupule site in Chambal basin in Bhanpura-Gandhisagar region, district Mandsaur, Madhya Pradesh (exact location is not given because of protection issues but the precise GPS co-ordinates have been recorded; Kumar 1996, 2002) (Fig. 7.1). It is a small, narrow and deep cave in the upper strata of quartzitic buttresses of Indragarh Hill which are broken into big blocks by vertical fracturing (Fig. 7.2). The site, located at an elevation of 420 m a.m.s.l., is among a complex of painted rockshelters in Indragarh Hill which on its top bears a fort of the Rashtrakuta period (seventh century A.D.), and near its base has yielded remains of an early Historic period habitation. This historic site was excavated by H.V. Trivedi and V.S. Wakankar in 1959–60 (1958–59: 27–28; 1959–60: 22–24). Indragarh Hill is a part of the Pariyatra Hill valley system, which comprises further rock art and Stone Age sites.

Daraki-Chattan is facing almost due west, with an entrance orientation at 10° NE and 190° SW. It overlooks

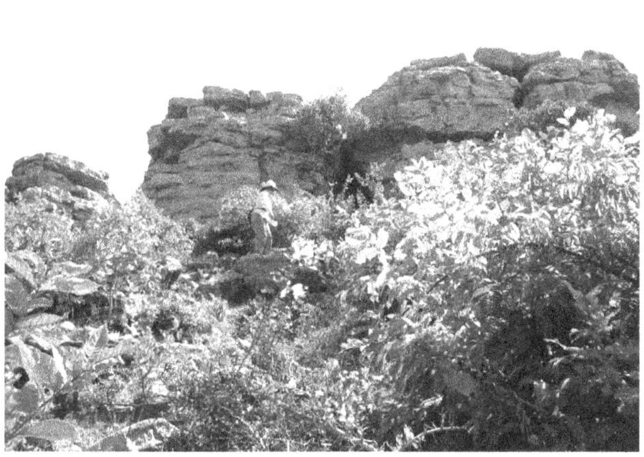

Figure 7.2. Indragarh Hill, with the entrance of Daraki-Chattan Cave up in the centre.

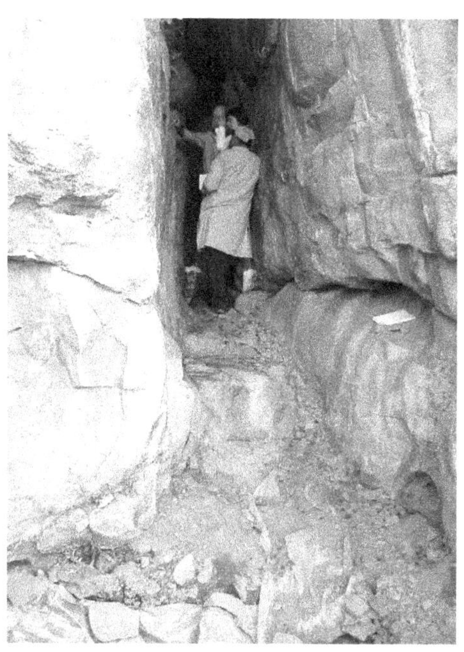

Figure 7.3. The entrance of Daraki-Chattan Cave.

a 1.5-km-wide beautiful and fertile valley of river Rewa which is bounded on both sides by Vindhyan escarpments, locally called hills. The valley opens into 3.5 to 4-km-wide plains of fertile agricultural fields and betel farms (*panvaris*). Deccan trap escarpments with laterite caps at places join the hill on the northwestern side of the valley. Through the valley flows a small perennial river, the Rewa. The valley is still a forest reserve, which provided sanctuary to tigers and other wild fauna up to the 1960s and 1970s. Close to Daraki-Chattan the Indragarh water reservoir has been made by constructing a dam across the valley in 2002.

Daraki-Chattan Cave was discovered by Ramesh Kumar Pancholi in 1993, but he could not recognise its great archaeological importance and published only four lines along with his other regular discoveries of petroglyphs (Pancholi 1994: 75). The cave was scientifically studied by Giriraj Kumar assisted by his son Ramkrishna in 1995 (Kumar 1996). On the basis of archaeological remains obtained from the surface of the cave, cupule patterns and patination on them, Kumar claimed that the cupules in the cave belong either to the late phase of Lower Palaeolithic or the transitional phase of Lower Palaeolithic-Middle Palaeolithic (Kumar 1996). It was a bold and extraordinary claim at that time (Kumar 2000–2001: 49–68). He was proved right by further scientific research through the EIP Project in the following years (Kumar *et al.* 2005; Bednarik *et al.* 2005).

The entrance of Daraki-Chattan is located in the upper strata of quartzite buttresses broken into big blocks with vertical fracturing. The cave is of tapered shape both in its depth and height. It is 4.0 m wide at the drip line, and 1.4 m wide at its mouth (Fig. 7.3). From here it continuously narrows down in width, to 34 cm at a depth of 7.4 m, it then becomes slightly wider, up to 40 cm, and finally closes at a depth of 8.4 m from its mouth. The cave is maximal 7.75 m in height. In its upper half, rock faces are tilting towards the northern side and converge at the top. The small gap between them has been sealed by boulders, cobbles and pebbles. The rock mass of both faces of the cave is divided into three strata of unequal thickness. The lowermost stratum of both walls bears cupule groups mostly on its upper two thirds. A few cupules can also be seen close to the bedrock of the cave. The cave walls bear over 500 cupules. I initially documented 498 cupules on its vertical walls in 1995, out of which five were doubtful (Kumar 1996, 2002). Afterwards I discovered four more cupules on the southern wall in 2002, out of these two were on the upper stratum (Fig. 7.4). They occur in four groups on the northern face and in six groups on the southern one. On the southern face there is also one solitary cupule on the lower part of the first stratum in the front of the cave, while two cupules were observed on the upper part of the second strata at a height of nearly 3.5 m from the cave floor on the southern face in 1995. Two more cupules were discovered on the bedrock inside the main body of the cave in 2004. In addition, 28 cupules were discovered on slabs exfoliated from the walls of the cave in the excavations during 2002 to 2005. The cobbles and rubble scattered on the cave floor yielded Middle Palaeolithic-Lower Palaeolithic artefacts when I studied the cave in 1995.

The cave floor slopes 1.4 m over a distance of 6.7 m (21%), then it suddenly dips to 60 cm. From there it slopes down at about 20%. The entire cave floor is littered with quartzite rubbles forming a 10 to 20-cm-thick deposit, together with fine sediment and humus. Some of this deposit might have been washed in by rainwater from above. The thickness of the deposit appears much greater at the mouth of the cave, until the floor suddenly slopes down outside the drip line. This floor deposit bears some scrapers and other tools of Middle Palaeolithic and

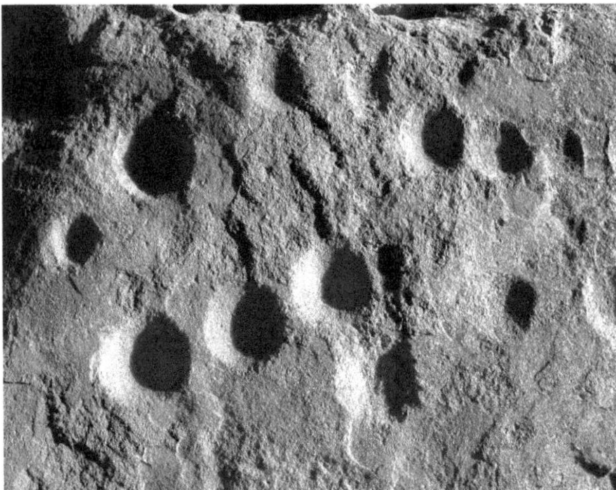

Figure 7.4. Cupules on the wall of Daraki-Chattan Cave.

Acheulian traditions. Some of them might have been brought in by rainwater from the hill above. Microliths and pottery pieces, which occur in profusion elsewhere in the region, could not be observed inside or outside the cave when surveyed in 1995. Acheulian and Middle Palaeolithic tools of early tradition on quartzite were also found on the hill above the cave. The foothills surrounding the area, the Rewa river valley and even the riverbed itself provide ample Acheulian and some Middle Palaeolithic tools of early tradition on quartzite, where as Upper Palaeolithic microliths are rare in the surrounding region.

THE EIP PROJECT

The name EIP Project is a short form of the major multidisciplinary project on 'Early Indian Petroglyphs: Scientific Investigations and Dating by International Commission'. It is a joint venture by the Rock Art Society of India (RASI) and Australian Rock Art Research Association (AURA) under the aegis of the International Federation of Rock Art Organisations (IFRAO). It was established by Giriraj Kumar, then President, RASI, and Robert G. Bednarik, Secretary, AURA, as the joint Project Directors in 1999. The work of the EIP Project has enjoyed the support from the Archaeological Survey of India, the Indian Council of Historical Research and the Australia-India Council. The Commission is to investigate all matters concerning the very early rock art of India including that of Daraki-Chattan thoroughly, using methods such as carbon isotope analysis, optically stimulated luminescence dating, microerosion analysis, uranium-thorium analysis and archaeological excavation. The Commission consists of geologists, archaeologists, rock art scientists and archaeometrists from India and Australia. The fieldwork of the EIP Project was commenced in mid-2001 by G. Kumar and several colleagues and expanded in the following years with an intensive campaign involving several specialists. A project web-page was established by Bednarik at *http://mc2.vicnet.net.au/home/eip1/web/index.html*. The first tangible findings were presented at the RASI-IFRAO Congress in Agra at the end of November 2004 and have been published in 2005 (Kumar *et al.* 2005, Bednarik *et al.* 2005), but fieldwork has continued, and will take several more years to complete.

THE EIP PROJECT TEAM

Patrons
The Director General, Archaeological Survey of India
The Chairman, Indian Council of Historical Research

Advisors
Dr A. Sundara, Dharwar, Dr S.P. Gupta, New Delhi, Dr R.C. Agrawal, New Delhi,
Dr R.S. Bisht, Dr Amarendranath and Shri P.B.S. Sengar, ASI, New Delhi

Directors
Dr Giriraj Kumar and Mr Robert G. Bednarik, the Indian and Australian directors of the project respectively.
Dr Narayan Vyas was, the official representative of the ASI, Bhopal Circle and co-director of the excavation at Daraki-Chattan

Executive team
Dr Giriraj Kumar, RASI; Shri Arakhita Pradhan, ASI, Agra Circle; Dr Pradymn Kumar Bhatt, Dr B.L. Bamboria, Dr Ashvini Kumar Sharma, Shri Aniruddha Kumar Bhatt and Shri Ramkrishna (RASI).

Australian team
Prof. Alan Watchman, AURA
Prof. Richard G. Roberts, Wollongong University
Dr Ewan Lawson, AURA

Visiting scientists and rock art scholars
Dr Carol Patterson, U.S.A.; Prof. V.N. Misra, Pune; Dr R.K. Sharma, Deharadun; Shri Ramesh Kumar Pancholi, Prof. G.L. Badam, Dr R.K. Ganjoo, Shri S.B. Ota, Dr M.L. Sharma, Shri M.L. Meena.

EXCAVATIONS AT DARAKI-CHATTAN 2002 TO 2006

Excavations at Daraki-Chattan have been the major aspect of the EIP Project. It was excavated under the direction of Giriraj Kumar from 2002 to 2006. Narayan Vyas was the official representative of the Archaeological Survey of India and was nominated as the co-director of the excavation.

When we decided to excavate at Daraki-Chattan Cave Kumar observed that a deposit of sediments, up to more than 6 m length, was lying in front of it. Beyond that the hill slopes steeply. Secondly, the majority of cupules are distributed in the first half of the cave, after which they become sparse. In front of the cave we can see the exfoliated surface on both the wall faces of the cave, most prominent on the southern face, where exfoliation scars can be seen quite deep into the cave, and made the face devoid of cupules. These exfoliated slab pieces must have been lying in the deposit in front of the cave. Thirdly, some of the hammerstones used for the creation of cupules in the cave must have been lying buried in the sediments of the cave. Considering these factors, the sediments in front of the cave and in the associated rockshelter in the north appeared to be the most promising area for excavation, and we laid down the trench there. Besides, only minimal work was also done within the actual cave passage.

Objectives

The initial objectives of the excavations and explorations at and around Daraki-Chattan were as follows:

1. To establish the stratigraphy of the sediments and the palaeoclimatic and cultural history of Daraki-Chattan.
2. To find evidence related to the production of cupules in the cave, and other art objects and artefacts, if any, from the sediments.
3. To obtain scientific dates for different levels of sediments exposed in the excavations and bearing artefacts and other antiquities related with human creation, including cupule production, by using the OSL dating method. AMS ^{14}C method will be employed for obtaining dates from the accretions and patination on the cupules. If possible, microerosion analysis will also be employed for dating of the cupules.
4. To establish the cultural sequence and Pleistocene history of the region.

Layout of the trench

A sketch plan of the area inside and in front of the cave and that in the associated rockshelter towards its north was prepared. A central line was drawn from the tip of the cave, through and in front of it. It was marked at one metre intervals. The mark of the 6th m was taken as the centre point of the Trench, and a grid of 1 m^2 was prepared around it. By considering the square of the 6th metre point as A1 we prepared the layout of the trench as given in Figure 7.5.

Area of excavations

The total area excavated in the Daraki-Chattan excava-tions during the five seasons from 2002 to 2006 was 33 square meters: in the entrance part or vestibule of the cave, in the associated rockshelter to the cave's immediate north, with only minimal work within the actual cave passage (Fig. 7.5). It also includes the area of 8 square metres of the trench extended in square XA7, A7 to XA10, A10 in 2006. Measurements of depth are of two types: (1) from the surface, and (2) from the datum A1. Mostly both are stated simultaneously here. Besides advancing in the excavation slowly but steadily in every season, we also explored the

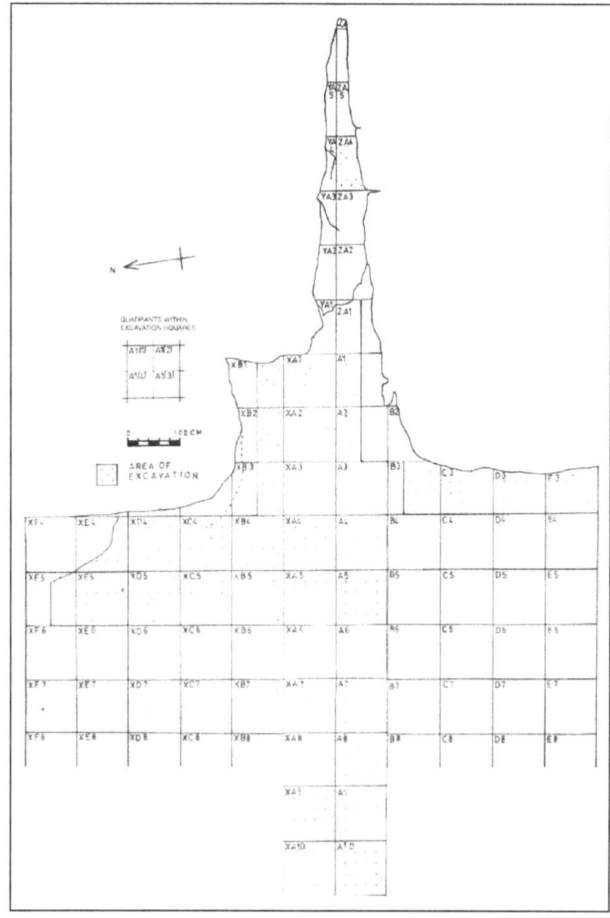

Figure 7.5. Floor plan of Daraki-Chattan, with excavation squares indicated.

surrounding region in order to better understand the problems posed by the excavations.

The excavated squares (Numbers in bracket represent quadrants):

YA4(2), ZA4 (1&4), ZA1(1&4),

XB1(2&3), XA1, A1(1&4),

XB2(2&3), XA2, A2(1&4),

XB3(2&3), XA3, A3, B3(2&3 and a part of 1&4), C3, D3, E3

Parts of XB4, XA4, a little bit in A4(1&4),

XB5, XA5, A5 (1&4, parts of XD5(2&3) and XC5 (1&4),

And also in sq. XA7, A7 to XA 10,A 10 in front of the cave.

The maximum depth we reached at bedrock or slabs lying on bedrock in the main trench:

In XB2 (2/3): -311 cm from datum A1 and -280 cm from section facing South.

In XC4 (3): -284 cm from datum A1 and -180 cm from section facing West.

In XB5 (3): -311 cm from datum A1 and -137 cm from section facing East.

In XA4: -256 cm from datum A1 and -171 cm from section facing South.

In the excavated western part of the trench in front of the cave the sediment is sharply sloping down from A6 to A8 from -168 cm to -249cm from Datum A1, then up to -368 cm at A10 (from Datum A1) i.e. 200 cm in a distance of 4 m. Bedrock/slabs on bedrock appeared at depth -280 cm from datum A1 in A7 and goes down to -413 cm from A1 in A10. In XA7 it appeared at depth -271 from datum A1 and goes down to -390 cm from A1 in XA10.

The maximum sediment depth on bedrock or slabs laying on bedrock in this area of working is as follows:

A7 -38 cm, XA7 -64 cm
A8 -64 cm, XA8 -58 cm
A9 -19 cm, XA9 -16 cm
A10 -45 cm, XA10 -45 cm

The excavations and explorations have solved our major problems. Scientific analysis and dating of the samples to establish the antiquity of the sediments yielding evidences scientifically is in progress.

STRATIGRAPHY

In the excavations at Daraki-Chattan, during five season's work (2002 to 2006), we have exposed sediments up to a depth of -311 cm from A1 in the main trench (Fig. 7.6). The sediments slope towards west by 150 cm over a distance of 5 m, i.e. up to XB6(2). The nature of the sediment so far exposed in the excavation is fairly uniform with gradations of colour, size of the exfoliated flakes, stones, blocks and slabs. However, for convenience of study the sediments have been divided broadly in two parts, a lower deposit with sub-pseudo-layers 6, 5 and 4; and an upper deposit with sub-pseudo-layers 3, 2 and 1 (see Table 7.1).

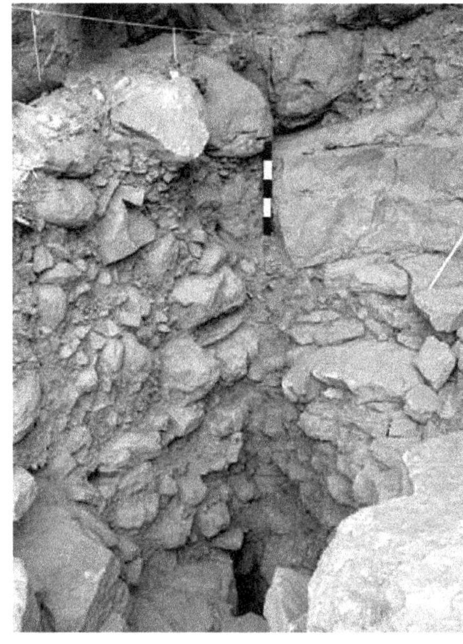

Figure 7.6. Main excavation trench, Daraki-Chattan.

Table 7.1. Stratigraphy and tool typology, section facing south, main trench. Layers 1 and 2 are visible only in the area of XB3 and XB4 and are almost indistinguishable.

Layer No.	Depth	Nature	Associated cultural material.
1.	A few -10 cm	Surface humus	Artefacts representing transitional phase from Lower Palaeolithic to Middle Palaeolithic.
2.	15 -24 cm including layer 1	Loose brown soil	
3.	37-110 cm	Loose brown soil with exfoliated flakes and stones	Lower Palaeolithic flake artefacts, some on pebbles and cobbles.
4.	26-50 cm	Compact calcareous yellowish-brown soil	Lower Palaeolithic flake tools along with artefacts on pebble and cobble tools. Cupules, petroglyphs and arranged stones.
5	25-28 cm	Compact brownish-red soil	Lower Palaeolithic. More artefacts on quartzite cobbles, pebbles and thick nodules (Fig. 7.7), some also on natural flakes, split pebbles and manmade flakes on quartzite, a few on chert also. Rare occurrence of handaxe like artefacts, only one cleaver, some hammerstones and slabs bearing cupules. Patinated chert flakes and artefacts continued. Hammerstones found from the upper part of the red laterite soil, layer 6, overlain by layer 5 (18-06-05).
6.	25-76 cm	Comparatively loose lateritic red soil	A few artefacts were obtained from the upper part of the red laterite soil, layer 6, overlain by layer 5 (18-06-05). Otherwise most of the lower portion of this lateritic red soil is devoid of stone artefacts. It corroborates the evidence of Lower Palaeolithic artefacts obtained from only upper layer of laterite deposit at Barodia-Navali Fanta on Gandhisagar road. Artefacts are on quartzite cobbles and pebbles, some also on natural and man made flakes and split pebbles on quartzite, a few on chert also.

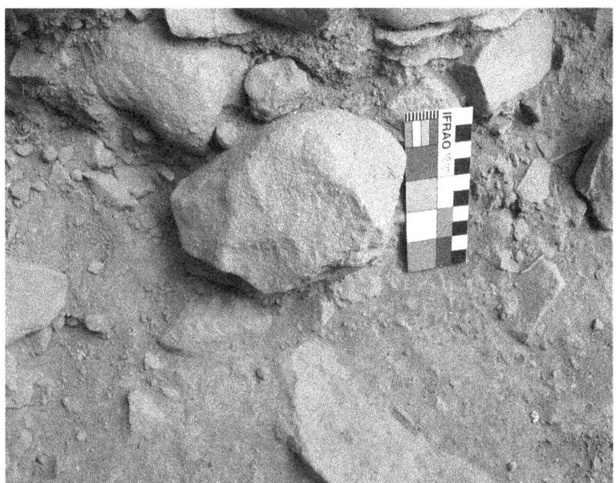

Figure 7.7. Lower Palaeolithic stone artefact in layer No. 5.

1. Lower deposit: The lowermost sediment is lateritic red soil that became slightly loose because of rainwater. It grades into the following compact brownish red soil and again into compact calcareous yellowish-brown soil (sub-pseudo-layers 6, 5 and 4). These sediments also comprise fallen large slabs and stone blocks. Most of these slabs have been weathered deeply and became highly patinated with dark-brown mineral accretion. Such weathered rocks are locally known as *barbarya bhata*. These sediments bear Lower Palaeolithic artefacts. Their stratigraphic-typological variation has been given in Table 7.1.

2. Upper deposit: It is composed of loose brown sediment with exfoliated flakes and stones, generally of comparatively small size and progressively of lower number. It consists of the upper three sub-pseudo-layers (3, 2 and 1). The top 20 to 24 cm sediment grades into greyish-brown pseudo layer (2) and thin humus layer (1). At places sub-pseudo-layers 1 and 2 have been washed away by rainwater.

Observations on the stratigraphy

1. From the very beginning of the excavation in 2002, the artefact assemblage represents a late phase of Lower Palaeolithic or transitional phase from the Lower Palaeolithic to the Middle Palaeolithic. However, the proportion of Lower Palaeolithic typology increases with depth.
2. Polyhedrons and discoid cores of quartzite are found from the lower level of layer 3. Cobble artefacts, like spheroids, were also found from the lower part of layers 3 and 4. Layers 6 and 5 revealed artefacts mostly of quartzite cobbles and thick nodules (cobble tools, discoids and spheroids). Patinated chert flakes and artefacts of chert nodules are found even up to the last level of the excavated sediment but their number decreases with increasing depth. Microliths of chalcedony and chert are rarely found in the loose sediments of the upper layers.
3. Tiny granules of haematite were found throughout the depth of the sediments.
4. The thin humus layer 1 contains some pottery shards, brick fragments, microliths and chert and chalcedony flakes.
5. In layer 3, the size and number of the stone blocks increase with the depth of the sediment. Huge blocks were found lying at a depth of -135 cm from A1 (-85 cm from surface) and continuing up to the depth of -177 cm from A1 (-127 cm from surface). Besides the huge collapsed boulder in the centre of the trench, a big block measuring 104 × 46 × 21 cm was lying at a depth of -135 cm from A1 in A3 and XA3. Lower Palaeolithic artefacts of quartzite are numerous, mostly in mint condition, only a few bearing abrasion marks. Patinated chert flakes and nodules are also found. The concentration of Lower Palaeolithic artefact assemblage is greatest in its lower half. Highly patinated utilised chert flakes and nodules occur there.
6. In layer 4, a 20-cm-thick floor made of well arranged, flat and thick rock slabs has been exposed in the main trench in XB4, XA4, XB5, XA5. It is preceded by three layers of arranged slabs, which are highly weathered and extend deep down to bedrock at the bottom of layer 6. Similarly, three layers of arranged flat slabs have also been exposed in the adjacent rockshelter in XC4, XC5, XD4, XD5, XE4(2), XE5(2).

Excavated cupules, 2002

Many slab pieces were recovered from squares A2, XA2, XA1 and A1, distributed mostly around point A2 at depth -26 cm to -43 cm from A2 (-38 cm to -55 cm from A1). Out of these, seven fragments joined perfectly to form a slab measuring 95 × 50 × 5–10 cm (Fig. 7.8). Its three big pieces bore seven cupules. One of its large pieces was covering a portion of another one in the excavation. These were found with a southward orientation at an inclination of nearly 25°. The inclination might indicate a former hollow space below. After removing them, one more piece was discovered 10 cm below them. Besides, four more slab pieces (including the vertical slab in the southeast corner of the trench) were found bearing one cupule each. The dimensions of the cupules range from 26.1 × 29.0 × 1.85 mm to 50.5 × 51.9 × 7.4 mm. Stone artefacts representing the transitional phase from the Lower Palaeolithic to the Middle Palaeolithic were discovered both above and below these slabs.

Another slab piece bearing three cupules was discovered from A2(2) at the time of collecting soil sample No. DC-1 on 27 September 2002. The soil sample was collected at a depth of -50 cm from the surface. The cupule slab fragment came out while digging horizontally into the section facing north. This fragment is roughly rectangular in shape, with one corner curved and another side obliquely cut towards the end. The maximum dimensions of the slab are 22.0 × 13.5 × 5.5/2.6 cm. The upper surface of the slab is sloping, while its lower surface is

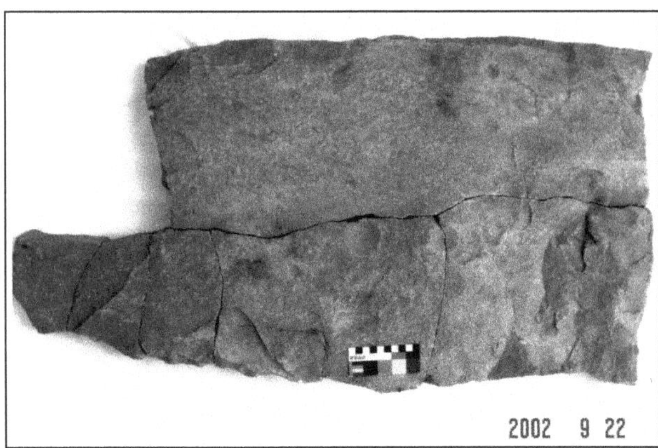

Figure 7.8. Exfoliated slab excavated in seven fragments, bearing seven cupules.

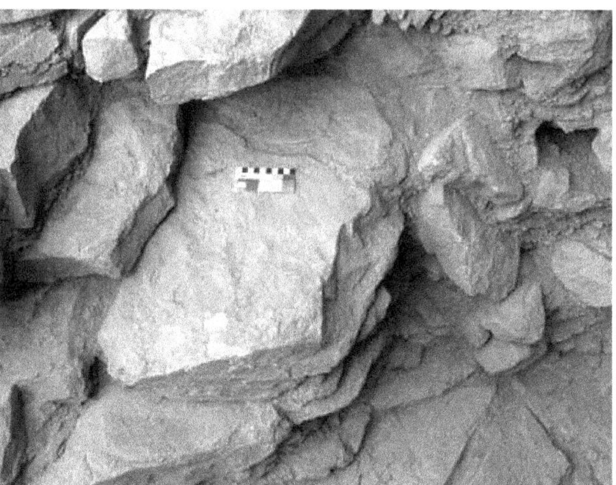

Figure 7.9. Cupule slab in situ, cupule was found on its underside.

almost plain with a shallow depression in the centre. The slab piece bears three cupules:

1. At the 'left' side, 45.8 × 37.7 (broken) × 6.7 mm.
2. In the 'right' half of the slab, 41.0 × 35.0 (broken) × 8.8 mm.
3. At the extreme end of the 'upper right' corner. The cupule is broken, only one-quarter of it remains. It is 16.0 mm deep.

Excavated cupules, 2003

1. A piece of cupule-bearing slab was found in XB(3) at depth -63 cm to -70 cm from A1. It is 18 × 16 cm in size and was inclined towards north. It bears two deep cupules and two shallow ones. It comes from slightly below the level from which cupule slabs were obtained from the Daraki-Chattan excavation in the previous year. Stone artefacts obtained from around it were of quart-zite. In the month of December 2003 a team of Stone Age archaeologists, consisting of S.B. Ota, R.K. Ganjoo, G. Kumar and A. Pradhan, studied the mate-rial. The team came to the conclusion that the assemblage obtained in the excavation till 2003 repre-sents a late Acheulian tradition. Two fine chalcedony blades were also obtained close to this slab, one from towards its east and another from towards its south.
2. A small piece of cupule slab was found lying upside down in XB2(2) at a depth of -72 cm from A1 (Fig. 7.9). Two stone artefacts of quartzite were obtained close to it.
3. Another small slab piece with two broken cupules was obtained from XA2(1) at a locus 55 cm from XA2, 81 cm from XA3, at a depth of -85 cm from A1 (-55 cm from surface).

Excavated cupules, 2004

1. A slab piece of quartzite bearing two cupules was found upside down in XC5(1) in the adjacent rockshelter at a locus 36 cm from XC5 and 74 cm from XB5, at a depth of -17 cm from the surface (-127 cm from A1 datum), in a Lower Palaeolithic context. The cupule surface is weathered, the cupules' dimensions are as follows: cupule 1, 31.0 × 25.0 mm (broken) x 4.7 mm; cupule 2, 40.6 × 36.8 mm (broken) × 5.0 mm.
2. A small cupule slab piece of quartzite was found in XC4(1) at a locus 59 cm from XB5, 59 cm from XC5, at a depth of -36 cm from XC4 (-142 cm from A1 datum). The cupule surface is smooth and patinated. It was found in the Lower Palaeolithic level. The dimensions of the cupule slab piece are 70 × 69.4 × 20.7 mm, and those of the cupule are 30.7 × 19.2 mm (broken) × 6.4 mm.
3. An irregularly broken thick slab was found lying along the slabs of the floor along the section facing south in XA3(1)/XB3(2) on 28 May 2004. The locus of the slab is 79 cm from XB4(2), 110 cm from XA4, depth -93 cm from surface and -164 cm from A1 datum. The sediment covering it yielded four Lower Palaeolithic artefacts, out of these three were of quartzite and one of highly patinated chert. When we removed this slab we observed two broken cupules on its patinated and slightly weathered surface. The cupules are smooth and appear to be equally patinated with a little light-brown encrustation on them. The dimensions of the slab are: upper surface 13 × 13 cm, lower surface 26 × 17 cm. It bears two cupules: cupule 1, 42.5 mm × 42.7 mm (broken) × 7.8 mm, ovoid in shape; cupule 2, 41.7 mm × 30.7 mm (broken) × 7.0 mm.

Cupules on slabs still lying in the main trench

On 19 June 2005 we observed a cupule on a quartzite slab projecting from the section facing south in XB3(2) (Fig. 7.10). The locus of the cupule is 39 cm from XA3, 70 cm from XA4, 119 cm from A3, depth -129 cm from XB4 and -184 cm from A1 datum. The dimensions of the cupule are: 32 mm (broken) × 29 mm × 6 mm. The thickness of the cupule-bearing slab is 20 cm and its

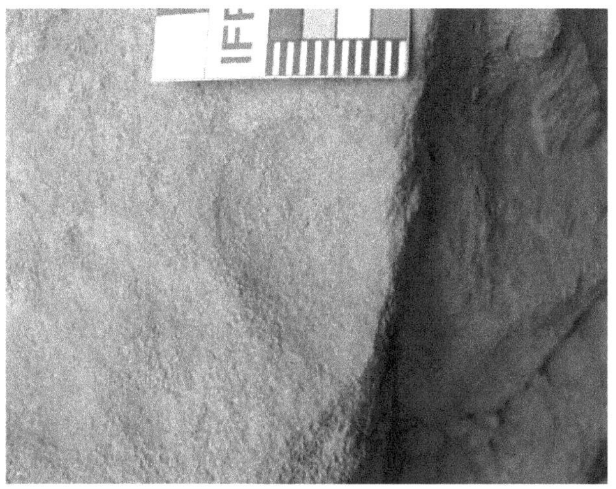

Figure 7.10. Lowest cupule found so far.

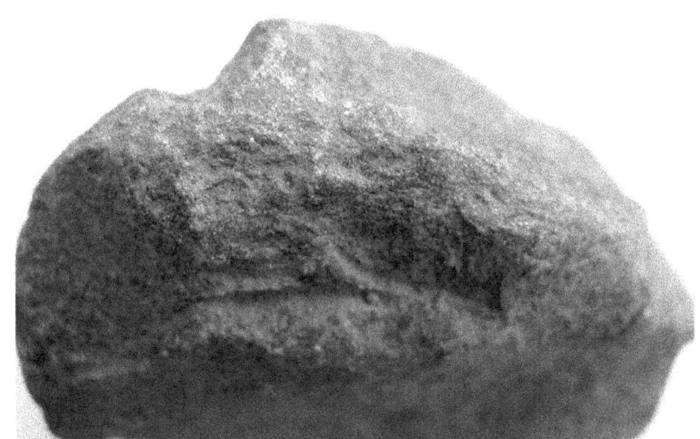

Figure 7.11. Quartzite hammerstone, used as a secondary artefact.

visible size is 49 × 45 cm. It is resting on another slab. Thus making the cupule-bearing surface 32 cm above bedrock in layer 5 (early phase). So far it represents the earliest cupule from the Daraki-Chattan excavation. Soil sample No. DC-5 for OSL dating was collected just above this slab on 9 and 10 December 2004.

Another cupule was observed on a very big fallen slab slanting NW in 2004, still lying in A2, A3 and A4 in layer 4. The cupule is slightly diagonal, with dimensions 32 (broken) × 34 × 16 mm. It is located just close to the section facing north, at locus 83 cm from A3, 124 cm from A4 and at depth -58 cm from surface of section facing north and -140 cm from A1 datum. The visible slab size is 118 × 93 × 34 cm.

HAMMERSTONES

Hammerstones used for the production of cupules were obtained from the excavation at Daraki-Chattan. A hammerstone fragment of a quartzite river cobble in XA2 (2) is from a locus 53 cm from XA2(3), 28 cm from XA2(2), at depth -37 cm from A1. It has a broad striking surface, which has been worn smooth by impact, obtained just 5 cm below the two major Acheulian artefacts in the same quadrant. It was found on 8 June 2002. The same sort of smooth crushed surface on hammerstones has been produced in the replication of cupule production.

A big sturdy hammerstone of quartzite from XA1(2) at a locus 50 cm from XA1, 50 cm from XA2, at depth -63 cm from the surface and A1 datum was discovered on 28 May 2003. In the same year, a second hammerstone of quartzite used for cupule production was found. It had been split after use to produce a secondary artefact, and occurred in XA1(2), 70 cm from XA1, 85 cm from XA2, at depth -127 cm from A1 (Fig. 7.11). It was lying just on the bedrock, hence it represents one of the earliest evidence of cupule production in the cave. It was discovered on 16 June 2003. This level yielded a rich concentration of Lower Palaeolithic artefacts, one of them is a 30-cm-long flake of quartzite.

Five more hammerstones were recovered in 2004. In XA3(1), a pointed hammerstone of quartzite from the Lower Palaeolithic floor level was left in situ for inspection by members of the EIP Commission, and removed in their presence. It was found 5 cm from XA3, 96 cm from XA4, at depth -111 cm from surface (-164 cm from A1 datum). In XA3(4)/XA4(1), a quartzite hammerstone was obtained from the extended trench at 30 cm in line from XA4 towards A4, at depth -107 cm from A1 datum. Another specimen was found in association with large Lower Palaeolithic artefacts of quartzite in XA4(1), at a locus 86 cm from A4, 65 cm from XB4(2), at depth -42 cm from the surface in XB4(2). A long quartzite hammerstone was excavated in XA3(2), in association with Lower Palaeolithic quartzite artefacts at 51 cm from XA3, 51 cm from A3, at depth -145 cm from surface (-190 cm from A1 datum). The fifth specimen found in 2004 came from XA5(1). It was a long hammerstone of quartzite, Lower Palaeolithic, also left in situ for reference (removed later on). It was found 60 cm from XA5, 85 cm from XA6, at depth -67 cm from XA5.

Finally, three further hammerstones were discovered in the lower strata in 2005. The first was an example with a good battering facet obtained from XA4(3) at a depth of -10 cm to -20 cm from surface, found in loose sediment on 30 May 2005. This was followed by a hammerstone of a quartzite cobble from XC4(2) at a locus XB4 -42 cm, XC4 -80 cm depth, -40 cm from surface, found 14 cm towards south of the fallen big rock in the rockshelter and 8 cm below it (obtained on 3 June). The most recently secured hammerstone, also a quartzite cobble, was found in XB4(4) at locus XB4 -80 cm, XA5 -80 cm, on 18 June. It occurred at a depth of -140 cm from XB4, where the sediment changes from lateritic red to brownish red soil. Its dimensions are 97 × 81 × 64 mm. It was found along with a Lower Palaeolithic artefact made from a quartzite cobble, a hematite pigment nodule and another cobble tool. All of these four objects come from an area measuring 17 × 16 cm in XB4(4), at -132 to -140 cm depth from XB4. One more artefact of a quartzite flake, Lower Palaeolithic, comes from nearly 20 cm away from the hammerstone. All these artefacts were found surrounded by decomposed quartzite stone blocks (*barbarya bhatas*).

OTHER PETROGLYPHS

Two engraved lines were observed on a boulder lying obliquely in XB4(2), XA4 (1&2), XB3(3), XA3(3&4) (Figs 7.12 and 7.13). The rock was removed to enable further excavation. Nearly twenty Lower Palaeolithic artefacts were found from above and alongside of this slab. About 15 cm below its tilted lower end were the arranged slabs of the floor (see below). It was fully exposed on 3 June 2004 and was removed on 4 June 2004.

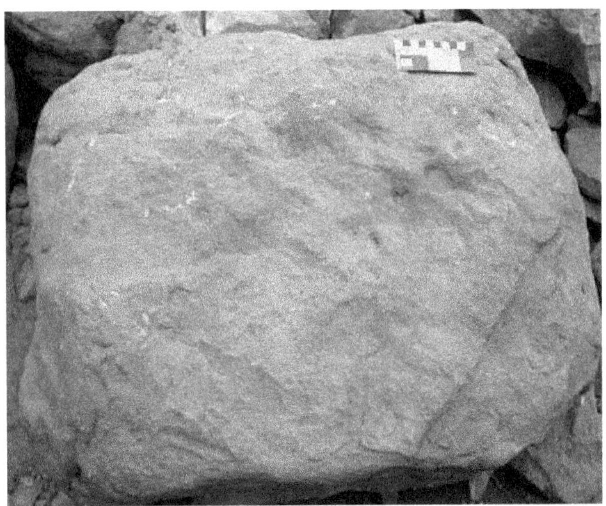

Figure 7.12. Quartzite block excavated from Lower Palaeolithic layer, bearing two engraved grooves.

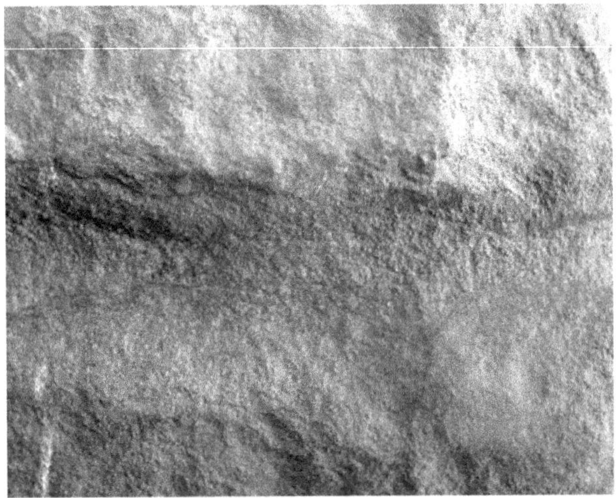

Figure 7.13. Close-up view of one of the engraved grooves from the Lower Palaeolithic deposit.

The boulder forms a rough rectangle when seen from above. One side of its lower surface is very thick in comparison with the other. Its upper surface measures 64.5 × 50.0 cm, the lower surface 60.0 × 44.0 cm, the thickness on its thick side is 35.0 cm and on its thin side 18.0 cm. The upper surface of the rock bears thick brown patina, in places it appears glossy. A similar patina also runs through the engraved lines, indicating their great antiquity. The engraved two lines are smooth and run obliquely at two corners of the slab. The 'left' groove (southern) is big and the 'right' one (northern) is small. They show fractured crystals of the rock under the magnifying glass. Their detailed measurements are as follows:

Engraved long line on the 'left' corner (southern) of the slab: length 295 mm, running obliquely on southern upper corner of the slab with dark-brown patina. Widths at different points: 14.2 mm, 20.3 mm, 19.0 mm, 14.0 mm, 19.0 mm, 18.4 mm, 18.2 mm, 14 mm. Depths at different points: 5.0 mm, 4.7 mm, 4.8 mm, 5.3 mm and 5.1 mm.

Engraved short line on the 'right' corner (northern) of the slab: widths at different points are 8.4 mm, 10.0 mm, 11.3 mm, 8.0 mm. Depths at different points: 2.0 mm, 3.0 mm, 2.0 mm.

A small piece of slab with a broad groove was found in A3(1) at a locus 5 cm from A3, 97 cm from B3, at a depth of -187 cm from A1 datum, on 9 June 2004. It is also of the Lower Palaeolithic. The slab measures 110 × 117 × 42 mm, the groove varies from 15.5 to 18.0 mm in width and 2.8 to 3.3 mm in depth.

REPLICATION OF CUPULE CREATION

In order to understand the nature and fracturing of hammerstones we conducted experiments to replicate cupules in 2002 and 2003. Three cupules were produced at a site 7 m to the south of the cave entrance, under a small overhang, located at a convenient height (about chest high) (Fig. 7.14). Hammerstones used and cupules made were examined at intervals of 15 minutes. It was observed that most of the hammering surface flakes off if striking is forceful. This is the reason why we find small hammering surfaces on the hammerstones obtained from the excavation. The time of making one cupule, spread over two days, was six hours, but only one person, a strong Gurjar youth, worked on it. Its diameters in any direction are from 56 to 57 mm; it is nearly perfectly circular. Also, the cupule is nearly symmetrical, i.e. its deepest point is equidistant, both vertically and horizontally. The maximum depth ranges from 7.9 mm to 9.7 mm, depending on which opposing rim locations are used as reference. This provides a fair indication of the great labour effort in making well over 500 cupules, most of which are deeper than 10 mm, and many of which are smaller than 56 mm. Most modern humans would not be able to match the required skill in precise percussion, and considerable physical strength and determination are indicated.

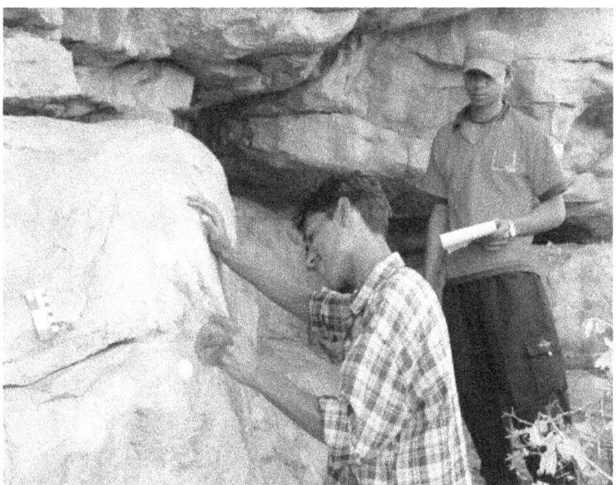

Figure 7.14. Replication experiment of cupule making.

Some hammerstones from Lower Palaeolithic levels are specially prepared from stout, pointed stone pieces. Comparatively deep cupules with good circular shape may be assigned to such hammerstones of Lower Palaeolithic/ Acheulian age.

STUDY AND OBSERVATIONS

The centrally lying big rock was part of the bedrock at the mouth of the cave. It got detached and slid north-westwards even before the humans visited the cave for the first time.

The Lower Palaeolithic big chopper on a cobble in A1(4) and other artefacts on cores in A1(1) lying in situ on bedrock at depth -135 cm from datum A1 and -124 cm from surface of section facing north represent the earliest material cultural remains left by the early humans at this site.

The solid but weathered strata exposed after removing this big rock and running diagonally from NE to SW appears the weathered bedrock in part of XA1, A1, part of XA2, and A2, extending in A3. The portion apposite to it was deep. We observed bedrock/slabs lying on bedrock at maximum depth in Sq. XB2(2/3) at -311 cm from datum A1, and -280 cm from surface of the section facing south. In Sq. A4 it is at -256 cm from datum A1 and -171 cm from surface of the section facing south.

Daraki-Chattan is almost solely a Lower Palaeolithic cultural site. We start getting Lower Palaeolithic artefacts right from near the surface of the sediment. Of course from the top humus layer and the following brown soil layer we also found some pottery pieces, brick fragments and microliths which renders it obvious that the site must have been visited by man in the later periods also.

The northern side of the rockshelter associated to the northern side of the cave yielded many Lower Palaeolithic artefacts from the surface and from the loose pebbly humus sediment up to a depth of more than 10 cm. A fine spearhead like artefact on quartzite from Sq XF6(3) was obtained at depth -10 cm from the northwestern corner of the trench.

We also obtained an artefact on quartzite with angular and smooth facets. The general archaeological trend indicates that it may be a Neolithic artefact, but its form, nature, patination and weathering indicate perhaps its Palaeolithic antiquity (16-6-2006).

Cupule surface in the cave

The thin exfoliation of the rock surface has resulted in the loss of cupule dimensions and ultimately the cupules. The loss of cupules is clearly visible on both walls of the cave. Generally, the smaller diameter and shallowness of the round cupules is because of exfoliation of the surrounding surface. Hence, any metrical analysis based on simply cupule dimensions will not help in reaching the proper conclusion.

Why we got comparatively young AMS ^{14}C dates (nearly 12,000 B.P.) for encrustation collected from outside a cupule by Alan Watchman in 2002 (Bednarik *et al.* 2005: 63–64) was a question to be answered scientifically. Kumar minutely studied the cave walls from 12 to 14 June 2006 and observed that the surrounding surface of the cupule has been continuously exfoliating in thin layers. Hence, older deposit of encrustation goes off with the exfoliation of the rock surface. Then a new process of encrustation sets in. It has been better observed on one place on the northern wall where recent deposit of encrustation is overlapping or concealing both the older and new surfaces of the rock. Deposition on the new surface means comparatively younger age, hence, we got younger AMS ^{14}C dates.

Nature of the sediments

The study of the sediments in the sections exposed in the excavation indicates that most of the sedimentation at the site is due to exfoliation of the standing and overhanging rocks. A little portion of the sediment is in situ development, while a little bit has been deposited by rain water in the form of a narrow strip of loose soil particularly in the north east corner, visible in the corner of Sq. XB1(2) and XB 2(2), then in the narrow gully running slightly diagonally from south to north-west, along the side of the big and thick slab bearing a cupule. The flow of both channels joins and then runs diagonally through XB4 from where we took soil sample DC4 for OSL dating in December 2004. That is why we are getting loose soil along this course. This narrow course of water was there even before the visit of the humans to this site. Hence, we can observe a deposit of lateritic red soil on the bedrock in the sections facing east and north in XA4., while in the section facing south in XA4 the soil is loose yellowish-red.

Activity area

The major activity area in front of the cave and in the shelter as revealed by the concentration of the Lower Palaeolithic artefacts obtained in the excavations appears to be the area covered by Sq XD4, 5, XC4, 5, XB3, 4, 5, XA1, 3, 4, 5, and A 1, 4, 5, in 11.5 sq m.

The extended trench in the west revealed the thick and high step-like bedrock/slabs on bedrock approaching the cave. They grade 200 cm in a distance of 4 m.

CORRELATION OF THE OBSERVATIONS IN THE FIELD AND EXCAVATIONS

In order to consider the cultural material in its total perspective and to understand problems posed by the excavation we thoroughly explored the region and discovered many cupule sites on the Indragarh-Chanchalamata hills, at Kanwala, Modi, Arnyabhau and Polabhata, in the exploration of the region in 2004. Lower Palaeolithic implements and cobbles occur in profusion around rock buttresses, and especially at Kanwala a lot of choppers and cobble tools were found along with Acheulian artefacts (Kumar *et al.* 2006: 13–34).

We also observed that fresh Acheulian artefacts occur in the exposed layer of lateritic soil at Barodia-Fanta crossing on Gandhi Sagar Road, nearly 18 km from Bhanpura. Artefacts made from cobbles, like spheroids (*bolas*), choppers, pointed choppers etc. were also found in the surrounding region. We are trying to understand the correlation between the evidence obtained in the excavation and that observed in the nearby region.

Daraki-Chattan is a Lower Palaeolithic site, yielding Lower Palaeolithic artefacts right from the surface and from all layers below it. From the top humus and to some extent from the following brown soil layers we also found some pottery and brick pieces, and microliths, which indicate that the site was visited by man in these late periods also.

In the early phase of the Lower Palaeolithic, the cave was a tool-manufacturing site. It yielded cobbles used as cores, flakes, unfinished tools (from XB5(4) at depth -161 cm from XB4, red lateritic soil), reused artefacts etc. A few artefacts from layer 3 upwards, particularly from the rockshelter trench and from the western part of the main trench, were also re-utilised. In the upper part of the stratigraphy, XA4 (4&3) and XA4(1) yielded a good number of fine Lower Palaeolithic artefacts at depths of -20 to -40 cm from the surface. Lower Palaeolithic patinated chert flakes and chert artefacts also occur right from the base of the excavation to its uppermost horizon. They include a patinated chert artefact from XA3(2), 64 cm from XA3, 45 cm from A3, at -127 cm depth from surface (-180 cm from A1); and a utilised and retouched knife-like artefact of a patinated Acheulian chert flake from XA5(3), 44 cm from A6, 75 cm from A5, at -10 cm from surface (-166 cm from A1).

The excavation at Daraki-Chattan has yielded definite evidence of human visual creation from the Lower Palaeolithic in the form of petroglyphs, both cupules and engraved lines, and also as hammerstones used for producing cupules. This is evident from the discovery of slabs bearing cupules and engraved lines, and of hammerstones right from the lowest layer 6 onwards. Although many hammerstones used for the production of the cupules were found, they are not in proportion to the very numerous cupules present in the cave. Acheulian floors or stone structures are rare features in the Lower Palaeolithic.

Detailed study of the excavated material is continuing.

CONCLUSIONS

The excavations at Daraki-Chattan in particular and the EIP Project (Bednarik 2001b; Kumar 2000/01; Kumar *et al.* 2002; Kumar *et al.* 2005) in general is endeavouring to secure the first comprehensive data of Lower and Middle Palaeolithic petroglyphs. The present preliminary report of the excavations at Daraki-Chattan provides unambiguous evidence of petroglyphs, mostly cupules, from archaeological occupation strata of Lower Palaeolithic age. It endorses the similar evidence previously presented from the Auditorium Cave at Bhimbetka. At Daraki-Chattan petroglyphs recovered from the excavations consist of a total of 28 cupules exfoliated from the cave wall, and two linear grooves. The lack of cupules on exfoliation scars on the cave walls implies that the remaining wall cupules are of ages similar to those in the excavation. The actual age of the cupules must have been much greater than that of their archaeological-stratigraphic age, as they must have been exfoliated much later than their production on the cave wall. The same relationship has been suggested for the cupules above ground in Auditorium Cave.

The recent research has shown that our understanding of art origins is rapidly changing. More than any other evidence during the last 100 years, the evidence produced by the EIP Project, especially from the excavations at Daraki-Chattan, has shown that we have misjudged the time depth of palaeoart and human cognition, creative ability and symbolism. Now the time has come to change our mindset. The evidence is so important that it is set to affect not only our concepts of Pleistocene hominin development in southern Asia, but it will influence the way we view cognitive evolution generally.

Acknowledgments

I am sincerely thankful to Mr Robert G. Bednarik for his guidance, co-operation and support for research in rock art with a new vision, as a friend and as the co-director of the EIP Project with me. The work of the EIP Project has enjoyed the financial support of the Archaeological Survey of India, the Indian Council of Historical Research and the Australia-India Council. I thank the heads and staff of these three sponsors, especially Prof. M.G.K. Narayanan, Dr R.S. Bisht and Dr R.C. Agrawal.

My special thanks are due to the Director General, Archaeological Survey of India, for granting us permission for the excavation at Daraki-Chattan and for sample collection from the early Indian petroglyph and rock painting sites. We have also benefited greatly from the collaboration of Dr Narayan Vyas, Dr P.K. Bhatt, Arakhita Prahran, Dr A. Sundara, Dr S.P. Gupta, Dr R.K. Sharma, Dr Amarendra Nath, P. B.S. Sengar, Ram Krishna, Dr S. Pradhan, K.K. Muhammed, Alok Tripathi, Dr B.L. Bamboria and Dr Ashvini Kumar Sharma. I heartily thank Dr Alan Watchman and Prof. Richard G. Roberts for carrying out scientific investigations of samples for AMS ^{14}C and OSL dating respectively. I also wish to thank the visiting scholars of this project for their invaluable participation and contributions: Dr Ewan Lawson (carbon isotope analysis), Dr Carol Patterson (rock art research), Professor V.N. Misra (Pleistocene archaeology), Dr R.K. Choudhury (nuclear physics), Professor S.N. Behera (nuclear physics), R.K. Pancholi (rock art research), Dr G.L. Badam (palaeontology), Dr R.K. Ganjoo (geology), S.B. Ota (archaeology), M.L. Sharma and M.L. Meena (both rock art research). Their co-operation has greatly facilitated the success of this endeavour. My special thanks are due to my wife Gita Devi with out whose co-operation this project could not have been done smoothly.

References

BEDNARIK, R.G. (1992) – Palaeoart and archaeological myths. *Cambridge Archaeological Journal*. Cambridge. 2: 1, p. 27–43.

BEDNARIK, R.G. (1993a) – Palaeolithic art in India. *Man and Environment*. Puna. 18: 2, p. 33–40.

BEDNARIK, R.G. (1993b) – About cupules. *Rock Art Research*. Melbourne. 10: 2, p. 138–139.

BEDNARIK, R.G. (1994) – The Pleistocene art of Asia. *Journal of World Prehistory* 8: 4, p. 351–375.

BEDNARIK, R.G. (2001a) – Cupules: the oldest surviving rock art. *International Newsletter on Rock Art*. Foix. 30, p. 18–23.

BEDNARIK, R.G. (2001b) – The Early Indian Petroglyphs Project (EIP). *Rock Art Research*. Melbourne. 18: 1, p. 72.

BEDNARIK, R.G. (2002a) – An outline of Middle Pleistocene palaeoart. *Purakala*. Agra. 13: 1–2, p. 39–44.

BEDNARIK, R.G. (2003) – The earliest evidence of palaeoart. *Rock Art Research*. Melbourne. 20, p. 89–135.

BEDNARIK, R.G.; KUMAR, G.; WATCHMAN, A.; ROBERTS, R.G. (2005) – Preliminary results of the EIP Project. *Rock Art Research*. Melbourne. 22, p. 147–197.

FOLEY, R.; LAHR, M.M. (1997) – Mode 3 technologies and the evolution of modern humans. *Cambridge Archaeological Journal*. Cambridge. 7, p. 3–36.

KUMAR, G. (1996) – Daraki-Chattan: a Palaeolithic cupule site in India. *Rock Art Research*. Melbourne. 13, p. 38–46.

KUMAR, G. (2000–01) – Early Indian Petroglyphs: scientific investigations and dating by international commission, April 2001 to March 2004. *Purakala*. Agra. 11/12, p. 49–68.

KUMAR, G. (2002) – EIP Project Report-I: Archaeological excavation and explorations at Daraki-Chattan-2002: a preliminary report. *Purakala*. Agra. 13: 1–2, p. 5–20.

KUMAR, G. (2005) – Preliminary report of the excavation at Daraki-Chattan for the session 2004-2005, send to the office of the D.G. Archaeological Survey of India. Unpublished.

KUMAR, G.; SHARMA, M. (1995) – Petroglyph sites in Kalapahad and Ganesh Hill: documentation and observations. *Purakala*. Agra. 6, p. 56–59.

KUMAR, G.; BEDNARIK, R.G.; WATCHMAN, A.; ROBERTS, R.G. (2005) – The EIP Project in 2005: A progress report. *Purakala*. Agra. 14–15, p. 13–68.

KUMAR, G.; PRADYUMN, N.; BHATT, K.; PRADHAN, A.; KRISHNA, R. (2006) – Discovery of early petro-glyphs in Chambal valley, Madhya Pradesh. *Purakala*. Agra. 16, p. 13–34.

PANCHOLI, R. K. (1994) – Bhanpura khetra me navin shodha (Hindi). *Purakala*. Agra. 5: 1–2, p. 75.

PEYRONY, D. (1934) – La Ferrassie. *Préhistoire* 3, p. 1–92.

TRIVEDI, H.V.; WAKANKAR, V.S. (1958–59) – Excavations at Indragarh, M.P. *Indian Archaeology 1958–59: A Review*, New Delhi.

TRIVEDI, H.V.; WAKANKAR, V.S. (1959–60) – Excavations at Indragarh, M.P. *Indian Archaeology 1959–60: A Review*, New Delhi.

www.ingramcontent.com/pod-product-compliance
Lightning Source LLC
LaVergne TN
LVHW070533110826
845147LV00017BA/982

* 9 7 8 1 4 0 7 3 0 2 9 1 1 *